SON OF MAN

SON OF MAN

The interpretation and influence
of Daniel 7

MAURICE CASEY

LONDON
SPCK

First published 1979
SPCK
Holy Trinity Church
Marylebone Road
London NW1 4DU

Printed in Great Britain by
R. & R. Clark Ltd, Edinburgh

ISBN 0 281 03697 7

For
Janice Casey

Contents

Preface   ix

List of Abbreviations   xi

1   Introduction   1

2   Daniel 7   7

3   The Syrian Tradition   51

4   The Western Tradition   71

5   Apocrypha and Pseudepigrapha   99

6   The New Testament:
the Book of Revelation   142

7   The New Testament Epistles   151

8   The Gospels and Acts   157

9   The Son of Man Problem   224

Select Bibliography   241

Index of Primary Sources   261

Index of Names and Subjects   269

Preface

This book is a completely revised and rewritten version of a thesis accepted for the degree of Ph.D. at the University of Durham in 1977. I would like to thank all those many people who have helped me to produce it. I would particularly like to mention Professor C. K. Barrett, who supervised the research with a very rare combination of real help with the ability to leave my mind independent; my mother, Mrs F. Casey, without whose financial assistance I could not have begun research in 1971; the University of Durham, who awarded me a Research Studentship in 1972; and my family, who have helped in many ways, practical and otherwise.

I have reused material from articles published in *ZNW* 67 (1976), pp. 147–54; *JThS* NS XXVII (1976), pp. 15–33; *JSJ* VII (1976), pp. 11–29; and *NT* XVIII (1976), pp. 159–73; I am grateful to Dr E. Lohse, Dr H. F. D. Sparks, Prof. A. S. van der Woude, The Clarendon Press, and E. J. Brill for permission to do this.

Ufford, England   15 August 1978

Abbreviations

Abr-n	*Abr-nahrain*
Adv. Marc.	*Against Marcion*
Agg. Ber.	Aggadath *Bereshith*
A.J.	*Jewish Antiquities*
ALBO	Analecta Lovaniensia Biblica et Orientalia
Apoc.	Apocalypse
Aphr.	Aphrahat
App.	Appendix
ASTI	*Annual of the Swedish Theological Institute*
Barn.	The Epistle of Barnabas
BASOR	*Bulletin of the American Schools of Oriental Research*
BCES	*Bulletin du Comité des études* (Compagnie de S. Sulpice)
BEThL	Bibliotheca ephemeridum theologicarum Lovaniensium
BGBH	Beiträge zur Geschichte der biblischen Exegese
Bib	*Biblica*
B.J.	*Jewish War*
BJRL	*Bulletin of the John Rylands Library*
BSt(F)	Biblische Studien (Freiburg)
BSNTS	*Bulletin of the Studiorum Novi Testamenti Societas*
bT	Babylonian Talmud
bT *AZ*	Babylonian Talmud, tractate *Abodah Zarah*
bT *Hag*	Babylonian Talmud, tractate *Hagiga*
bT *Meg*	Babylonian Talmud, tractate *Megillah*
bT *Qid*	Babylonian Talmud, tractate *Qiddushin*
bT *San*	Babylonian Talmud, tractate *Sanhedrin*
BZ	*Biblische Zeitschrift*
BZAW	Beihefte zur Zeitschrift für die alttestamentliche Wissenschaft

BZNW	Beihefte zur Zeitschrift für die neutestamentliche Wissenschaft
CBQ	*Catholic Biblical Quarterly*
CChr. SL	Corpus Christianorum, Series Latina
CD	The Damascus Document
Chrys. *Hom. de Res.*	Chrysostom, *Homily on the Resurrection*
CI	Cosmas Indicopleustes
Clem. Alex.	Clement of Alexandria
1 Clem.	First Epistle of Clement
CP	Classical Philology
CSCO. SS	Corpus scriptorum christianorum orientalium. Scriptores syriaci.
CSEL	Corpus scriptorum ecclesiasticorum latinorum.
Dem.	*Demonstration*
Dem. Ev.	*Demonstration of the Gospel*
Dial.	*Dialogue*
Div. Inst.	*Divine Institutes*
Eccl. R.	*Ecclesiastes Rabbah*
Eph.	Ephraem
Esth. R.	*Esther Rabbah*
ET	English Translation
EThL	Ephemerides theologicae Lovanienses
EvTh	*Evangelische Theologie*
ExpT	*Expository Times*
Exod. R.	*Exodus Rabbah*
FRLANT	Forschungen zur Religion und Literatur des Alten und Neuen Testaments
Gal.	Galipapa
GCS	Die griechischen christlichen Schriftsteller der ersten drei Jahrhunderte
Gen. R.	*Genesis Rabbah*
Gr	Gregorianum
HAT	Handkommentar zum Alten Testament
HUCA	*Hebrew Union College Annual*
ICC	International Critical Commentary
Interp.	Interpretation

Ish.	Isho'dad of Merw
Isr Or St	Israel Oriental Studies
JBL	*Journal of Biblical Literature*
JJS	*Journal of Jewish Studies*
JQR	*Jewish Quarterly Review*
JR	*Journal of Religion*
JSJ	*Journal for the Study of Judaism*
JSS	*Journal of Semitic Studies*
JThS	*Journal of Theological Studies*
KAT	Kommentar zum Alten Testament
Lev. R.	*Leviticus Rabbah*
LXX	Septuagint
Mekh. *Baḥ.*	Mekhilta, tractate *Baḥodesh*
Mekh. *Shir.*	Mekhilta, tractate *Shirata*
MGWJ	*Monatsschrift für Geschichte und Wissenschaft des Judentums*
Midr.	Midrash
Midr. *Ps.*	Midrash on Psalms
Ms(s).	Manuscript(s)
MT	Massoretic Text
NS	New Series
NT	New Testament
NT	Novum Testamentum
NTS	*New Testament Studies*
NT. S	*Novum Testamentum, Supplements*
NTT	*Nieuw Theologisch Tijdschrift*
Num. R.	*Numbers Rabbah*
OrChr	*Oriens Christianum*
OT	Old Testament
OTS	*Oudtestamentliche Studien*
Pesh.	Peshitta
Pes. R.	Pesikta Rabbati
Pol.	Polychronius
Por.	Porphyry
pT	Palestinian Talmud
pT *Sheb*	Palestinian Talmud, tractate *Shebiith*
P.V.T.G.	Pseudepigrapha veteris testamenti Graece

Q	Material common to Matthew and Luke
R	Rabbi
RB	*Revue Biblique*
RScR	*Recherches de Sciences religieuses*
SBL	Society of Biblical Literature
SBM	Stuttgarter biblischer Monographien
SBT	Studies in Biblical Theology (SCM Press)
SC	Sources Chrétiennes
Sem	Semitica
Sib.Or.	Sibylline Oracles
SimE	Similitudes of Enoch
SJTh	*Scottish Journal of Theology*
Soc Bib Lit MS	Society of Biblical Literature, Monograph Series
Soph. *Oed. T.*	Sophocles, *Oedipus Tyrannus*
StTh	*Studia Theologica*
StudEv	*Studia evangelica*
StUNT	Studien zur Umwelt des Neuen Testaments
S.V.T.P.	Studia in veteris testamenti pseudepigrapha
Tanch. *Miš.*	Tanchuman, *Mišpat*
Tanch. *Tol.*	Tanchuma, *Toledoth*
Tanch. *Ts.*	Tanchuma, *Tso*
Tanch. *Qed.*	Tanchuma, *Qedoshim*
TDNT	*Theological Dictionary of the New Testament* Tr. and ed. G. W. Bromiley. London/Michigan, Eerdmans, 1964–74
TED	Translations of Early Documents
Test. Abr.	Testament of Abraham
Test. Dan	Testament of Dan
Test. Jos.	Testament of Joseph
Test. Levi	Testament of Levi
Tg	Targum
Theod.	Theodotion
ThR	*Theologische Rundschau*
ThStKr	Theologische Studien und Kritiken
ThZ	Theologische Zeitschrift
TK	Theodore bar Koni
Tr.	Translated

TU	Texte und Untersuchungen zur Geschichte der altchristlichen Literatur
TWNT	*Theologische Wörterbuch zum Neuen Testament.* Ed. G. Kittel and G. Friedrich. 9 vols, Stuttgart, Kohlhammer, 1933–73.
VigChr	*Vigiliae Christianae*
VT	*Vetus Testamentum*
VT. S.	*Vetus Testamentum, Supplements*
WMANT	Wissenschaftliche Monographien zum Alten und Neuen Testament
ZAW	*Zeitschrift für die alttestamentliche Wissenschaft*
ZNW	*Zeitschrift für die neutestamentliche Wissenschaft und die Kunde der älteren Kirche*
ZThK	*Zeitschrift für Theologie und Kirche*
1QApGen	The Genesis Apocryphon
1QH	The Qumran Hymns
1QpHab	The Habakkuk Commentary
1QS	The Community Rule
1QSa	The Rule of the Congregation
4QOrNab	The Nabonidus Prayer from Qumran, Cave 4
4Qps-Dan	Pseudo-Daniel from Qumran, Cave 4
4Q184	Document 184 from Qumran, Cave 4
11QMelch	Melchizedek document from Qumran, Cave 11
11QTgJob	The Job Targum from Qumran, Cave 11

1
Introduction

The origin and meaning of the Gospel term 'Son of man' is a
central problem for research into the Gospel traditions of the
teaching of Jesus. None of the proposed solutions has won
general acceptance. According to one widespread theory, the
use of the term 'Son of man' in the Gospels is derived ultimately
from Dan. 7.13, where Daniel saw 'one like a Son of man
coming with the clouds of heaven'. In recent years this theory
has taken a significant new turn, with the suggestion that it is
written in Dan. 7 that the Son of man should suffer. If this
theory had been right, it would have been of the utmost
importance for our understanding of Jesus himself and for the
interpretation of a fundamental group of Gospel sayings. Moreover, the failure of investigations of the Aramaic term בר אנש,
and of 'man' concepts in the ancient Near East, to lead to a
satisfactory solution of the Son of man problem made it all the
more imperative that a thorough investigation of the interpretation of Dan. 7 and the Son of man problem should be
carried out. This book is the result.

For this purpose I collected and analysed evidence of ancient
interpretation of Dan. 7, for it was evident from current scholarship that our knowledge of this was insufficient. The whole
chapter was taken as a unit, to provide a complete context for
the interpretation of the central verses 13 and 14. There were
three general questions for this research to answer. How was
Dan. 7 interpreted in the ancient world, especially in the time
of Jesus and the Gospel writers? How much was it used in the
very earliest period of Christianity? Thirdly, and most important of the three, what was the connection between its
interpretation and use and the Son of man problem, both in
Judaism and Christianity?

The first of these questions required the survey of a considerable quantity of material. All published Jewish apocrypha and
pseudepigrapha which might date from approximately the

1

period of Christian origins were read, a procedure which showed that earlier scholars had found every single reference to Dan. 7 in this literature. Rabbinical literature was also surveyed. It was not possible to study only early sayings, because existing methods were not adequate for dating individual sayings which use Dan. 7. The whole rabbinical period was therefore covered, though the investigation was limited to published works, and the material was not read again; the investigation proceeded by means of collecting references from existing indexes and from previous scholarship. Some use was also made of medieval Jewish commentators, who occasionally preserved some very early interpretative material.

For patristic evidence, all documents down to Eusebius were surveyed, and the Western Church's interpretation was filled out by reading the commentaries of Jerome and Theodoret. This was not however sufficient for the recovery of the author's original interpretation of Dan. 7, and for this purpose published commentaries and similar works from the Syriac-speaking Church were read, down to the end of the first millennium.

Thus the limits of the investigation were set at points which enabled me to lay down the lines of the different traditions of interpretation of Dan. 7 in the ancient world, as well as to assess the nature and extent of its use in the most important period. The results have dictated the order in which the evidence is discussed in this book. In ch. 2 I have surveyed the evidence of Dan. 7 itself, to set out the way in which it was interpreted by its author, and hence lay down a *terminus a quo* for his views. In ch. 3 I have dealt with the evidence of the Syrian Church, for it is here that there is most evidence of the author's original interpretation of the chapter, by means of which it can be shown that this interpretation was known at the time of Jesus. In ch. 4 I have dealt with the mass of evidence for the other interpretative tradition, held in the West by both Jews and Christians. The results discussed in these chapters are then utilized in the interpretation of evidence from the most important period. In ch. 5 the early Jewish evidence is surveyed, and chs. 6 and 7 discuss the Book of Revelation and the New Testament epistles. The results of all this research can then be used for the main attack on the Son of man problem in ch. 8. Here I have endeavoured to solve all the outstanding problems

2

concerned with the interpretation and use of Dan. 7 by Jesus himself, the earliest Church, and the Gospel writers. This has led me to propose a partial solution to the Son of man problem, and I have tried to demonstrate that, as far as it goes, it is right. However, a partial solution is not enough, especially since failure to find the real origin of the Gospel term 'Son of man' has always been a major factor in the persistent attempts to extract it from Dan. 7, so in ch. 9 I have completed the theory and proposed a complete solution to the Son of man problem. The significance of this for current christological debate will be evident.

The whole investigation had to contend with two serious problems of method. The first concerns the dating of the exegetical traditions. I have used evidence which must be dated after, and sometimes long after, the time of Jesus. The reason for doing this is obvious enough: earlier material required for answering the necessary questions has long since disappeared. This observation does not remove the problem. For this investigation, however, analysis of the evidence can in large measure provide the necessary substitute for early date. The techniques proposed here are not new. They are the normal techniques of modern historical research. The gap in time thus spanned is great, but not unique in historical work on the ancient world. What is less common is the application of these techniques to enable us to tap the resources of late Jewish and patristic exegetical works, and apply the results to the study of Christian origins.

The second serious problem of method concerns the definition of 'literary dependence'. What criteria should be used in deciding when an author is dependent on Dan. 7? The answer to this question is difficult, but for this investigation we can get somewhere by drawing the two lines which can be precisely drawn. When an author cites and quotes Dan. 7, he must be said to have had it in mind. When an author's remarks have no verbal connection with Dan. 7 and have no contact with it in thought, it may safely be assumed that he did not have it in mind. These definitions may look so simple and obvious as to be otiose. However, the scope of this investigation was extended more than once to cover works which are explicitly commentaries on Daniel. One reason for their usefulness is that they fall

3

on the easy side of the first of these lines—there is no room for doubt that their authors have the Danielic text in mind.

It is the area between these two lines which is difficult. For almost the whole of this investigation, I was concerned with conscious literary dependence, that is, dependence of which an author was aware and which is such that the author could, if he had so desired, have given an account of his interpretation of the Old Testament passage on which he was dependent. It is not a consequence of this definition that the account which an author could have given of his interpretation of an Old Testament passage should be consistent or should not be atomistic; only that he should have had an interpretation of which he could have given an account. By contrast I have made no attempt to uncover possible echoes of Dan. 7 which might be attributed to the subconscious mind of an author who knew the chapter very well, because the hypothesis that such an echo is present in a given verse is of no use, partly because it cannot be tested and partly because the workings of the subconscious mind are sufficiently devious to render any deduction that might be made from the presence of a supposed reminiscence of this type to an author's interpretation of the Old Testament passage in question dubious in the extreme. This definition does not of course exclude the possibility that an author did know Dan. 7 as well as this; it assumes only that in order to reach the conclusion that he did have such knowledge we must have more straightforward evidence that he knew it. I have diverged from this procedure only in ch. 8, where I have found criteria on the basis of which it was possible to conclude that in some cases there has been dependence on Dan. 7.13 at an earlier stage in the development of the synoptic tradition, but that the actual Gospel writers cannot be shown to have been aware of this dependence. This is the only section of the material where conclusions of this kind could be usefully sought and established. Here it was important to do so, both to answer the question as to the extent that Dan. 7 was used in early Christianity, and to take seriously the possibility that the term 'Son of man' might have been derived from Dan. 7 by Jesus himself, or at a stage in the development of traditions about him prior to the writing down of the Gospels. The situation was thus different from that involved in trying to assess the amount of use of Dan. 7 in the intertestamental period and in early patristic literature. Here demonstrable use of Dan. 7 by the authors of the documents is a satisfactory index of the amount of its use, whereas in the Gospel evidence it was necessary to examine the possibility that Dan. 7 had been influential in a manner unknown to the authors of the Gospels.

Throughout the investigation, I used two criteria in considering cases of possible literary dependence. The first is verbal similarity. The second is that the thought of the dependent passage shall not be such as to be inconsistent with the hypothesis of literary dependence on the Old Testament passage in question. Similarity of thought on its own is not a sufficient guarantee of literary dependence, particularly where the thought in question occurs in documents other than those being considered. The application of such a criterion would moreover be especially hazardous in dealing with a period of history such as the intertestamental period, where most documents have long since perished, and an item of thought found in two documents written two hundred years apart may have been expressed in lost documents in the intervening years. Furthermore, the question as to what the authors of documents studied imagined the thoughts in Dan. 7 to be is to some extent at issue.

It is unfortunate, but unavoidable, that the two criteria selected for use are lacking in mathematical precision. However, I do not think that, in the case of the material surveyed in this book, the results of this are serious. There are, it is true, cases where the question of literary dependence has not been finally resolved: 2 Baruch is the outstanding example. Usually, however, this is not the case. It is important that, while it is, both theoretically and practically, impossible to draw an accurate line in a specified place between literary dependence on the one side and lack of it on the other, it is contingently true that it is often possible to place a given document on one side or the other of that imaginary line. That is what is of practical importance, and it has been successfully achieved with almost all documents discussed, and in all cases that should be considered to be genuinely important. In doing it, I have provided more detailed discussions of the practical application of these criteria to particular sections of the evidence, and I have examined the outstanding efforts of previous scholars to do the same. Moreover, in the central example, the use of Dan. 7.13 in the Gospels, I was able to employ a completely different set of arguments to show that the group of Son of man sayings dependent on Dan. 7.13 was not significantly larger than careful employment of these two criteria had suggested. This confirmed the appropriateness of careful use of these two criteria.

We may now begin by establishing the original author's interpretation of Dan. 7.

2
Daniel 7

The place of Dan. 7 within the book of Daniel as a whole has been a major source of difficulty. While the book appears to divide into two parts at the end of ch. 6, chs. 1–6 consisting of stories and chs. 7–12 of visions, it is written in two languages, Dan. 1–2.4a, 8–12 being in Hebrew and 2.4b–7 in Aramaic, and this division puts Dan. 7 with the stories of 2–6 instead of with the visions. This linguistic division is fundamental, and formal grounds can now be found for classifying 7 with 2–6. If we view Dan. 2–7 as a unit, its stories appear to be chiastically arranged. On the outside are two dreams embodying the four kingdom theory, according to which the destruction of the fourth world kingdom will be followed by the divinely ordained triumph of the kingdom of God. Next, Dan. 3 and 6 are martyrologies, in which however the self-sacrifice of the heroes leads, not to their death, but to their deliverance by God. Thirdly, Dan. 4–5 correspond in the middle. Both concern rebellious kings. Nebuchadnezzar repented and obeyed, and was pardoned. Belshazzar did not, and was therefore destroyed.

This complete collection puts forward a simple and unified message. While some, at least, of the stories depend on old traditions, all have very simple, straightforward, and vital relevance for a single author who used them when he and his fellows suffered persecution and war. God is supreme and faithful: he will punish our enemies, and deliver us. The different groups of stories stress different facets, though one should be careful not to analyse too strictly a form of expression whose whole nature is dramatic and illustrative rather than analytical. In 4 and 5 the judgement of the kings of the ruling empire by God stresses the supremacy of God himself. In 3 and 6, the accent is on the deliverance of the individual. In 2 and 7, the stress is on the destruction of the oppressors and the deliverance of the community.

The correspondence of 2 and 7 is especially important for this

7

investigation. All ancient commentators make much of it, and anyone who finds that dreams and stories are natural modes of expression would regard it as more important than any formal distinction between 1–6 on the one hand and 7 on the other. The importance of Dan. 2 lies in 2.31–45, which consists of a dream and its interpretation, corresponding to the dream and interpretation of Dan. 7. It is not wrong to point out also that Dan. 7 has actually got a narrative framework, vss. 1 and 28, corresponding to the narrative framework of Dan. 2.1–30, 46–9, but it does no good to minimize the fact that 2.1–30, 46–9 is a fine story, whereas 7.1, 28 is only just there. The explanation of this difference lies in the contents of 2.31–45 and the nature of our author. Dan. 2.31–45 presents a pagan king having a dream of the future Jewish triumph. That is remarkable, and demands some sort of narrative setting. Dan. 3–6 shows clearly enough that the author had a natural gift for telling stories, so it is not surprising that the setting of 2.31–45 is a story of some length and considerable artistry, which has always attracted widespread admiration. The dream and its interpretation form a very good climax.

Dan. 7 is somewhat different. The dreamer is the main hero, whose character and attainments are so clear that it is no surprise to find him too dreaming dreams. All that is necessary is therefore a statement that he did so on a particular occasion, and some sort of conclusion (Dan. 7.1, 28). A story is not necessary on grounds of content, because the general setting is already clear enough and the point is the dream and its interpretation, and a story is not necessary on grounds of form because the author's ideas of form were not as rigid as that. To get his chiastic structure he needed another dream of the four kingdoms and the Jewish triumph, together with its interpretation, and this is what he has supplied; to a natural story-teller it did not matter that he had put a good story round the first dream and interpretation.

These two dreams correspond in what they symbolize. There will be a sequence of four kingdoms, of which Nebuchadnezzar's is the first. The fourth will be the most terrible, but at length it will be destroyed, and the Jewish people will triumph, by the ordinance of their God. That the symbolism of the two separate dreams should correspond need not be maintained, and for the most part it is clearly not the case. That the metals of the image in Dan. 2 decline in preciousness is probably due simply to the use of ancient symbolism, since the author does not stress this decline. Certainly the correspondence between Dan. 2 and Dan. 7 should not be forced by seeing the four beasts in a declining sequence too. The fourth beast was intended to be worse than the other three, but this does not establish a complete declining sequence of four. A decisive factor is the lack of any indication, symbolic or real, that the third beast is worse than the second. To suggest that the bear and leopard mark a decline from the lion and eagle, the kings of beasts and birds, is to point out that there is no decline from bear to leopard, and to stress that the Babylonian kingdom was more favourable to Israel both shifts the argument from symbolism to reality and points up the lack of evidence that the Persians are considered to mark a decline from the Medes. Attempts to demonstrate more detailed correspondence in the symbolism of the two chapters are open to more obvious criticism. For example, the append-ages of the first beast have no parallel in Dan. 2—there is no reason why they should have. Finally there is some development in Dan. 7 over Dan. 2: Dan. 7 has more ample description, especially in its picture and interpretation of the little horn. None of this is sufficient to upset the basic literary structure of Dan. 2–7. Dan. 2 and 7 broadly correspond in all important matters; there is no reason to imagine that they should have corresponded at the level of more precise detail.

Dan. 2–7 may therefore be seen as a unified literary structure, the work of a single author. But what of Dan. 1, 8–12? Were they written by the same man? The matter is difficult to resolve, but the two languages suggest two authors, and a reasonable hypothesis may begin from the unified literary structure of Dan. 2–7. This was written first. Its message is simple, as we have seen, and its function in time of persecution is clear and well known, that of fortifying the faithful. Aramaic was the natural language in which to write this material because it was intended to have popular appeal and Aramaic was the *lingua franca* of the time. The choice of Hebrew for the remaining material may be ascribed to deliberate nationalism. It is most natural to ascribe this change of policy to a change of author. In time of war and persecution, change of authorship in such an

9

important and successful religious work may have a simple and unavoidable cause—the death of the first author.

If this conjecture is right, the author of Dan. 2–7 left behind him a unified collection of stories and dreams. Someone else, writing now in the Jewish national tongue, furnished them with an introduction. He made a little beginning to the first of the original stories in Hebrew, but his Hebrew was not of the most brilliant, and everyone admired the existing collection of stories, so he left the transition at 'in Aramaic' (2.4). It is that kind of device—clever at the most mechanical level, dissatisfying to anyone literary. It reeks of someone who could not manage to translate 2.4b–7, though it may be he had respectable reasons, including lack of time. Then he, or other men, added the three sections of Dan. 8, 9, and 10–2. They are of unrelieved solemnity, perhaps unlikely to be the work of a natural story-teller (but not impossibly so, if he were constrained by recent disaster and an unfamiliar tongue).

This reconstruction is in a measure imaginative, but it does explain the basic evidence. More detailed investigation of the languages has been attempted, but it has been more learned than successful: the problems of method are severe, and compounded by the small quantity of both languages surviving for comparison, and this explains the failure to achieve any useful results. There is nothing here to overthrow the *prima facie* impression that the Hebrew is of different authorship from the Aramaic. Finally, the similarities between 7 and 8–12 may not be urged in favour of unity of authorship, since they are perfectly explicable on the assumption that the second author (and, if need be, the third and fourth) belonged to the same religious group as the first author and took up his work when he died.

Hence, probability is on the side of a separate author for Dan. 8–12, though certainty has not been achieved. It is therefore reasonable to use these chapters with caution to illustrate the religious environment and general viewpoint of the author of Dan. 7.

We can now establish the date of Dan. 7. When it was completed, the persecution of Antiochus Epiphanes was already under way, as is clear from the account and interpretation of the little horn. The date is therefore somewhat after December,

167 B.C. The three-and-a-half-year interval to the Maccabean victory is inaccurate: the expanded version of the story in 11.40ff. is certainly wrong. Therefore this is a genuine prediction, and the date is somewhat before December 164 B.C. Allowance has to be made for 1, 8–12 to be written early enough for 11.40ff. to seem plausible. From these factors it follows that Dan. 2–7 is to be dated in 166 or 165 B.C. The Qumran fragments of Daniel may not be held against this. It is very exciting that we have some fragments written so soon after the composition of this book, and verifying that already it was written in both languages just as we have it now. This does not, however, constitute proof that it was already regarded as Scripture in the full sense which that word later came to have, and we have no evidence that suggests that this period of time was too short for its acceptance as a sacred book. Interpretative traditions of this work also suggest that its pseudepigraphic device was successful. There is nothing wrong with the suggestion that it was successful quickly.

But have we now dated the composition of Dan. 7, or only its final redaction? There have been several theories of the redaction history of the chapter. They are important because they suggest the possibility of a written source in which the manlike figure was something other than a symbol of the Saints of the Most High. Some authors have thus been able to use this chapter as evidence that there once existed a 'Son of man Concept' in pre-Christian Judaism. The most important attempts in recent years to trace out the pre-history of the chapter have been those of Hölscher, Noth and Dequeker. These must therefore be examined in some detail.[1]

Hölscher argues that the pre-Maccabean version of Dan. 7 did not include vss. 7b, 8, 11a, 20–2, 24–5. He begins with vs. 11, where there is a genuine difficulty which has led some scholars who do not follow the view that this chapter has a complex literary history to suppose that something has gone wrong at this particular point. The versions are not helpful. The omission of vs. 11a in the Peshitta must be ascribed to *homoioarcton*: the repetition of 'I was looking' is unnecessary to the sense, so it is not surprising that LXX and Theodotion omitted the second occurrence of it. The main point is that מן must be taken as a temporal particle. This makes excellent sense, whereas in the

11

middle of such a dramatic vision there is no need for an explanation of why Daniel should have continued to watch it. בֵּאדַיִן normally occurs at the beginning of a sentence in Daniel because elsewhere it introduces a statement of an event subsequent to those previously related, but here it is in a different position because it picks up the events of vs. 8. An interruption in the account of the activity of the little horn was desirable so that the scene could be set for the passing of judgement, but Daniel did not cease to notice the blasphemy of the little horn. בֵּאדַיִן here denotes events which began to take place before the events of vss. 9–10, and this accounts for its unusual position, for which there is a good parallel in 1QApGen XXII, 2

ואברם באדין הוא יתב בחברון

'Now at that time Abram was living in Hebron.' Dan. 7.11 may therefore be translated 'I was watching then, from the time when I heard the blasphemous words which the horn was speaking, I was watching until the beast was slain . . .'. Dequeker complains that the 'regular transitional formula' חָזֵה הֲוֵית עַד דִּי is interrupted:[2] it will be argued that his ideas of transitional formulae are more rigid than those of our author. The effect of the repetition of 'I was watching' is to quicken the tempo of the narrative just at the point where the terrible enemy is to be destroyed. The author's Aramaic has been misunderstood, and here as elsewhere his resolution of a literary problem by means of a formulation which deliberately seeks a literary effect has remained unappreciated.

Hölscher then argues for the omission of vs. 8, on the ground that אֵלֶּין is used here only in Dan. 7 instead of אֲרוּ. Haller added that אֲרוּ was the older form. Rowley replied, pointing out that the *prima facie* evidence of the book of Daniel is that the author used both forms, as אֵלֶּין occurs also in 2.31, 4.7, 10. Dequeker remains unconvinced. 'They do not explain however the *variation* of the formulas in Dan. 7. Dan. 2 and 4 have only *'lw*. That means that the basic text of Dan. 7, which has *'rw*, may be older than Dan. 2 and 4. . . .'[3] We may now add the information that אֲרוּ is still used in 11QTgJob, 1QApGen and 4Q Giants.[4] Dequeker's argument is unsound for two reasons. Firstly, if אֲרוּ was replaced by אֵלֶּין as the Aramaic language developed, there will have been a period of transition in which either form might be used. We do not have sufficient evidence outside the book of Daniel to enable us to date any transition, but it is now evident that ארן continued to be used after the time when Dan. 7 was finally written down. During any such transition period, the possibility has to be admitted that an author may use both forms. The contrary has to be demonstrated, not simply assumed. Rowley already pointed this out, citing the use of ארקא and ארעא side by side at Jer. 10.11 and in the Elephantine papyri, which provide many examples of the same phenomenon. Secondly, the number of occurrences of each form is too small for observations such as 'Dan. 2 and 4 have only 'lw' to have any real force. It is to be concluded that Rowley's arguments stand. The author used ארן and אלו, five times each. The demand that he should have been consistent has never been justified.

Dequeker further objects to משתכל instead of the 'regular' חזה. But the variation is deliberate, to concentrate attention on the little horn. שכל has a different semantic field from חזה and the difference is really well used here, as Plöger had already seen. Dequeker's reply is mere reference to 'the structure and the style'. He could better have cited Procrustes. Dequeker next objects to the perfect סלקת; he thinks we should have a participle, as after ארן in vss. 2, 3, 5 and 7. 'Montgomery and Ginsberg have seen the difficulty, changing the aorist of the Massoretic text into a participle.'[5] This misrepresents Montgomery, who showed proper philological concern about the MT סלקת and suggested that the original consonantal text סלקת might have been intended to be a participial form, which he vocalized סלקת. Delcor had already replied to Ginsberg. The use of the perfect is quite normal. It may be added that the variation in tense increases the dramatic quality of the description and helps to focus the reader's attention on to the little horn, which is just where the author intended to focus it. Dequeker's final argument from the 'syntaxis' is to object to the *hithpeel* (sic) passive אתעקרו instead of the 'regular' passive *qal* and *hophal* forms. But his base for determining what is 'regular' is far too narrow: he has given no reason at all for regarding this kind of variation as abnormal within the work of a single writer. Finally these arguments should not be held to carry cumulative weight, because none of them carries any weight on

13

its own. It will be noted that I have supposed two kinds of variation in the author's work, random variation of a kind which normally occurs, and deliberate variation for literary effect. Neither Dequeker nor anyone else has really got down to arguing that these kinds of variation do not occur in the work of normal authors. Yet only if this assumption is made can the persistent attempts of these literary critics to point out (usually with perfect accuracy) that there are variations between vs. 8 and other verses of this chapter actually constitute evidence of separate authorship.

Hölscher turns next to 7.20–2, which are, in his view, rather pointlessly repetitive. He objects particularly to 7.21, on the ground that this does not offer any interpretation of the dream but forms a later addition to it, one which would have been better placed after 7.8. Putting it there illustrates well enough the prosaic and unimaginative mind of the critic, far removed from the creative histrionics of our author. The effect of vs. 21 in its present position is to increase the dramatic quality of the narrative. Moreover we shall see that the position of vss. 20–2 was necessitated by the author's choice of symbolism. The man-like figure cannot suffer, and it is only when he has been identified as the Saints of the Most High that Daniel can see them humiliated. This could not be said at vs. 8.[6] Finally it should be remembered that this is not the sudden occurrence of part of a vision in the middle of its interpretation: Daniel is dreaming throughout the chapter. Hölscher adds two arguments from the vocabulary: דִינָא in vs. 22 has a different sense from דִינָא in 7.10, 26, and חֲזָו in vs. 20 a different sense from its occurrences in 7.1–15. Again the observation is sound, but the conclusions do not follow. Words have semantic fields, not single meanings, and authors habitually make use of them. The author of Dan. 7 is in this respect simply normal, and a very precise parallel to his use of חֲזָו in two senses is now to be found in 4Q 'Amram[b] I, 10–4.

Hölscher next attacks vss. 24–5, on the ground that here the 'other king', that is, the little horn, is described as different from his predecessors, whereas at 7.7 it is the fourth beast which is said to be different from its predecessors. And why not? The author had very good reason to believe it of both. Hölscher then tries to use Dan. 8–12 to bolster his argument: but that their contents correspond with the verses he wants to excise is equally consistent with unity of authorship and with the conjecture that 8–12 was written after 7 by someone else. He then excises vs. 7b 'and it had ten horns', but his argument derives what little plausibility it possesses from his omission of the climax to the description of the fourth beast by excising vs. 8.

Haller used Hölscher's critical position to date Dan. 7 earlier than Dan. 2, at about the time of Alexander the Great. One more of his arguments is worthy of mention, because it illustrates how much the literary criticism of this chapter has fed on itself. He argues that the author of Dan. 2 had more knowledge of the Greek kingdom than had the author of Dan. 7. The reason for that judgement was that Hölscher and Haller had excised most of what ch. 7 has to say about the Greek kingdom.

Noth based himself on the earlier work of Hölscher and Haller, and contributed a new argument from the structure of the chapter, which Dequeker still largely accepts. On the basis of the opening verses of this chapter Noth constructed a rigid structural schema: finding that the remainder of the chapter does not fit his schema, he resorted to the excision of the offending parts. But the method of this procedure is unsound. It is true that if vss. 2–8 are examined in isolation, they can be divided into four sections: three begin חָזֵה הֲוֵית ... וַאֲרוּ, as does vs. 13, and וַאֲרוּ in vs. 5 can plausibly be described as part of this same formula. It is also true that twice here, and again in vs. 11, events are introduced with the formula חָזֵה הֲוֵית עַד דִּי. But it is also very important from the structural point of view that already at this stage the operation of these formulae is flexible rather than rigid, and that Noth has to admit omission and abbreviation. When more striking variations from Noth's schema are found in the rest of the chapter, it should be concluded, not that the author's work has been upset, but that the author's ideas of introductory formulae were not as rigid as those of Noth. The occurrences of חָזֵה הֲוֵית עַד דִּי in vss. 9, 11b are just as much part of the primary evidence as the formulae in the opening verses. When all the primary evidence is taken into account, it becomes clear that the author was somewhat flexible in his use of these phrases. It is useful to compare 2Q24, which also has חֲזֵי הֲוֵית עַד דִּי at line 17, but at lines 11 and 15 has the variants חֲזֵית עַד דִּי and הֲוֵית עַד [חֲזֵי]. This is not

15

the same as Dan. 7, but the significant factor is that here too the formula is not inflexible.

Noth further developed his argument by trying to show that the author of the Similitudes of Enoch did use Dan. 7 but knew only vss. 9, 10 and 13. This is unconvincing: the author of the Similitudes gave Enoch the substance of vs. 14 and had no use for vss. 11 and 12, not because they were not there, but because he had no use for the four kingdom theory embodied in them.[7] Noth's argument for a separate literary source behind Dan. 7.9ff. thus collapses. He develops his argument further with reference to the angelic interpretation. Obviously those parts of it which interpret secondary additions to the vision must themselves be secondary, so out goes most of the interpretation, and Noth finds himself left with vs. 17 alone. He then concludes that this is too short! This is a classic example of the catastrophic results that can follow from the rigid application of the techniques of some literary critics. This brevity has nothing to do with the author, but is the achievement of Noth, whose critical operations were so arbitrary and so remote from the literature he was dealing with that they could not possibly demonstrate anything.

Dequeker continues to adhere in general to Noth's analysis, but his opinion that 'Noth's surgical operation is too radical' only serves to underline the fact that the criteria which he uses for making decisions about authenticity and redaction are no less arbitrary than those of Noth. He is able to make only one effective point against earlier defenders of the unity of the book of Daniel, in that he does give a convincing outline of circumstances under which what he regards as the original substratum of Dan. 7 might have been written. For this purpose he makes use of mostly recent work on the 'opposition history' of the Hellenistic period. However, this general point demonstrates no more than that this kind of writing could have been done at an earlier period; it does not show that Dan. 7 is actually based on an earlier literary source.

It is to be concluded that attempts to find an older literary source behind Dan. 7 have not been successful. They are less numerous than at first appears, because they depend on each other. All fail because of the inadequacy of the criteria which they use. Most assume that the author's habits were extremely rigid, and can be deduced from a small proportion of his work and then applied to the rest. None takes sufficiently seriously the variation and flexibility found in the work of real authors, whether in random variation or for deliberate effect. This does not of course preclude the possibility that the author used old stories and old ideas. We shall see that in ch. 7 he did indeed make use of older material, though not in the way that literary critics assume. The real importance of this result is twofold. First, the present text of Dan. 7 does not provide evidence of an older source which dealt with the supreme figure of 'the Son of man'. Secondly, the only interpretation of vss. 2–14 which we have is the angelic interpretation in vss. 17–27: it tells us what the author meant by his symbolism.

We can now establish the original author's interpretation of Dan. 7. It falls naturally into two main parts: first in vss. 2–14 Daniel sees a symbolic dream, then in vss. 17–27 one of the angels in his dream interprets it for him. It begins, however, with a brief narrative framework. Since Daniel has the dream, an angelic interpreter is required: he is put in the dream, and the opening verse gives us the basic information of the date and the authenticating information that Daniel wrote the dream himself. The date under Belshazzar has provoked comment because so far the stories of Dan. 2–6 have appeared to be set in chronological order. Dan. 2 is dated in the second year of Nebuchadnezzar, Dan. 4 must be placed later in his reign, and it is natural to suppose that Dan. 3 took place in the meantime. Dan. 5 is then set under Belshazzar, and Dan. 6 under Darius. However, chronological sequence cannot be followed further, because the destruction of Babylon is not to be foretold after it occurred, and the setting of Dan. 5 and 6 under different kings from those of Dan. 4 and 3 is also to be related to the chiastic literary structure of Dan. 2–7. For these reasons Dan. 7 was to be set under a Babylonian king other than Nebuchadnezzar, and this makes Belshazzar a natural choice.

The symbolic part of the vision falls naturally into two sections. In vss. 2–8 four beasts rise from the turbulent sea; in vss. 9–14 the fourth is destroyed in a divine judgement and sovereignty is given to the man-like figure. The location of the whole scene has been problematical. I shall argue that the beasts come out of the Mediterranean Sea on to the shore of the land of Israel, and that it is here in Israel that the judgement takes place.

The identification of the 'big sea' as the Mediterranean is crucial. There are two points. The Jews were acquainted with several seas, of which the Mediterranean is the biggest, and genuinely big, so it is natural that they should term it 'the big sea'. Secondly, OT evidence, simple and straightforward, shows abundantly that they actually did so, and this is now further confirmed by 1QApGen 21, 16 where 'the big sea' is again clearly the Mediterranean. To explain why the author brings the beasts out of the Mediterranean we must consider the matter from a different perspective. In the OT the sea is used to symbolize the turbulent world and peoples, Isa. 17.12f., Jer. 46.7f. More than that, the sea has mythological overtones—it is the domain of all that is opposed to God. Hence it forms a perfect contrast to the clouds of Dan. 7.13. If Babylonian material lies behind this, it is a long way behind. Nearer at hand (and more recently discovered and canvassed) are the Ugaritic texts, in which Baal does battle with Yamm the sea monster. Above all, clear evidence of this way of thought occurs in the OT, notably at Isa. 27.1; 51.9–10; Pss. 74.13f; 89.10–1. If we consider this now, as we should, from the author's own perspective, it means that in using the sea as a symbol of hostility to God he was drawing on native Israelite imagery, as a conservative defender of the traditional faith might be expected to. Finally there is no inconsistency in locating the dream in a definite place while using material with mythological overtones. It is useful to compare Ps. 104.25–6, where the great sea has Leviathan (the terrible Chaostier l-t-n in his home the Chaosmeer) in it and ships on it. The dramatic imagery is heightened by the use of the four winds to whip up the sea into a storm. The winds are the four cardinal winds. It is not surprising that they are found in the Babylonian epic of creation, but it is more relevant that they were already in use in Israel (Jer. 49.36; Zech. 2.6; 6.5; cf. also Dan. 8.8; 11.4).

In vs. 3 the four beasts come out of the sea on to the land. It may be assumed that they came in a line, because this harmonizes so well with the following description as a whole and especially with the fact that they are described simply as 'first', 'second', 'third', and 'fourth'. That they do come on to the land

18

is not stated explicitly in vs. 3, but it can be deduced from the detailed description of them in vss. 4–8. In vs. 4 the first beast is lifted off the ground; this could happen only if it was on the ground. It is put back on the ground when it is stood on its feet. The fourth beast must also have been on the ground to indulge in its terrifying activities, 'devouring, shattering and trampling the residue with its feet'. The total situation of the second beast, and particularly its position raised up on one side, is also best accounted for by supposing that it is depicted on land in vs. 5. The description of the third beast is perfectly consistent with the supposition that it too was on land.

It is clear from this evidence that when the author described the beasts in vs. 3 as coming up from the sea he actually meant that they came up from the sea on to the land. סלק is a natural word to describe this process, and it will never have occurred to the author that his words could be taken to mean that the beasts might ascend in a mysterious and unfamiliar manner from the middle of the sea. Since he was a Jew, it may be assumed that the land in question is the land of Israel, and this assumption will be confirmed by the location of the scene of judgement in vss. 9ff.

The four beasts symbolize four kingdoms, and Rowley has conclusively demonstrated the correctness of the normal critical identification of them as Babylon, Media, Persia, and Greece.[8] That there was a sequence of four kingdoms which would be succeeded by a fifth is one of the older ideas which our author used. The sequence, which originated in oriental political and religious circles, had earlier begun with Assyria, but the Jews had replaced Assyria with Babylon, a step which led to historical errors in dealing with the kingdom of the Medes.[9] Since this is the reason for the sequence Babylon, Media, Persia, Greece, we should not associate it with the order of the winds in Enuma Elish IV, 40. This illustrates the fragile nature of some of the parallels drawn from Babylonia.

In choosing beasts to symbolize all these foreign kingdoms, the author made use of the traditional Israelite idea that rebellion against God is beastlike rather than manly.[10] The use of beasts to symbolize gentile nations is common enough in the OT, e.g. Jer. 4.7; 5.6; Ezek. 29.3f.; Pss. 68.31; 80.14. The general idea of *Mischwesen* rather than more straightforward

19

animals was widespread in oriental art. For the selection of these particular beasts to symbolize these particular kingdoms the author appears to have been dependent on current astrological symbolism, as this theory explains the choice of all the beasts.[11]

For Babylon, however, the author could look back to the OT to confirm his choice of a lion and even add the symbolism of the eagle—Jer. 4.7; 49.19; 50.17; 49.22; Lam. 4.19; Hab. 1.8; Ezek. 17.3ff. The events of this verse recall the story of Nebuchadnezzar in Dan. 4. This is not coincidental: the beast becomes more like a man to symbolize Nebuchadnezzar's repentance. The symbolism of the first beast is the only one that can provide any events to form a realistic counterbalance to vss. 7–8. This should not be surprising, since most of the stories of Dan. 2–7 are set in Babylon which therefore looms large in this book, and it is not in any way unsatisfactory that the first beast should most nearly balance the last with two less weighty descriptions in between. The only event in vs. 5 is the command to 'eat much flesh', which hardly amounts to more than recognition of Median destructiveness. The rest of the description makes best sense as a colourful description of a voracious bear, rather than an allegory of the Medes. The third beast is another of the *Mischwesen*, being in this respect like the first and fourth, and its details should probably be regarded like those of the second, as riotous description rather than as allegorical detail.

The fourth beast is different from the others, as we are told, so terrible that it is not likened to any real beast. Its details really are allegorical, to enable the author to expound contemporary history with the assumption that the End is at hand. He concentrates our attention on the fourth beast, and above all on the little horn, whose identification as Antiochus Epiphanes is rightly unquestioned among serious critical scholars. The ten horns are the Seleucid line—Alexander the Great, Seleucus I Nicator, Antiochus I Soter, Antiochus II Theos, Seleucus II Callinicus, Seleucus III Ceraunus, Antiochus III the Great, Seleucus IV Philopator, Demetrius I Soter, and Antiochus. The last three are the three horns uprooted before the little horn. Verse 24 explains that this means that the last king (viz. the little horn, Antiochus IV Epiphanes) will put down three of the kings of the fourth kingdom. Seleucus IV was murdered by Heliodorus: clearly our author believed that Antiochus IV Epiphanes was behind it. This belief is reflected also in Dan. 11.21, and was not unreasonable. Demetrius I Soter did not become king until 162. Our author was not aware that this would happen, as he wrote in 166–5, but he classified Demetrius among the kings because he was the eldest son of, and hence the rightful heir to, his father Seleucus IV Philopator. He was a hostage in Rome at the time of Seleucus' murder, so Antiochus IV Epiphanes was able to seize power. This situation fits 'uproot' (אתעקרו, vs. 8) and 'put down' (יהשפיל, vs. 24), the latter a general term deliberately chosen to include this usurpation as well as two murders. For the remaining horn was murdered too. He was a young boy, co-regent of Antiochus IV Epiphanes, done to death on Antiochus' orders in 170 BC. His name too was Antiochus. Probably he was a younger son of Seleucus IV, adopted at the age of 4 or 5 by Antiochus IV Epiphanes when he seized the throne, but some uncertainty over detail must not be allowed to obscure the basic identification.[12]

With this Antiochus we have a coherent and convincing identification for all the fourth beast's horns. A little uncertainty must remain about the beginning of the list. Since the fourth beast is the Macedonian kingdom, it probably began with Alexander, the first Macedonian king and the real destroyer of the third kingdom. The author is not the sort of historian who is likely to have been worried by the fact that the Seleucid era was reckoned from Seleucus I in 312, or by the gap between 323 and 312 (if he knew of it). However the uncertain situation in these years may have led him to take a different view, reckoning the fourth beast as the Macedonian kingdom which destroyed the Persians, and bringing up a list of eleven Syro-Macedonian kings starting perhaps with Antigonus. This degree of uncertainty is due to the looseness of the author's criteria, which will have enabled him to take whichever of these views appeared to him to be historically accurate, and to our ignorance of his precise views of the history of that period. It does not affect the basic identification of the horns as the Seleucid line, nor the detailed working out of the last three of the ten horns. As always, our author speaks with the greatest clarity and detail of his own period. He will have found all his information in earlier sources. Whether they were written or oral we do not know, but at this level we can demonstrate that he used them. They bear no resemblance to Dan. 7 itself, and they help to obviate any need to be vague about the older material which our author used.

Verses 9–14 deal with the divine judgement of the fourth beast and the triumph of the man-like figure. In vss. 3–8 the beasts came out of the Mediterranean Sea on to the land, presumably, we conjectured, the land of Israel. No change of scene is marked at the beginning of vs. 9. We have no right to suppose one, and this is confirmed by the use of the formula 'I was watching until', which elsewhere in this chapter always denotes an action which takes place against the background of the existing scenery—it is difficult to see how it could do otherwise. It follows that the judgement in vss. 9–12 takes place on earth. There are other examples of this at 1 Enoch 1.3–9; 90.20ff.; 4Q Giants; cf. 1 Enoch 25.3. At 1 Enoch 90.20 the land of Israel is specified as the place of judgement, a predictable view among Jews. Thus we have independent contemporary evidence of the view which I have attributed to the author of Dan. 7. If the judgement is on earth, God will have to come to earth in order to carry it out. This is not explicitly stated at vs. 9, because it is not an important aspect of what the author wanted to say. The scene is sufficiently sketched out by declaring that the thrones were put in position and an Ancient of Days took his seat, his arrival for that purpose being assumed. It is stated explicitly in the summary at vs. 22: 'until the Ancient of Days came'. The coming of God for judgement was already part of Old Testament belief (cf. Zech. 14.5; Ps. 96.13; Joel 3. 12).

This interpretation provides an excellent connection between vss. 2–8 and vss. 9–14, and we shall see that from the point of view of their content vss. 9–14 make an organically connected whole. Some scholars have however argued on metrical grounds that a separate source is to be distinguished behind vss. 9, 10, 13 and 14, and Perrin has recently distinguished these verses from the rest of the chapter on the basis of their metric structure alone.[13] This argument is unconvincing, because our understanding of the metre of Semitic poetry is not exact enough to form a sound basis for emending texts or distinguishing literary sources.[14]

22

At vs. 9 the Ancient of Days appears for the first time. He is clearly God, and the description is that of an old man. He is not likened to an ancient of days, for the beings described as 'like' something are all pure symbols; God really exists. Moreover he had existed for a very long time, and this piece of imagery should not be held to imply that he had not existed for ever before—we are still dealing with imagery rather than precise description, and a being who was 'from of old' (Ps. 118.2) was necessarily ancient of days. If there are echoes of Ugarit they are far behind. Man was made in the image of God, and there were old men in Israel, so that the use of imagery taken from the dignity of old age should not cause surprise.

The plural 'thrones' are for the heavenly court to sit on (vs. 10b). Mowinckel[15] used them to argue that the man-like figure originally took part in the judgement, but this left him with nowhere for the court to sit, and it should be accepted that the man-like figure does not take part in the judgement because the text does not give him this function. The divine throne is altogether more splendid and fiery; the imagery is in the tradition of Ezekiel, and had been Israelite for some time. So had the heavenly host, seen already by Micaiah ben Imlah (1 Kings 22.19): God would not come alone for judgement (e.g. Zech. 14.5).

Elsewhere in our meagre sources דִּינָא means 'judgement', but here 'the abstract passes into the concrete', as Montgomery notes, comparing κριτήριον and *iudicium*.[16] The meaning must be that 'the court sat'. The existence of a heavenly court should be no surprise in view of the common OT idea that God has a heavenly council associated with him (e.g. Job 1, Ps. 82). As on earth, the court does not sit down until the Judge has done so; the intervening lines are simply an extended description of the Judge, together with his many attendants. The judgement then proceeds with the opening of the books. Divine books were a traditional item widespread in the ancient Near East and found also in the OT (e.g. Isa. 4.3; Mal. 3.16; Ps. 69.29).

With the scene thus set, the narrative proceeds without further ado, let alone any change of scenery, straight to the destruction of the fourth beast. Vs. 11a picks up the events of vs. 8, the description of the fourth beast and in particular its little horn having been interrupted only for the setting of the judgement scene.[17] The whole narrative is therefore perfectly coherent, and could not be much tauter without detracting from the splendour of the judging deity and his court. The whole of the fourth beast is necessarily destroyed. It should be clear that the destruction of the little horn itself would not have been sufficient, as it would have left the hated Macedonians still in power, and that the destruction of the whole fourth beast necessarily involves the destruction of its little horn. The first three beasts are not destroyed; no interpretation is given, but one may be surmised. Babylon, Media, and Persia will remain as separate states, serving Israel, whereas the Seleucid empire will actually be destroyed. The mention of this completes the symbolic picture of the judgement in vs. 12, and was desirable after the symbolic grandeur of the appearance of the first three beasts in the vision, but the reality of the survival of these states was not important enough to the author to warrant separate mention in the interpretation where, as in Dan. 2, it is subsumed in the general picture of the triumph of Israel, who are then served by all nations.

The destruction of the fourth beast is the essential point of the judgement, and an essential preliminary to the passing of sovereignty to the man-like figure in vss. 13–4. The full introductory formula at the beginning of vs. 13 marks an important event, but not a change of scenery. Since the scene is set on earth it follows that the man-like figure comes downwards with the clouds. But who is he? His identification has been the subject of lengthy debate, and this is an appropriate place to try to bring that debate to an end.

In vss. 13–4 the man-like figure is brought before the Ancient of Days and given sovereignty: all nations will serve him and his kingdom will last for ever. This is summarized briefly in what is said of the Saints of the Most High in vss. 18 and 22, and it is explicitly stated of the people of the Saints of the Most High in vs. 27. It is natural, and it is important that it is the case, that this longest formulation of the triumph of the Saints echoes the language of vs. 14 most accurately. What the man-like figure gets in vs. 14, the people of the Saints of the Most High get in vs. 27; they get nothing which was not granted to him. He corresponds to them also in the structure of the dream and its interpretation. He receives the kingdom from

God after the destruction of the fourth beast: they receive the kingdom from God after the destruction of Antiochus Epiphanes, who was to be the last king of the kingdom which the fourth beast symbolized. It follows from this that the man-like figure is a symbol of the Saints of the Most High. Moreover he is a pure symbol, that is to say, he is not a real being who exists outside Daniel's dream; he is only a symbolic being within the dream. This is clear for two reasons. In the first place, the author provided an interpretation of the symbolism of this dream, which reaches a climax with the full description of the triumph of the people of the Saints of the Most High in vs. 27. This triumph was very important to the author, and it corresponds precisely to what is said of the man-like figure in vs. 14, but it does not mention him. If the author had viewed him as a real being who would lead or deliver the Saints, he must have mentioned him here. The second reason is that on this view the basic structure of the symbolism is consistent. The first four kingdoms are represented by beast-like figures, the fifth by a man-like figure. It is not suggested that the beast-like figures really existed somewhere; we only attribute consistency to the symbolism by concluding that the man-like figure was not a real being either.

The author evidently thought that in interpreting the man-like figure as the Saints of the Most High he was making his meaning clear. Unfortunately, however, the meaning of this term is also a subject of considerable debate. I shall argue that he meant the Jewish people, specifically the faithful Jews attacked by Antiochus Epiphanes,[18] and I assume this result now. In selecting a man to symbolize the true Israel, the author was making use of some of the simplest and most basic concepts of his native Israelite religion. He believed that Israel was the chosen people of the only God, who was faithful and would deliver them. They were a holy people, and if they had done wrong (cf. Dan. 9) they repented, and because they were a righteous remnant not rebelling against God they would soon be triumphant. To symbolize this the author made use of the traditional Israelite idea that man is superior to the beasts, an idea which is expressed with great clarity in the creation narrative of Gen. 1 and in Ps. 8.6–8. From it grew the symbolism of opposition to God as brutish, and obedience to him as manly

25

(e.g. Ps. 73.21f.).[19] The author had used these ideas already in Dan. 4, where Nebuchadnezzar's pride led to his condemnation to a beast-like existence. When he repented and acknowledged the sovereignty of God, Nebuchadnezzar was restored to manhood. This incident is reflected in Dan. 7.4, and these same Israelite ideas explain the author's choice of a man as a symbol of the true and obedient Israel in 7.13. Moreover the fact that man is traditionally superior to the beasts explains why the author chose the man-like figure as a symbol of the Jews only when they are in triumph, not when they suffer.

It is this symbolism, consistently maintained, which explains the apparently anomalous position of vss. 21–2, and which necessitated the summary interpretation of the symbolic part of the dream in vss. 17–18. If he was to maintain this symbolism, the author could not portray the man-like figure as suffering and humiliated by a beast. Therefore there is no mention of the suffering of Israel in the account of the fourth beast and its little horn at vss. 7–8, even though this account is relatively prolonged. The author had no symbol for Israel suffering, so the sufferings of Israel could not be portrayed until the man-like figure had been interpreted. This is the main function of the summary interpretation of vss. 17–18. The author, living among and writing for the Saints of the Most High, provided in these verses the interpretation of the man-like figure in a way which will have been much clearer to his readers than it has been to contemporary scholarship. Once this interpretation was supplied, Daniel could see the suffering of the Saints, and this follows immediately, tacked on to his question in vss. 19–20. This lengthy repetition of the description of the fourth beast and especially its little horn, in the form of Daniel's question to the interpreting angel, thus has two functions. It draws attention to the fourth beast and particularly to its little horn, and it prepares the way directly for the new piece of visionary material in vs. 21. Now that the man-like figure has been interpreted as the Saints of the Most High, Daniel can see the little horn making war on them, a piece of visionary material symbolizing the persecutions and war brought on them by Antiochus Epiphanes. Verse 22 brings added clarity and emphasis to the most important event of the chapter, the triumph of the Saints.

Thus a proper understanding of the author's symbolism

enables us to see clearly the point of the structure of this chapter. The order of events in vss. 17ff. also increases the dramatic effect of the narrative, drawing attention as it does so to the activities of the little horn, under whom the author and his comrades lived and suffered. It results in the final triumph of the Saints being emphatically stated three times in the second half of the chapter. The author will no doubt have been well satisfied with his literary and dramatic solution of the problem he set himself by his choice of the man-like figure to represent the true Israel.

His choice was not a necessary one, in the sense that other possibilities were open to him. The author of 1 Enoch 89–110, like the later author of 4 Ezra 12, used animals in a different and more essentially neutral symbolic sense, and our author could have done the same. He had known many people martyred, so he might have produced a suffering man. However, his choice of the man-like figure as a suitable symbol for the triumph of the true Israel, is, as we have seen, a perfectly intelligible choice made on the basis of ideas found elsewhere in Jewish theology and used by him elsewhere in his book. That this was the choice that he made is demonstrated by the evidence of the text of this chapter, whose symbolism and structure are otherwise unintelligible.

What about כ? 'כ retains its original nominal character as "the like of" '.[20] It was 'like' a human being because in Daniel's dream it looked like one: however it was not in fact a human being, it was a purely symbolical being. This is true also of the first and third beasts in vss. 4 and 6, though it is easily over-looked because of their peculiar features. It is true also of the second beast, which has none, but our author's habitual flexi-bility of expression resulted in his using a different expression here, though it is one with the same meaning, דמיה ל. The same is not said of the fourth beast because it is to be portrayed as so awful that there is nothing to compare it with, in appearance as in frightfulness. The other important being in the dream is the Ancient of Days; here there is no כ because this being in fact exists.

Thus the use of כ in this chapter is consistent. It is true that it is used a little differently in the description of angels in 8–12, but this does not matter, even if these chapters are from the

27

same author. How different the usage is, is a function of the finesse of the analytical technique employed, not only of the primary evidence. If we are content to say that here too כ is used in expressions of comparison, then the uses in 8.15 etc. are the same as in 7.13. If we employ a finer analytical technique which differentiates between the use of כ in 7.13 to describe a being which looked like a man in every way but did not in fact exist outside Daniel's dream, in 8.15 etc. to describe the real appearance of real angels, and in 7.4, 6 to describe beings which looked partly like and partly unlike something, we must add that all this falls within the semantic area of כ, and that variation within the normal semantic area of any word is normal in any author. Such an analysis cannot therefore constitute a valid argument either against the interpretation I have proposed or against the common authorship of all these passages.

בר אנש was described by Driver as 'a choice semi-poetical expression'.[21] Evidence subsequently gathered, though still meagre, has made it clear that it was a normal term for 'man'.[22] The singular does not recur in Daniel, but the plural is found twice, 2.38; 5.21. Reasons for the author's choice of it here can be plausibly surmised. Against אנש, he wanted an individual rather than the species: against גבר, the less definite expression is perhaps the more suitable for a pure symbol. Montgomery's judgement appears sound: 'the expression of both category and individual was best expressed by בר אנש'.[23] Ps. 8 may have been in mind, but it is not the coincidence of בן אדם that suggests this so much as the content of vs. 6, an expression of that sentiment which explains our author's choice of a man as a symbol of Israel.

Daniel saw the man-like figure coming down 'with the clouds of heaven'. His heavenly origin is right and proper for a symbol of the chosen people of God; the idea that it makes him a divine being results from too rigid an interpretation of other texts. There are no previous examples of purely symbolic beings coming with the clouds in the OT because there are no previous examples of purely symbolic beings coming at all. It marks a perfect contrast with the beasts emerging from the sea. They are forces basically hostile to God; the chosen people symbolized by the man-like figure are God's own. The position of 'with the clouds of heaven' immediately after 'behold' properly draws the eye of the reader like that of the visionary up into the sky—the scene so far has been set entirely down on earth. This does not usually happen after אֲרוּ, and hence the unusual order of words. At vs. 2 an identical order of words was not required because the author began with a statement about the sea, which corresponds symbolically to the clouds, and could thus use 'and' to add the information that the beast emerged from it.

There is insufficient reason to suppose that the author avoided putting the man-like figure on the clouds. Since he is coming down to earth it may be that the author considered his passage most naturally rendered with עִם, but neither he nor the LXX translator can be shown to have had the finesse to see substantial difference between עִם and עַל, ἐπί and μετά. The LXX translator used ἐπί because that was how he saw the man-like figure coming, and *religionsgeschichtlich* evidence makes his view unsurprising. The subsequent exegetical tradition shows a good variety of prepositions, and this does not appear to have any organic connection with different interpretations of the man-like figure. He is then brought before the Ancient of Days by some of the divine servants already mentioned in vs. 10. The LXX says this explicitly, but this must be the meaning of the Aramaic text as well, for they are the appropriate beings for this task, and there is no one else there to do it.

The man-like figure is then given dominion, glory, and sovereignty. He cannot represent 'the rule of the saints, or the saints as invested with authority'[24] because he comes first and then is invested with kingship and authority. As the interpretation makes clear, he simply represents the Saints. Despite being invested with such dominion, glory, and sovereignty, he is not enthroned. He is not in any way confused with the heavenly beings who constitute the court, and who do indeed sit on thrones. He is given the sovereignty to symbolize the giving of sovereignty to Israel, and every Jew knew that, so far from detracting from the sovereignty of God, this would demonstrate that God was in fact king of all the world.

Thus the corporate interpretation of the man-like figure as a symbol of the Saints of the Most High enables us to give a coherent and consistent account of the symbolism and structure of the whole of Dan. 7. Other identifications have, however, been so abundant in the scholarship of recent years that a critical survey of them is a necessary complement to the exposition of the Danielic text. The commonest of these other views is that the man-like figure is the Messiah. This view has a long tradition from the pre-critical era. One of the best recent expositions of it is that of Dhanis.[25]

Dhanis recognizes that the man-like figure represents Israel, but he argues that it represents the Messiah too. He notes that in the angelic interpretation the beasts are interpreted as kings (מלכין, vs. 17, where the reading מלכן with versional support is unlikely to be correct) as well as kingdoms. The author could in fact say 'kings' in his summary because like everyone else at that time he believed that a king was representative of his kingdom.[26] Dhanis quotes two straightforward examples from the book of Daniel: 2.39 from the same author, and, what is perhaps the most striking of all, from the Hebrew part of the book, 8.21, 'And the he-goat is the king of Greece; and the great horn between its eyes is the first king'. It does not however follow from this that our author believed that Israel would have a king at all. Messianic beliefs were not universal, and the fact that our author did not share them is demonstrated by his failure to mention the Messiah anywhere, above all in his interpretation of the man-like figure. The author of the longer account of Israel's deliverance in Dan. 12 does not mention any Messiah either. It is to be concluded therefore that our author belonged to a group which did not expect a Messiah. From Dan. 10–12 we may conclude that Michael was thought of as the guardian angel of Israel; but her only king, in our author's view, will have been God. Transcendental features of the symbolism cannot be held against this because in themselves they need not involve transcendence in the being symbolized, and the author's interpretation shows that no transcendental being is involved in this particular case, but only God's chosen people whom he held in the highest possible regard. Some scholars have made use of the idea of 'corporate personality' to explain how the man-like figure can symbolize both the Messiah and the people of Israel, but this idea cannot be helpful until it is shown that the man-like figure is in fact an individual as well as a symbol of a corporate entity.[27]

Dhanis further observes that the interpreting angel never

makes statements such as 'The Son of man is the Saints of the Most High', or 'Those who receive the kingdom are the Saints of the Most High', but he says only 'The Saints of the Most High will receive the kingdom'. This observation, which recurs throughout the modern literature on Dan. 7, is perfectly correct but leads nowhere very significant. In the same way the author never says 'Now the little horn is another king'. His style of writing interpretations is not to do this with every item. Having set up the ten horns and briefly interpreted them, he assumes quite correctly that he simply has to proceed 'and another one will arise after them' and we shall all know that he is referring to the little horn. Similarly he assumes that, if he proceeds from the beasts in vs. 17 to the triumph of the Saints of the Most High, and from the destruction of the little horn in vs. 26 to the triumph of the people of the Saints of the Most High in vs. 27 in language very similar to that of vs. 14, we shall all know he is interpreting the man-like figure. His was not an unreasonable assumption, and it has been called into question only by interpreters who do not share his ideas. He did not imagine that the man-like figure would be interpreted as the Messiah because he and the other members of his group did not expect the Messiah, because he assumed everyone would realize that the interpretation he wrote was really intended to explain what his symbolism meant, and because his interpretation supplies the expected triumph of his group as a very precise equivalent of the triumph of the man-like figure.

Another suggestion is that the man-like figure should be identified as Michael. The classical exposition of this view is that of N. Schmidt, and it has been revived recently by Collins.[28] In a passage which has exercised considerable influence on subsequent scholarship, Schmidt notes the examples of expressions of the type 'one like a son of man' used in the Book of Daniel to designate angels. At 8.15 Gabriel is described as 'like the appearance of a man'; at 8.16 he has the 'voice of a man'; at 10.16 he is described as 'like the resemblance of the sons of man', at 10.18 'like the appearance of a man'; at 3.25 one of the four 'men' is likened to a son of God; at 9.21 the angel is referred to as 'the man Gabriel'; at 10.5 he is 'a man clothed in linen' and likewise at 12.6, 7. Schmidt adds references to Rev. 19.14; Ezek. 1.26; 1 Enoch 87.2, to show that the representation of angels in human form is comprehensible in the thought and usage of this period, and he deduces that the man-like figure in Dan. 7.13 is an angel too.

As applied to Dan. 7.13, this argument is logically unsound. Let us first grant Schmidt's supposition that Dan. 7 was written by the same man as Dan. 8–12. From the fact that the author described angels in human terms, it does not follow that he could not describe anything else as 'man-like' as well. On this logical point Schmidt's argument collapses. It is even less improbable that a different author should use the same image for a piece of pure symbolism. That Michael is the heavenly prince of Israel in Dan. 10.21; 12.1 is to be granted, but it follows from the evidence of Dan. 7 itself that the author of Dan. 7 did not regard him as important enough to mention.

Collins' argument differs chiefly in that he regards the 'holy ones' in Dan. 7.18, 22 as the angels, though this leads him into some difficulty at 7.27.[29] This makes it more natural for him to interpret the man-like figure as their representative, but his argument is no real improvement on that of Schmidt. He repeats the references to Dan. 8.15; 9.21; 10.5; 12.6, and does not explain the absence of Michael in Dan. 7.27.

Zevitt has interpreted the man-like figure as Gabriel,[30] but his argument suffers from the fatal flaw of being dependent on Schmidt to show that the man-like figure is an angel. His interpretation of Dan. 9.21, 'the man Gabriel whom I saw in the vision at the beginning', as a reference to Dan. 7.13 is based on a definition of 'vision' (חָזוֹן) remote from the book of Daniel. The reference is to Dan. 8.16, where the appearance of the angel Gabriel to interpret the symbolism is still part of the vision. It need hardly be added that Zevitt does not explain the absence of Gabriel from the interpretative section of Dan. 7.

Black has used the biblical application of terms such as 'one like the appearance of a man' together with Feuillet's assertion of direct dependence on Ezek. 1 to support his belief that 'in effect . . . Dan. 7 knows of two divinities, the Head of Days and the Son of Man'.[31] The author of Dan. 7 was a pious Jew, so that clear evidence would be required for us to suppose that he had produced a second divinity, but no purely divine terms are used of the man-like figure, and he is clearly subordinate to the Ancient of Days. Feuillet exaggerated the dependence on

Ezekiel, partly because he still believed that the term 'Son of man' was an abnormal semi-poetic expression. The phrase 'like the appearance of a man' is suitable for comparing anything to a man, and the early biblical examples could not limit its potential in the work of any native speaker of Hebrew or Aramaic. Consequently the increasing quantity of non-biblical material has produced an example of its application to a phenomenon quite different from the *numen praesens et visibile* of Yahweh theophany or an angelic theophany, namely the appearance of the moon during the night (1 Enoch 78.17). Dan. 7.9ff. really does contain a throne theophany of Yahweh in the old Israelite tradition found especially also in the book of Ezekiel, and it is a theophany of the one God, not of two; moreover the symbolic heavenly origin of the man-like figure may not be applied to produce the deification of the Saints because it symbolizes them but does not describe them.

Apart from the anonymous Messiah, three human beings have been suggested as candidates for the man-like figure. Gaster suggested Moses.[32] His unsatisfactory approach typifies all too many attempts to get behind the text of Daniel. He comments on vss. 9–18, 'It is absolutely incoherent and confused. In order to understand it properly, some order must be put into that confusion so characteristic of a dream told incoherently'.[33] But the incoherence and confusion lie in the mind of the researcher who cannot understand the text, and the function of such remarks is to permit an arbitrariness in method whereby the scholar reads into or behind the text what he first expected to find there. His comment on vs. 9 is reminiscent of his ancient predecessors: 'Evidently the word thrones is not to be taken as plural'.[34] Equally arbitrary is the comment on vs. 14: 'The glory of God, His might and power, is described in Dan. 7.14, which has nothing to do with the Son of man, and should follow immediately after God sitting in judgement'. This is not interpretation of the Danielic text, but simple rejection of it. The identification of the man-like figure as Moses follows on the most general of grounds, its only particularity being the unconvincing assertion of direct dependence on Deut. 32.2–4. Gaster uses very late evidence to fill out his picture of Moses, without the careful discrimination which must be employed if such late material is to be handled convincingly, and his

33

production of Moses on a cloud suffers from the same fault as more orthodox attempts to identify the figure by means of its cloud. Yet the late date of some of Gaster's evidence is a less fundamental fault than the way in which he distorts and in the last analysis brushes aside the evidence of the Danielic text which he is supposed to be interpreting.

Sahlin has suggested that the man-like figure is Judas Maccabaeus.[35] The fact that the author never mentions Judas Maccabaeus is a fatal objection to this view. Also the disappearance of this view is especially difficult to explain because it fits so beautifully into the Syrian tradition of interpretation, which saw the Maccabean victory under Judas as the meaning of the triumph of the Saints of the Most High, and could easily have seen Judas Maccabaeus as a type of Christ.[36]

Schmid has suggested that the man-like figure is none other than Daniel himself.[37] Schmid's view is dependent on his redaction history of Dan. 7, which is similar to those discussed above, and unconvincing for the same reasons.[38] It is precisely the removal of the interpretation of the man-like figure which makes its interpretation difficult. Schmid then seeks the source of the designation 'one like a son of man' in Dan. 8.17 where Daniel is addressed as 'son of man'. But this term is not a title nor an exclusive description of anyone, and the fact that it is applied to Daniel (probably by a later author, but that is a separate point) does not supply the identification of the person involved when the description is used elsewhere. It is a normal term for man, and the fact that Daniel, like Ezekiel before him, could be addressed by means of it is not inconsistent with the use of human symbolism in a different way in a separate chapter.

The remaining identification of significance is that which regards the man-like figure as derived from widespread concepts of an *Urmensch* in the ancient Near East. This is important because if the author of Daniel knew a glorious individual figure, 'the Man' or 'the Son of man', it could be this figure which was known to later sources and referred to by Jesus himself, and this could be the case even if our author has used this individual figure as a symbol in Dan. 7 itself. The weakness of this view is that this 'Son of man' figure does not actually occur in any Jewish source. I shall argue here that the present

34

text of Daniel does not provide sufficient evidence of its existence in Israel. I shall argue similarly in the case of other texts as I deal with them, and draw the results of these discussions together at the end of ch. 5, where I shall argue that there was no Son of man concept in Judaism.

How far this interpretative school depended on its own inability to understand the Danielic text is evident in the seminal work of Gunkel, who used the incomprehensibility and un-Jewish nature of the man-like figure as a major argument for his conjecture that in the myth 'Son of man' was the title for the conqueror of God.[39] But the outstanding difficulties listed by Gunkel have now all been solved, and the structure and symbolism of the chapter have become clear when it is seen against its native Jewish background. Thus the ground is removed from Gunkel's conjecture. Little enough evidence could in any case be drawn on in its favour. The number of genuine similarities between Dan. 7 and the Babylonian material, whether assessed in its original form or as it supposedly recurred in Israel, were too few to demonstrate dependence, and some of them, such as the use of רוּחַ, are in themselves common use of material so widespread that its recurrence in independent works was inevitable.

This same mythological background was also utilized by Schmidt, who in suggesting that the man-like figure was Michael argued that his prototype was Marduk.[40] Subsequent scholars have produced a series of different suggestions, which underlines the methodological inadequacy of their work. Beginning from an inability to understand the origin of the man-like figure in Daniel and the 'Son of man' in the Similitudes of Enoch, they have pointed out similarities to Dan. 7 in a variety of mythological sources in the ancient Near East. But a few similarities are not proof of origin, and the uncontrolled nature of the use of this evidence is decisively against all these views. In recent years Canaan has replaced Babylon as the main source of influence to be suggested. This is instructive. The similarities with the Babylonian material are still there, but now appear as inadequate, which they always were. But the Canaanite arguments are of the same type, relying on a few similarities, and having to posit an Israelite conception different from that found in any source because existing Israelite sources

35

do not have any concept sufficiently like that of the earlier myths. Moreover the assembling of an apparently imposing list of differing myths as evidence of a widespread concept of an *Urmensch* used by Daniel is misleading; the need to assemble such a list of foreign material is really due to the absence of sufficiently clear evidence of the requisite kind anywhere.

A few examples will suffice. C. H. Kraeling,[41] beginning from the assumption that there was a Son of man concept in Judaism, argued that in order to demonstrate that the Anthropos constituted the origin of the Son of man he had to show (1) that the Jewish figure in question cannot be explained adequately as a product of Hebrew thought; (2) that it and the proposed foreign prototype are basically homogeneous; (3) that the suggested prototype was actually adaptable to the expression of those Jewish ideas which it served to convey in the new environment. The trouble here lies right at the beginning, where his assumption that there was a Jewish Son of man concept which cannot be explained adequately as a product of Hebrew thought rests on his inability to understand Dan. 7 and the Similitudes of Enoch. With the failure of (1) the foreign prototype becomes irrelevant. Then 'basically homogeneous' conceals so many differences that only his difficulties in understanding the Jewish documents themselves could make his second point look even plausible.

Bentzen has suggested that Dan. 7 is an eschatologizing of Ps. 2, which he thinks is derived from the enthronement ceremony celebrated at the New Year in Israel.[42] There is some uncertainty as to whether there ever was an Israelite enthronement festival; there is no doubt that when Daniel was written no such ceremony had been celebrated in Israel for centuries. Dan. 7 has important contacts of thought with Ps. 2, but there is not sufficient evidence of the direct dependence that Bentzen seeks. On the contrary, there are important differences which he has to minimize. Above all Dan. 7 has no proper equivalent to the Anointed One in the psalm: it is simply tendentious to claim that the man-like figure is his equivalent, when he is a symbol of the Saints and is not enthroned at all. Bentzen supposes that one of the thrones mentioned in vs. 9 is reserved for him, but this is not stated in Daniel and has to be assumed to make Dan. 7 more like its posited source.

Bentzen's position has been further developed by J. A. Emerton.[43] Here again failure to understand the Similitudes of Enoch and 4 Ezra 13 is important, for Emerton puts them together with Dan. 7 and Sib. Or. V, 414–33 to get the Son of man imagery whose origin he seeks. Emerton then assimilates 'the Son of man' to a divine figure. This is just what the man-like figure is not. The author of Dan. 7 was a traditionalist defending the ancient Israelite faith against foreign encroachment; nothing he says leads one to the improbable notion that he chose a time of desperate persecution for his faith to introduce a second deity into the monotheistic faith of Israel. The clouds function as a means of transport for the man-like figure and symbolize the fact that Israel was the chosen people of God. That in the Old Testament God comes with them is no excuse for turning another figure coming with them into a deity. God may be likened to a man in Ezek. 1.26; that men are like men is more obvious, that angels are likened to men in Daniel and elsewhere is well-known, and that the author used a man as a pure symbol of the people of Israel is now comprehensible. Jebusite conjectures cannot be determinative for the views of a second-century conservative and Emerton's reliance on Canaanite evidence leads him to make a classic formulation of the faults of this line of investigation. 'It is not explicitly stated that the Son of man kills the fourth beast, but the Canaanite parallels suggest that this occurred in the underlying myth.'[44] This is to twist Daniel forcibly in a Canaanite direction. The fact is that in the Danielic text the man-like figure does not kill the fourth beast at all. The judgement is carried out by God alone, with the assistance of such assessors as may be. But the man-like figure does not come on stage until after the destruction of the fourth beast, so that he can symbolize the Israelite triumph. Canaanite parallels suggest otherwise because they are not sufficiently parallel; above all the pious Jew has not given us a second God.

Mowinckel argues from the fact that 'with the clouds of heaven' is not interpreted that the author must have been using an existing mythological figure from which he got this item that he did not use.[45] But from this it follows only that our author's interpretative style was not as rigid as Mowinckel imagines it should have been. The clouds perform an important symbolic function, associating the Saints of the Most High with God by providing their symbol with a heavenly origin, and they function as a means of transport. They are not interpreted simply because the author was not constructing a precise allegory. The origin of the beasts 'from the sea' is not interpreted, the peculiar features of the first three beasts are not interpreted, much of the symbolism of vss. 9–10 is not interpreted either. This is not because the author could not understand his own symbolism, or took it over wholesale from a previous source. It is because he had sufficient literary and dramatic sense to construct a colourful dream to put forward his message. In the interpretation he concentrates on essentials. If the symbolic part of his dream were deprived of all features that do not appear in the interpretative part, it would be too feeble to form an effective piece of literature. That the author drew on previous sources for his imagery is true enough, but we should not assume he lacked creative originality by supposing that he must have drawn it wholesale in large units.

The mythological interpretation of the man-like figure is therefore to be rejected. Beginning from an inability to interpret Jewish texts against a background of Jewish thought, it has utilized weak similarities in order to assert dependence on foreign material so alien as to necessitate frequent assumptions that the Danielic and other texts must once have meant something other than what they mean in their surviving form. These assumptions have not been justified.

One of the most important recent theories about the man-like figure is that in some real sense he suffers. This theory arises from the Son of man problem in the New Testament, and its application to the text of Daniel is forced and unconvincing. It appears to have been broached first by C. F. D. Moule.[46] He argues that in Dan. 7, as it now stands, 'the saints are *symbolized by the Human One*—not identified with, but represented by him: and if the saints are partially and temporarily eclipsed, only to be subsequently glorified, then exactly the same may be presumed to be appropriately predicated of the Human Figure'. It may not be presumed at all. It is nowhere stated, and it is inconsistent with his choice of a man as a symbol of triumph. The author could easily have said it in a further extension at vs. 8, which he could have had instead of the present insertion

38

at vss. 21–2. He did not do so, both for dramatic effect and because he in fact chose his man symbol as a symbol to portray Israel's triumph. 'If so, then "the Son of Man" already means "the representative of God's chosen people, destined through suffering to be exalted".' There are two further reasons why it does not: one is that the man-like figure is a pure symbol, so that the term 'representative' conceals an important difference between this figure and what Moule regards as the 'Son of man' in the Gospels. The second is that '*the* Son of man' does not occur in Daniel at all: כבר אנש is a figure like a son of man.

Moule's position has been further developed by M. D. Hooker.[47] Hooker realizes that the author 'may well have felt that the human figure was an inappropriate symbol for the people of Israel during their tribulation', but she nevertheless continues 'but the Son of man clearly represents in some way the saints of the Most High, and there can be no doubt at all that they suffered'. They did; but when the author meant this he said it, in vs. 21. She goes on 'unless we detach him from them and regard him as a separate figure with independent experiences we cannot dissociate him from what happens to them'. But it is not that the man-like figure has independent experiences; he is a pure symbol with no experiences at all, other than the symbolic ones in vss. 13–14. To that extent he is a separate figure and he is to be dissociated from the sufferings of the Saints. The author's hope of deliverance by God was not 'based on the fact that Israel is already Son of man'. It was based on his faith in a reliable God who would deliver his people. Our author did not believe that Israel is, was, or would be 'the Son of man', he simply chose a man-like figure to symbolize Israel in triumph. We should not suppose that he believed Israel was 'the Son of man' because that is not what he says; and he does not say that 'the Son of man', or the man-like figure, suffers either.

The conclusions of this discussion may now be summarized. The man-like figure is a pure symbol of the 'Saints of the Most High', the faithful people of Israel. In choosing this symbol of them our author used old and simple Jewish ideas. He chose it to represent them coming in triumph, so that they are not mentioned as suffering under the little horn until the man-like figure has been interpreted as the Saints of the Most High. His coming in triumph to be given sovereignty by God symbolizes the forthcoming triumph of the Jews over Antiochus Epiphanes and the Macedonians, a triumph which was to be achieved by means of divine intervention.

An interpreting angel now appears in Daniel's dream. He undertakes to provide the interpretation of what Daniel has seen, and goes straight into the summary interpretation of vss. 17–18, where he says that the four beasts represent four kings who will arise from the earth. This is simply a way of saying that they represent the four kingdoms. The king represented his kingdom in a very straightforward way, and Daniel's interpreters often identify the beasts either as kingdoms or by means of their most outstanding kings, evidently regarding both as symbolically interchangeable.[48] The main function of this summary interpretation is to identify the man-like figure as the Saints of the Most High, so that Daniel can see them suffer under the little horn before a fuller interpretation is supplied.[49] Most interpreters have supposed that the Saints of the Most High are the Jewish people, but in recent years their identification has been a subject of considerable debate, and the opinion has been growing that they are in fact angels. Stated by Procksh, this view has been properly developed by Noth and Dequeker, and refuted by Brekelmans and Hasel.[50] One of the most significant statements of the evidence is that of Dequeker, who in his second attempt to advocate the view that the 'Saints' are angels has to admit 'Reading the verses 21 and 25 for themselves, without taking into account the *Redaktionsgeschichte* of the chapter, one comes necessarily to the conclusion that "the Saints" must be understood as the faithful Jewish people, persecuted by Antiochus Epiphanes'. Quite so, and Noth had already admitted as much.[51] This is important, because it means that even if Noth and Dequeker are right, the interpretation of the Saints as the Jews was held in 166–165 B.C., and this supplies a *terminus a quo* for the corporate interpretation of the man-like figure as a symbol of the Jewish people. It is also an admission which undermines much of their argument.

The fundamental statement is that of 7.27. It is the author's longest and most explicit statement of the triumph of the Saints, and here he calls them 'the people of the Saints of the Most High'. The use of the term עַם, 'people', enables us to deduce

that this is the Jewish people in triumph. Noth argued that
עַם here means 'host', and sought to justify this by appealing
to 1QH III, 21. In that passage, however, we must follow
most scholars (including Dequeker) in interpreting עַם as עִם,
'with'. This makes excellent sense, saying that the psalmist will
be united in community with the angels.[52] עַם is never employed
either at Qumran or in the OT with reference to angels or
celestial beings. In Dan. 7.27 it should be taken in a straightforward way as a reference to the Jewish people. The triumph
of 'the people of the Saints of the Most High' in vs. 27 is clearly
the same event as the triumph of 'the Saints of the Most High'
in vss. 18 and 22, and of 'the Saints' in vs. 22. Therefore these
phrases also refer to the Jewish people. Therefore the expression
עַם קְדִישֵׁי עֶלְיוֹנִין in vs. 27 begins with a use of the construct
state equivalent to an epexegetical genitive and it may be
rendered (overliterally, to bring out the construction and
meaning) 'the people which consists of the Saints of the Most
High'.

This makes excellent sense of all the author's statements
about the Saints of the Most High. The summary interpretation
of vss. 17–18 provides a summary statement of their triumph.
At vs. 21 Daniel sees the little horn making war on the Saints.
Antiochus' persecution of and war against the Jewish people
called forth the Book of Daniel, so that prominent mention of the
war is entirely natural. Verse 22 has the controversial statement

וְדִינָא יְהִב לְקַדִּישֵׁי עֶלְיוֹנִין

Most scholars have argued that it means that judgement was
given in favour of the Saints of the Most High, but some have
suggested that it means that judgement was given into the hands
of the Saints of the Most High, that is, they became the judges.
Both are sound Aramaic, and there is no justification for
emending the text. LXX and Theod. both imply יְהַב, but
none of the versions helps with the point in dispute. Parallels
are adduced from Wisd. 3.8; Matt. 19.28; 1 Cor. 6.2; Rev. 20.4:
the first especially suggests what our author might have
believed, but none tells us what he in fact meant, for this must
be extracted from the text of Daniel, which is decisively in
favour of the first possibility. That judgement was entered in
favour of the man-like figure is presupposed by the symbolism

of vss. 13–14. That judgement was given in favour of the Saints is presupposed in their triumph in vss. 18 and 27. The same cannot be said of the other view. In the symbolic account, God judges with the assistance of his angelic court. The man-like figure does not judge at all. In the interpretative comments, there is no suggestion of the Saints becoming the judges in vs. 18, which might be dismissed as too short for that purpose, or in vss. 26–7, where its absence would be remarkable. Moreover, the destruction is the result of a judgement that must be given before the destruction can take place. The Saints of the Most High would be in no position to be judges until they had been delivered.

The next statement about the Saints is at 7.25,

ולקדישי עליונין יבלא.

'and he will wear out the Saints of the Most High'. This is the interpretation of vs. 21, so that some reference to Antiochus' activity against the Jewish people is required, and comparative philology provides an appropriate sense for יבלא. Brekelmans pointed out that the Akkadian balu/belu is used in the intensive of destroying people, and Hasel notes the similar use of the Hebrew בלה. Noth's objection that יבלא in the sense of 'wear out, destroy' should not have a personal object is therefore inaccurate.[53] Antiochus offended God and attacked the people of God, so that the parallelism here is perfectly sound and may not be held to favour the view that the Saints are angels. It is difficult to be certain whether this verse concludes with another statement about the Saints, because the subject of 'and they shall be given' is problematical. Is it the Saints of the Most High from vs. 25a, or is it the previous words 'times and the Law'? On balance, it is perhaps better to take the Saints as the subject, on the ground that this makes the more straightforward sense. The whole verse now makes excellent sense in accordance with the view that the Saints of the Most High are the Jewish people.[54] To interpret them as the angels not only creates difficulties at this level, but also involves the omission of the sufferings of the Jewish people under Antiochus from the main interpretative section of the dream. On general grounds, that is not a probable result; when the text can be interpreted of them so easily, it is wilful to do otherwise.

There is no statement about the Saints in vs. 26, but this verse is directly relevant because it deals with the heavenly court. From the opening words 'and the court sat' it is clear that the court really exists and is not merely symbolism in vs. 10. The collocation of vss. 26 and 27 makes it clear that the Saints benefit from the decision, and do not constitute the court. If the Saints are the Jewish people, this is straightforward. The court are the reason for the plural number of יְהַעְדּוֹן, 'and they shall take away'. The destruction of the power of Antiochus for ever necessarily accomplishes the demise of the whole fourth kingdom, and the triumph of the people of the Saints of the Most High follows in vs. 27. The suffix in מַלְכוּתֵה picks up the last mentioned singular עַם so that we would translate 'their kingdom is an everlasting kingdom', and the remainder of the verse accurately portrays the situation symbolized in vs. 14 in much the same language. Dequeker asserts that it refers to the Most High, but his assertion is accompanied by more dogma than argument.[55] Dan. 3.33; Ps. 145.13 do not count against the usual view; it should be clear enough that the sovereignty which the Saints receive remains the sovereignty of God when they have received it, and it was celebrated elsewhere as such. To assert that פְלַח in Daniel refers only to the gods is arbitrary and of unsound method. The Aramaic word פְלַח has a semantic range which includes service to human beings (necessarily of unusually exalted status). To say that an author uses only part of a word's semantic area x times is not to demonstrate that he could not use the rest of it too (especially when x has a low value, here no more than 6). The evidence of the text before us is that Daniel used it of service to human beings in vs. 27, and symbolized this by his use of it in the case of a pure symbol in vs. 14. But the basic trouble with Dequeker's view is his failure to understand the man-like figure of vs. 13.

It is therefore to be concluded that all statements about the 'Saints', 'the Saints of the Most High' and 'the people of the Saints of the Most High' in Dan. 7 make excellent sense on the traditional view that they are the Jewish people. Some of them do not make sense on any other view, and the theories of redaction history on which these other views depend have been shown to be unsound.[56] The view that the 'Saints' are the Jewish people is therefore correct. It fits well with the evidence of the rest of the book, and with the general cultural background. A corresponding dream and interpretation, from the hand of the same author, is to be found in Dan. 2. God will set up his kingdom, 'and his kingdom will never pass to another people' (2.44) because the Jewish people, the chosen people of God, have got it for ever. There is no mention of angels at all. Dan. 8.24 is difficult because of textual uncertainty, but at least it is clear that Antiochus will be persecuting 'the people of the Saints', that is, again, the Jewish people. The parallelism of the dream and the interpretation cannot require that the people of the Saints are the host and the stars in the dream, though they may indeed be symbolized by them. Ch. 12 supports the same picture: it is the Jewish people who will be delivered in 12.1, 'the holy people' as they are called in 12.7.

This evidence is completely consistent. Only the terminology, 'Saints', 'Saints of the Most High', 'people of the Saints of the Most High', 'people of the Saints', 'holy people', is variable, and no one has yet given any satisfactory reason for thinking that the author should have been consistent. Nor should the terminology be regarded as surprising. The Jews had regarded themselves as a holy people for a very long time. The Hebrew language always permitted but never demanded that this be expressed by means of a nominal adjective קְדוֹשִׁים in isolation. This certainly occurs, used of the pious, in Ps. 34.10. Some of them certainly termed themselves 'holy ones' in the intertestamental period, as even Dequeker says. Even Noth and Dequeker think that קַדִּישִׁין was so understood by the Maccabean redactor of Dan. 7. This is sufficient to undermine any argument that קַדִּישִׁין on its own ought to be understood of angels rather than men. Yet the main thrust of the argument has been towards showing that קַדִּישִׁין on its own *could* denote 'angels'. Certainly it could; it has next to be shown that it actually did so in this chapter. Perhaps the most remarkable feature of that version of Dan. 7 which emerges from the work of Noth and Dequeker is that the Jewish people are left out of it altogether. This has suited some Gentile scholars, but it was hardly the purpose of a Jewish writer, nor is it a likely outcome of the use of 'opposition history'.

The general background material has finally been straightened out by Hasel. He concludes his survey of it: 'From the traditio-historical perspective the dual attribution of holiness to beings in the celestial and terrestrial realms not only ante-dates the usage of adjectives derived from the root *q d s* in the book of Daniel but is also reflected in later extra-canonical Jewish literature of the pre-Christian era'.[57] Noth's attempt to limit consideration of the evidence to the substantival use of the adjective is linguistically absurd and generally of unsound method. Any attempt to set up a general presumption in favour of 'the holy ones' being angels is therefore unsound. The decision as to whether they are angelic or human beings must therefore be made on the basis of the evidence of Dan. 7 alone, and we have seen that this demonstrates decisively that the reference is to the Jewish people.

It would be useful to determine what kind of triumph the author had in mind. Did he expect the Jews to win a military victory? There is no mention of it in the interpretation of this chapter. The parallel 2.44 is not explicit. On the one hand God is very clearly the subject of the statement 'the God of heaven will raise up a kingdom which will last for ever'; on the other hand this need not preclude a military victory as the means by which he did so, and this might be suggested by 'it will shatter and destroy all those kingdoms', a statement of which this new kingdom appears to be the subject. 8.25 produces a purely supernatural intervention to bring about the end of Antiochus, an event which in this context clearly involves the deliverance of Israel. 12.1–3 similarly envisages the deliverance of Israel, and this deliverance certainly includes supernatural inter-vention, though the possibility of military action by earthly or heavenly hosts, or both, cannot be ruled out. In view of these factors, we may conclude that the author of Dan. 7 appears to have envisaged deliverance by supernatural means. It is to be noted, however, that the military view, which will therefore have come into being after the Maccabean victory, does not directly contradict anything in Dan. 2 or 7, and the difficulties which it ran into at 12.1–3 are chiefly due to its assumption that this is a record of the Maccabean triumph only, rather than to any direct contradiction between these verses and the notion that a military victory was involved as well.[58]

The climax of the chapter, then, comes with the destruction of Antiochus Epiphanes and the triumph of the Jews by means of supernatural intervention. Not only will their kingdom be eternal, but all other nations will serve and obey them. There is no mention of the resurrection of the dead, an idea which does not occur in this book until ch. 12. If the author believed in it, this is rather surprising. It is therefore probable that, if we are right in supposing that 8–12 were written by a different author, the reason why it is not mentioned in ch. 7 is that its author did not believe in it. The idea of a personal resurrection was developing and gaining wider acceptance at this period, so that there is nothing intrinsically improbable about this view, though it may be felt to fall short of certainty. Probably, then, the author's idea of the Jewish triumph is that after the supernatural intervention the Jewish people will continue to live and die in their kingdom which God had established. The important unit which triumphs is thus the nation, which is delivered and survives for ever, rather than the individual rising from the dead. This fits very well the 'opposition history' from which the author derived the sequence of four kingdoms and a fifth. It utilizes ancient Israelite ideas of Israel as the people of God. That God will care for his people and look after them, delivering them in time of distress, is writ large over the whole OT. When the historical context is borne in mind, it is not fanciful to mention also the idea of the righteous remnant.[59] Many in Israel had apostatized, and it was the pious who were left. The author does not explicitly refer to this, but it may lie behind his description of the triumphant group as 'Saints'. It is God's holy ones who have been faithful to him who will be delivered: these are the true Israel, to be described as 'the people of the Saints of the Most High'. The ideas of 'opposition history' have been brought into the framework of traditional Israelite ideas. These traditional ideas constitute the framework and the essence of the author's message.

With the identification of the Saints of the Most High established and the forthcoming Jewish triumph clarified, we can now deal with some of the details of the interpretative section of the dream. The description of the fourth beast in Daniel's question says of the little horn 'and its appearance was bigger than that of its companions' (vs. 20). This is not inconsistent with the evidence of 7.8. Like the little horn of 8.9f., this little horn came up and up and up, and 7.20 tells us that it finally became the biggest of all. The symbolism is natural and un-forced. Some would prefer the author to have said it all at 7.8, but it is intelligible that he should have sought after dramatic effect by leaving something for his second lengthy description of the fourth beast and its little horn.

Verses 23–7 give the detailed angelic interpretation. An out-line has already been supplied in 17–18, and in response to the dreamer's desire the angel can now concentrate on the fourth beast. Its identification is not specific, but will have escaped no one. The ten horns are identified as kings, and then a more prolonged account of the little horn is given. Again there is no direct identification, possibly because this was felt to be dangerous; perhaps more probably because our author's group saw the events of their time in old prophecies which they had to reinterpret for that purpose (e.g. Dan. 9, cf. e.g. 1QpHab). Seen like this the old prophecies were imprecise, and it may be this that our author was imitating.

Verse 25 records Antiochus' blasphemy, persecution, and war. We are told that he attempted to change 'times and the Law'. Some scholars[60] have dated Dan. 7 before the occupation of the sanctuary in 167 B.C., because of the lack of mention of the desecration of the Temple and the abolition of the sacrifices, contrasting 8.11; 9.26f.; 11.31; 12.11. 'The Law' is against this, and 'times' supports it. It is only Antiochus' measures of 167 B.C. that really justify the description of him as trying to change the Law (cf. 1 Macc. 1.41ff.). The complete expression forms a rather comprehensive general description of Antiochus' measures against the Jewish religion. 'Times' in particular will refer to the change of calendar involved in the abolition of Jewish festivals and the introduction of a different cultus in the Temple at Jerusalem. Thus vs. 25, despite being a brief descrip-tion of Antiochus' measures, effectively summarizes successively Antiochus' blasphemy, persecution, abolition of the Jewish festivals, measures against the Jewish religion, and success in persecution and war. Apocalyptic prophecies do not have to mention everything in detail: in the whole book of Daniel there is no specific mention of Antiochus' abolition of the sabbath and circumcision. The lack of mention of the desecration of the Temple here should not therefore be regarded as evidence that it had not yet taken place, especially when it is recalled that the

47

prophecies of Dan. 8–12 are in any case more specific than Dan. 2 and 7, a fact probably related to a change of authorship. This also makes the simplest sense of the period of time, $3\frac{1}{2}$ years, עִדָּנִין being taken as a dual. The reason for the precision is that it is half a week of years (Dan. 9.27); the prediction is the same length of time as twice given in Dan. 8–12 from the desecration of 167 B.C. onwards (Dan. 9.27; 12.7).

Verse 28 forms the concluding narrative framework. This time Daniel really has woken up. The concluding phrase is still in the first person and is no doubt intended deliberately as part of Daniel's account referred to in vs. 1.

This concludes our study of Dan. 7 in itself. It has emerged as a thoroughly Jewish chapter in a thoroughly Jewish book. When its Jewish basis, principles, and beliefs are taken for granted, its symbolism becomes clear and its structure for the first time genuinely intelligible as the work of a single author. It contains no 'Son of man concept', and its man-like figure does not suffer. An understanding of its symbolism and structure has removed all ground for supposing that the author ever knew a Son of man concept. Finally we have been able to see how this chapter was interpreted in 166–165 B.C. This provides a *terminus a quo* for correct interpretations. When they recur in late sources, the *terminus ad quem* thus provided will enable us to argue that these interpretations were in existence at the time of Jesus.

NOTES

1 G. Hölscher, *ThStKr* 92 (1919), 114–38; M. Noth, *ThStKr* 98/9 (1926), 143–63 = M. Noth, *Gesammelte Studien* II, 11–28; L. Dequeker, *EThL* 36 (1960), 353–92, reprinted in J. Coppens and L. Dequeker, *Le Fils de l'Homme et les Saints du Très-Haut en Daniel VII, dans les Apocryphes et dans le Nouveau Testament*; L. Dequeker, *OTS* XVIII (1973), 108–87. My references are all to Dequeker's most recent attempt, in *OTS* XVIII. In support, especially M. Haller, *ThStKr* 93 (1920–1), 83–7; J. Coppens, *Miscellanées Bibliques* XXVIII–XXXII (*ALBO* IV, 8: 1973); H. Schmid, *Judaica* 27 (1971), 193–9; U. B. Müller, *Messias und Menschensohn in jüdischen Apocalypsen und in der Offenbarung des Johannes* (1972), 19–36; P. Weimar in *Jesus und der Menschensohn*. Für Anton Vögtle (1976), 11–37; K. Müller, ibid., 38–80. Against them, especially H. H. Rowley, *HUCA* 23 (1950–1), 233–79 = H. H. Rowley, *The Servant of the Lord and Other Essays*, 235–68. For H. L. Ginsberg, *Studies*

in Daniel (1948), cf. H. H. Rowley, op. cit.; Ginsberg, *VT* 4 (1954), 246–75; Rowley, *VT* 5 (1955), 272–6.

2   Op. cit., 120.

3   Dequeker, op. cit., 115, with references.

4   Cf. M. Sokoloff, *The Targum to Job from Qumran Cave XI* (1974), 109–10; J. A. Fitzmyer, *The Genesis Apocryphon of Qumran Cave I* (²1971), 96.

5   Dequeker, op. cit., 115–6, with references.

6   Infra, 24–7.

7   On the use of Dan. 7 in the Similitudes, infra 99–112.

8   H. H. Rowley, *Darius the Mede and the Four World Empires* (1935).

9   On the theories of four kingdoms, J. Swain, *CP* XXXV (1940), 1–20; D. Flusser, *Isr Or St* 2 (1972), 148–75.

10 Cf. further infra, 25–7.

11 A. Caquot, *Sem* V (1955), 6–13: id., *Sem* XVII (1967), 37–71; cf. M. Delcor, *Le Livre de Daniel* (1971), 144–7.

12 O. Morkhølm, *Antiochus IV of Syria* (1966), especially 36–50.

13 E.g. H. H. Schaeder, *Studien zum antiken Synkretismus aus Iran und Griechenland* (with R. Reitzenstein, 1926), 337–8; N. Perrin, *Rediscovering the Teaching of Jesus* (1967), 166.

14 W. Baumgartner, *ThR* 11 (1939), 214; D. Broadribb, *Abr-n* 13 (1972–3), 66–87.

15 S. Mowinckel, *He That Cometh* (ET 1956), 352.

16 J. A. Montgomery, *A Critical and Exegetical Commentary on the Book of Daniel* (1927), ad loc.

17 On vs. 11a, supra 11–12.

18 Infra, 40–4.

19 Cf. M. D. Hooker, *The Son of Man in Mark* (1967), 15ff.

20 Montgomery, op. cit., ad loc.

21 S. R. Driver, *Daniel* (1900), ad loc.

22 G. Vermes, App. E in M. Black, *An Aramaic Approach to the Gospels and Acts* (³1967), 310–28.

23 Montgomery, op. cit., ad loc.

24 H. H. Rowley, op. cit., 63, n. 2 from p. 62.

25 E. Dhanis, *Gr* 45 (1964), 10–16.

26 Cf. D. Flusser, *Isr Or St* 2 (1972), 170.

27 In general cf. J. W. Rogerson, *JThS* XXI N.S. (1970), 1–16.

28 N. Schmidt, *JBL* 19 (1900), 22–8; J. J. Collins, *JBL* 93 (1974), 50–66.

29 Against this view, infra 40–5.

30 Z. Zevitt, *ZAW* 80 (1968), 385–96.

31 M. Black in *Jews, Greeks and Christians* . . . in Honour of W. D. Davies (1976), 61; A. Feuillet, *RB* 60 (1953), 170–202; cf. M. Black in *Jesus und der Menschensohn. Für Anton Vögtle* (1976), 92–9.

32 M. Gaster, *The Search* I (1931), 15–30.

33 Ibid., 21–2.

34 Ibid., 24–5: cf. infra, 86–8.

35 H. Sahlin, *StTh* 23 (1969), 41–68.

36 Cf. infra, ch. 3.

37 H. Schmid, *Judaica* 27 (1971), 192–200.

38 Supra, especially 11–17.

39 H. Gunkel, *Schöpfung und Chaos in Urzeit und Endzeit* (²1921).

40 N. Schmidt, op. cit.: supra, 31–2.

41 C. H. Kraeling, *Anthropos and Son of Man* (1927), ch. vi.

42 A. Bentzen, *King and Messiah* (1953), 74–5: id., *Daniel* (²1952), ad loc.

43 J. A. Emerton, *JThS* N.S. IX (1958), 225–42.

44 Emerton, op. cit., 32.

45 S. Mowinckel, op. cit., 348–53.

46 C. F. D. Moule, *BSNTS* 3 (1952), reprinted in C. F. D. Moule, *The Phenomenon of the New Testament*. I quote from the latter, p. 83.

47 M. D. Hooker, *The Son of Man in Mark* (1967), 11–32. Cf. also C. K. Barrett, *Jesus and the Gospel Tradition* (1967), 41ff.

48 Cf. supra, 30: infra 60.

49 Supra, 24–7.

50 M. Noth, *NTT* 56 (1955), 146–57 = M. Noth, *Gesammelte Studien zum Alten Testament* (1957), 274–90 (I cite the latter), ET in *The Laws in the Pentateuch and other Essays* (1966), 215–28; J. Coppens and L. Dequeker, *Le Fils de l'Homme et les Saints du Très-Haut en Daniel VII* (1961); L. Dequeker, *OTS* XVIII (1973), 108–87; C. H. W. Brekelmans, *OTS* XIV (1965), 305–29; G. F. Hasel, *Bib* 56 (1975), 173–92. Cf. also R. Hanhart, *VT.S* 16 (1967), 90–101; J. J. Collins, *JBL* 93 (1974), 50–66; V. S. Poythress, *VT* 26 (1976), 208–13.

51 Noth, op. cit., 289.

52 See further Hasel, op. cit., 186–8.

53 Noth, op. cit., 285–6; Brekelmans, op. cit., 329; Hasel, op. cit., 185–6; Brekelmans' argument is accepted by Dequeker, op. cit., 130. Cf. F. Brown, S. R. Driver, C. A. Briggs, *Hebrew and English Lexicon of the Old Testament* (1907), 115.

54 For more details of the interpretation of this verse, infra 47–8.

55 Dequeker, op. cit., 181–2.

56 Supra, 11–17.

57 Hasel, op. cit., 185.

58 Cf. infra, ch. 3.

59 Cf. Hasel, op. cit., especially 188ff.

60 E.g. E. W. Heaton, *The Book of Daniel* (1956), 50.

3

The Syrian Tradition

The original author's interpretation of Dan. 7 was never forgotten or superseded. It was preserved by a narrow stream of tradition which flowed through the desiccated synagogues and monasteries of an intellectual desert. I have called it the 'Syrian' tradition, because most of its witnesses are Syrian Christian exegetes. The existence of this tradition has not previously been observed, though pieces of evidence have been noted occasionally. These have been attributed to the influence of the Syrian tradition's earliest witness, Porphyry, famous as a Greek philosopher and more especially as one of the greatest intellectual opponents of Christianity in the ancient world. This erroneous attribution has made his demonstration that the book of Daniel was a Maccabean pseudepigraph seem not merely clever but beyond explanation. In fact Porphyry made use of this complete exegetical tradition. We must therefore begin by demonstrating its existence.

For this purpose all published commentaries from the Syriac-speaking Church were surveyed down to the end of the first millennium. Known discussions of Dan. 7 of any substantial length were also included, as was the Peshitta version of Daniel. The Syriac *Questions and Answers* of Theodore bar Koni was for this purpose defined as a commentary too. However, no attempt was made to examine other works of the Syrian Churches which are not commentaries. These limitations, and the employment of such late sources, were satisfactory from the point of view of this investigation because this is the stage of the argument at which the tradition must be shown to exist and these sources are ample for that purpose, and for the provision of an adequate description of it. I found also one medieval Jewish writer, R. Hayyim ben Galipapa, who adhered to this exegetical tradition. This gives us ten adherents of the tradition.

51

1   Porphyry, c. A.D. 270–320. Porphyry's exegesis was in the twelfth book of his famous work *Against the Christians* but since the Christians destroyed it, we are dependent for our knowledge of this part of his work on Jerome, *In Danielem*.

2   Aphrahat, *Demonstration* V, A.D. 337.

3   Ephraem, c. A.D. 360–73.

4   Polychronius, c. A.D. 430.

5   Cosmas Indicopleustes, c. A.D. 550, Christian Topography II, 66–73; V, 131–2.

6   Peshitta glosses, seventh century or earlier.

7   Theodore bar Koni, c. A.D. 790.

8   Isho'dad of Merw, ninth century.

9   An anonymous commentator on Dan. 7.7, published from a catena by Mai.[1]

10 R. Hayyim ben Galipapa, c. A.D. 1310–80. Galipapa's work is no longer extant, but is discussed by Joseph Albo, *Book of Principles* IV, 42.

Since the significance of this tradition for our purposes lies in the fact that it preserved an outline of the original author's interpretation of Dan. 7, it is useful to provide a rather conservative itemization of the authentic elements in this tradition, together with a list of those exegetes who adhere more or less explicitly to each item.[2]

Verses

3	The four beasts are the four kingdoms.	All
4	The first beast is the kingdom of Babylon.	All
5	The second beast is the Median kingdom.	Eph. Pol. CI Pesh. TK Ish. Anon. Gal.
6	The third beast is the kingdom of Persia.	Eph. Pol. CI Pesh. TK Ish. Anon. Gal.
7	The fourth beast is the Greek kingdom. Its ten horns are ten successive Macedonian kings.	All Aphr. Eph. Pol. TK Anon.
	The first horn is Alexander.	Pol. Anon.

52

8	The little horn is Antiochus Epiphanes. Its mouth speaking big things is his arrogance and blasphemy.	All Eph. Pol. TK
9ff.	Judgement is passed on the Macedonian kingdom.	Eph. Gal.
9	The 'Ancient of Days' is God.	Eph. Pol. Ish.
10	The 'thousand thousands' etc. are angels.	Pol.
11	The slaying of the fourth beast is the destruction of the Macedonian kingdom.	Pol.
12	The prolongation of the lives of the first three beasts means that the first three kingdoms were not destroyed but lost power.	Eph.
13	The man-like figure is a symbol of the Saints of the Most High.	Por. Eph. TK Ish.
16	Daniel approached one of the angels mentioned in his vision.	Pol.
17	Four 'kings' refers to the four kingdoms.	Eph.
18, 22, 27	The Saints of the Most High are the Maccabean Jews.	Por. Eph. TK Ish. Gal.
21, 25	The Saints of the Most High are the Maccabean Jews.	Por. Aphr. Eph. Pol. TK Ish. Gal.
21	The little horn making war on the Saints refers to Antiochus' measures against the Jews.	Aphr. Pol.
25	Changing 'times and the Law' refers to Antiochus' measures against Jewish religious practices. Time, times and half a time = $3\frac{1}{2}$ years.	Aphr. Eph. Pol. Ish. Por. Eph. Ish.

A few of these items show a shift of meaning away from the author's original interpretation, which they nevertheless clearly attest. This is because they were written so much later. For the author of Daniel the Saints of the Most High were the group of pious Israelites to which he belonged. The interpretation of them as the Maccabees involves some expansion of the author's group, but it nevertheless witnesses to the right sort of group. The author of Daniel did expect Antiochus Epiphanes and the Seleucids to be overcome, and the dominion to be given to the Jews, for whom the Maccabees fought.[3] Interpreters mentioned here effectively have in mind the Jews of this period. Similarly Ephraem and Galipapa have correctly preserved the author's intention in holding that in vss. 9ff. judgement is passed on the Macedonian kingdom. The author of Daniel, however, expected the end of the Seleucids to be the end of normal human history. I have nevertheless not included here witnesses who thought that the Saints of the Most High were the Jews at the End, because in fact they are invariably following an actualizing exegesis of the chapter. Nor have I included the Syrian tradition's interpretation of the Saints of the Most High receiving the kingdom. The older interpretation which they preserved was of the military victory of the Maccabees over the Seleucids, and this represents perhaps too much of a shift from the author's intentions to term it the preservation of them. Nevertheless, we must note here that these interpreters (Porphyry, Ephraem, Theodore bar Koni, Isho'dad and Galipapa) do in this way indirectly testify to the preservation of the original author's interpretation.

It is clear that evidence of the existence of this tradition is ample. There is much more than I have produced in an investigation of deliberately limited scope. For example, Theodoret, who adhered to the Western tradition of interpretation, regarded adherence to the Syrian tradition by his fellow Christians important enough to require refutation, and his critical comments reveal knowledge of more written commentaries than are extant now. The tradition is of course incomplete. Few Syrians knew that the ten horns were successive kings beginning from Alexander, and none of them knew the names of all ten. This is a minor weakness, though Theodoret made use of it to attack the Syrian tradition. Many additions were made by means of ancient exegetical methods, and the results are no better than Western efforts of this kind. For example, Ephraem believed that the second beast was raised on one side because Darius the Mede 'ruled only over his own kingdom, unlike Nebuchadnezzar, whose preceding kingdom held sway over the whole earth': Polychronius thought the four wings of the third beast symbolized Medes, Babylonians, Egyptians, and Persians. Occasionally, gaps in the tradition led to more straightforward mistakes, as when Ephraem comments on the three horns uprooted, 'It was not these three horns that were uprooted, but the descendants of these horns'. The need to maintain a full interpretation that accorded with received tradition led Galipapa to identify the Ancient of Days as Mattathias.

However, all this means only that the tradition was handed down by ancient exegetes, not by modern critical scholars, and it does not detract from the real value of the tradition. The important factor is that a complete outline has been preserved, with no more than the slight shift necessary to conform the Danielic predictions and the actual course of history to each other. The four kingdom theory was preserved as it was known to the author of Daniel—Babylon, Media, Persia, Macedonia. The account of the little horn was rightly remembered as the story of the persecution of Antiochus Epiphanes. The man-like figure was a symbol of the Saints of the Most High. Here the shift begins, to accommodate the interpretation to the facts of history. The Saints are the Maccabees, and their triumph begins with the Maccabean victory in 164 BC.

This outline is already to be deduced from the Syrian tradition's earliest witness, Aphrahat, but his interpretation of Dan. 7 is quite muddle-headed. He received more than one tradition; he expounded more than one tradition too, and the combination is less than successful. *Dem.* XXII, 26 gives advice to interpreters of Holy Writ who have got stuck, and it is a recipe for continued and comfortable muddle: 'Thus we say that what is written has been well written, but I do not see how to understand it'. Aphrahat supported Rome politically, and repeatedly follows the Western identification of the four kingdoms as the Babylonian, Medo-Persian, Macedonian, and Roman. He follows it in his interpretation of the Image of Dan. 2 at *Dem.* V, 12–14. A detailed interpretation of Dan. 7 is provided at V, 15ff., and as far as the beginning of V, 19 all is clear: the same Western interpretative tradition is employed, with the Western identification of all four kingdoms. Then it changes, and to see what has happened, it is simplest to begin by looking at V, 20, where we find a long account of the little horn interpreted as Antiochus Epiphanes. This is the Syrian tradition, with the fourth kingdom as the Macedonian. It is quite inconsistent with Aphrahat's previous remarks, and it indicates that the driving force of the preservation of the Syrian tradition of the interpretation of the four kingdoms was the memory that the little horn was Antiochus Epiphanes.

Aphrahat's efforts at a transition are to be found at V, 19. He begins with the Western tradition's identification of the fourth beast, which he has held consistently up to this point: 'Now this is the kingdom of the sons of Esau'. The next statement appears, from the lack of logical connection which the conjunction ought to indicate, to be derived from another source: 'Because from the time that Alexander the Macedonian ruled, he held the kingdom of the Greeks, for Alexander was one of the Greeks himself'. But it is the statement after this that takes us into the same by-form of the Syrian tradition as is to be found in Porphyry: 'But his vision of the third beast was fulfilled in him', that is, Daniel's vision of the third beast was completed in Alexander. There is no direct trace anywhere in Aphrahat's work of the pure form of the Syrian tradition in which the third kingdom is the Persian; in its context this statement must be supplying the alternative, that the third beast is Alexander and the fourth the rest of the Macedonian kingdom. This is odd, in that it puts Macedonians in both the third and the fourth kingdoms, so the explanation follows at once: 'For the third and the fourth are one'. If the statement that the vision of the third beast was fulfilled in Alexander were taken as an expression of the usual Western identification of the third kingdom as the Macedonian, this identification of the third and fourth kingdoms would not be necessary. It is not a notion that would occur to any innocent reader of Dan. 7: it is comprehensible only as an effort at solving an awkward exegetical problem. The need for Macedonians in the fourth kingdom derives from the vigorous survival of the interpretation of the little horn as Antiochus Epiphanes. To put the Romans in the same kingdom is very forced, but the Western tradition told Aphrahat that the fourth kingdom was the Roman and the contemporary useful-ness of this tradition made it difficult to discard. He goes straight through with it, concluding V, 19 with chronological data on Macedonian kings and Roman emperors. The identification recurs at *Dem.* XXII, 25 when Aphrahat is doing nothing more tendentious than supplying the date of his homilies. The last twelve were completed in the 655th year 'of the kingdom of the Greeks and the Romans, which is the kingdom of Alexander'. Thus Aphrahat's work constitutes evidence of the existence of no less than four interpretations of the four kingdoms: (1) The third is the Macedonian, the fourth is the Roman. (2) The third is Alexander, the fourth is the rest of the Macedonian and the Roman as well. (3) The third is Alexander, the fourth is the Macedonian kingdom from the Diadochi onwards. (4) The third is the Persian, the fourth the Macedonian. Aphrahat himself puts forward (1) and (2). They have two factors in common. Both have Alexander in or as the third kingdom, such that according to either tradition the third kingdom may be said to symbolize Alexander; secondly, both have the Romans in or as the fourth kingdom. These common factors do much to explain how Aphrahat was able to put forward both (1) and (2) without ever combining them properly. (3) is the view of Porphyry. (2) is a combination of (1) and (3); the ineptness of the combination suggests, but does not prove, that Aphrahat may have known (3) and have attempted the combination himself. In any case, he provides evidence, independent of Porphyry, that (3) was in existence before A.D. 337. (4) is the authentic tradition of interpretation, found in later Syrian interpreters. Aphrahat appears ignorant of it. However, (3) is a development of it. This is important, because it means that our first Syriac writer, by adopting a tradition which is a development of (4), provides evidence that other people held (4) before he wrote.

At *Dem.* V, 20 Aphrahat provides a substantial account of Antiochus Epiphanes, interpreted as the little horn. Having identified the ten horns in accordance with Dan. 7.24 as ten kings, and made it reasonably clear that he had in mind a chronological list going down to the time of Antiochus Epiphanes, Aphrahat likewise identifies the three horns cast down as three kings whom Antiochus put down. The Saints of the Most High at Dan. 7.21, 25 are identified as the Maccabean Jews persecuted by Antiochus. At V, 21 Aphrahat changes traditions again, identifying the triumphant Saints as the Christians, but his discussion in V, 21ff. makes it clear that other interpreters known to him were more consistent. His first reason for rejecting the view that the triumphant Saints were Jews is that they have not in fact received a kingdom, and this is amplified at V, 23, where Aphrahat points out that they were enslaved among the Gentiles. It is clear that the interpreters whom Aphrahat is refuting believed that the reception of the kingdom by the Saints of the Most High was a symbol of the Maccabean triumph; it must be a past event for the contemporary servitude of the Jews to be thought to constitute an objection to this interpretation, and the Maccabean triumph is the only past event that fits the evidence.

In his interpretation of the man-like figure Aphrahat again followed the Western Christian tradition, identifying the figure as Jesus at his second coming, and giving the whole of Dan. 7.9–14 an eschatological setting, concluding with Jesus' reception of his eternal kingdom at the End. This is clear from his remarks at *Dem.* V, 6, 22 (229, 25–231, 2); 23 (231, 23f.); 24 (233, 5–15). At V, 21, however, in rejecting the interpretation of the triumphant Saints as the Jews, he comments 'Have the children of Israel received the kingdom of the Most High? God forbid! Or has that people come on the clouds of heaven? This has passed away from them.' The interpretation which Aphrahat is rejecting regarded the man-like figure as a symbol of the Saints of the Most High, who were taken to be Jews. This is the only possible source of the polemical suggestion, which is deduced from that tradition in hostile fashion in order to be rejected, that the children of Israel might have come on the clouds of heaven. It is interesting moreover that the arguments which Aphrahat uses to reject this exegetical tradition are specifically Christian; they are eloquent testimony to the theological pressures which this tradition had to withstand in order to survive in Christian circles.

Aphrahat's fifth Demonstration thus provides clear evidence that in A.D. 337 there were other exegetes who held a pure form of the Syrian tradition, an accurate outline of the original author's interpretation of Dan. 7. This must have been transmitted to them by the Jewish communities in Syria. Edessa is the obvious centre for a whole area where Jewish communities are known from pre-Christian times. Some of their members were subsequently converted to Christianity, and the Jewish communities continued alongside the newly formed Christian groups. Hence the Syrian Churches had so much more exegetical material in common with the Jews than did the Churches of the West. This is the path travelled by the authentic interpretation of the Book of Daniel. Its plausibility is not diminished by the fact that we cannot tell the story in more detail—this simply reflects the lack of material coming from this environment in this period. There is no direct evidence of the existence of the authentic tradition of interpretation of Dan. 7 actually dateable during this period from this area because there are no comments on the Book of Daniel dateable during this period from this area at all. The first Syriac-speaking Father extant in any quantity is Aphrahat, who duly provides evidence of a large part of the tradition and of adherence to it by contemporaries and predecessors, some of whom clearly held it in a purer form than Aphrahat himself.

There is an alternative theory, so widespread that it must be examined.[4] According to this theory, the tradition was forgotten (or, according to the earlier adherents of this theory, never held), and revived (or produced) by Porphyry as part of his brilliant discovery (or wicked invention) that the Book of Daniel is a Maccabean pseudepigraph. Such items of the Syrian tradition as have been noted by previous scholarship have thus been attributed to Porphyry, and such adherents of it as have been observed have been accused of being his followers. This theory began in the pre-critical era, and that is where it belongs.

Firstly, if Syrian Christians already knew the Christian exegetical tradition such as we find it in the commentaries of Hippolytus and Jerome,[5] it is very unlikely that they would accept a different exegetical tradition from the author of an anti-Christian onslaught on the Book of Daniel itself. Secondly, this theory makes it impossible to explain how Porphyry could have originated the exegetical tradition, and how he found out that Daniel is a Maccabean pseudepigraph. Hence critical scholars have on the whole admitted that they do not know how Porphyry divined the Maccabean origin of Daniel. Once it is supposed, however, that he inherited the Syrian tradition of exegesis, the matter becomes clear. It was this tradition which told him that the Danielic prophecies went down to the death of Antiochus Epiphanes and the Maccabean victory. With his extensive knowledge of religious sects he knew that they produced pseudepigraphical works which they attributed to ancient figures. He can hardly have been unaware that Jews and Christians possessed pseudo-prophetical works which they wrongly attributed to their ancient heroes, and he will have perceived also the actualizing nature of some contemporary exegesis. Against this background, his refusal to accept the claim that Jewish prophets foretold the future far ahead of their time is not surprising. When the Syrian exegetical tradition is added to these general views, the Maccabean origin of Daniel follows straightforwardly.

These general considerations are supported by two points of detailed exegesis. The first concerns Porphyry's identification of the second and third kingdoms. To modern scholarship, occupied in identifying the fourth kingdom as the Greek and the little horn as Antiochus Epiphanes, as well as determining the Maccabean origin of the book, the dramatic thing about Porphyry has been how much he got right. Here, however, the important factor is that he got the identification wrong, being joined in this by Aphrahat, whereas the rest of the Syrian tradition got it right. For Porphyry, as for Aphrahat some of the time, the second kingdom was the Medo-Persian, and the third Alexander. Not only is this wrong, but the rest of the Syrian tradition knew that the second was the Median and the third the Persian. This is easy to explain if we suppose that the Syrians received the correct tradition of interpretation handed down to them, and that Porphyry and Aphrahat inherited a by-form of it created by Western influence. This by-form resulted from a combination of the usual view of this exegetical tradition that the little horn was Antiochus Epiphanes with the Western identification of the second kingdom as the Medo-Persian and the third as the Greek. The view that the third kingdom was the Greek was sometimes expressed by saying that the third kingdom was Alexander, and in this by-form of the tradition this proposition has been taken literally. It provides the means whereby the Western identification of the second and third kingdoms can be combined with a strong tradition identifying the little horn as Antiochus Epiphanes. This identification of the little horn requires that the fourth kingdom be the Macedonian; if the third kingdom is identified literally as Alexander, the fourth can then be the Macedonian kingdom from the Diadochi onwards.

If, therefore, we suppose that this exegetical tradition inherited the correct identification of the kingdoms, we can explain the view of Porphyry and Aphrahat as a by-form of it. But if Porphyry is held to have originated this exegetical tradition, we are in difficulties. Aphrahat's adherence to the view of Porphyry is odd, though this is but a detailed example of the general difficulties of having this exegetical tradition dependent on Porphyry. More fundamentally, it becomes impossible to explain how the other adherents of this tradition deduced the correct identification of these kingdoms. They had none of the resources of modern scholarship—like Porphyry, they simply swallowed Darius the Mede. In short, if they did not inherit a sounder tradition, they had neither the means nor the motive for altering Porphyry's view.

For the final argument we must leave ch. 7 for the exegesis of 11.40–12, where Porphyry and the Syrians all made the same mistakes. They continued to interpret it historically of the end of Antiochus Epiphanes, and took the beginning of ch. 12 as an account of the Maccabean victory of 164 B.C. Had Porphyry inherited a Western exegesis, which interpreted this of Anti-christ and the final resurrection, he would have had no reason to alter it. Since he did not accept the authority of the Old Testament, he could have been quite content to suppose that the Book of Daniel predicted the resurrection of the dead. Had he been able to deduce that it predicted that this would happen in 164 B.C., he would have been especially happy to argue that it was at this point that the author began to leave his *vaticinia ex eventu* and tell lies about the future. The exegesis which he in fact followed is not merely forced, and false to history. It has another important facet. It supposes that the account of the Book of Daniel is right, where we know it to be a prediction that was never fulfilled. That is not the mistake of an anti-Christian Neoplatonist; it is the mistake of men who believed that the Book of Daniel was the Word of God, and its prophecies true. Once this is supposed, Porphyry's exegesis becomes explicable. An unhistorical Egyptian expedition with undue Danielic colouring is found in his exegesis precisely because his exegesis follows the book of Daniel. The opening of ch. 12 has been forced in order to reconcile it with facts of history. After Antiochus' death people did not rise from their graves, but the Maccabeans did win a signal victory. Therefore that is what the prophet Daniel must have been referring to. It follows that Porphyry's exegesis was derived from the Syrian tradition already at work before him.

Thus we may safely conclude that the Syrian exegetical tradition preserved the outline of the original author's interpretation of Dan. 7. It was inherited, not originated, by Porphyry, from the Syriac-speaking Church, to whom it was transmitted by Syrian Jews. It must next be shown that this tradition retained the original corporate interpretation of the man-like figure.

We have already seen that Aphrahat, while himself following the Western Christian interpretation of the man-like figure as Jesus at his second coming, provided evidence that other interpreters regarded the man-like figure as a symbol of the Saints of the Most High, who were taken to be Jews. The latter interpretation was in fact adhered to by Porphyry, the earliest witness of its tradition, though some effort is required to disentangle Porphyry's view from Jerome's polemic. It is best to begin with the comparatively clear evidence of Jerome's comment on Dan. 11.44. Here Jerome was in difficulties. He interpreted the whole context as a genuine prophecy of Antichrist, while Porphyry took it to be a correct historical account of Antiochus Epiphanes, couched in terms of a prophecy. Jerome found it very difficult to prove his own view correct, and at 11.44 he appeals to 'clear' evidence from another place. 'Who can that stone be which, cut from the mountain without hands, grew into a large mountain, filled the world and shattered the fourfold image? Who is that son of man who will come with the clouds and stand before the Ancient of Days, to whom a kingdom is to be given which will have no end and all people and tribes of every language shall serve him?' The reference of both the stone of Dan. 2 and the man-like figure of Dan. 7.13 to Jesus is taken to be so obvious that Jerome, having said so ad loc., feels no need to repeat it here. He calls it 'clear' again in the next sentence, in which he tells us the view of Porphyry. 'He passes over the evidence which is clear and asserts that the prophecy concerns the Jews, whom we know are in a state of servitude until the present time.' This is very straightforward evidence that Porphyry held the corporate interpretation of both the stone and the man-like figure.

In the case of the stone, this is further confirmed by Jerome's comment on 2.35, 'which the Jews and wicked Porphyry wrongly refer to the people of Israel, which they believe will be powerful at the end of the ages and will shatter all kingdoms and reign for ever'. However, the interpretation here is eschatological, and in this single respect, if Jerome has represented him with precision, Porphyry did not hold the stone and the man-like figure in exact parallel. Porphyry's interpretation is clearly Jewish in spirit, though it also represents the Peshitta version (and the LXX) divested of the second level of interpretation given to it in the Syriac-speaking Church. At 11.44, Jerome brought an objection against Porphyry's corporate interpretations of the stone and the man-like figure as symbols of the Jews, 'whom we know are in a state of servitude until the present time'. This is not a sensible objection to the eschatological interpretation catalogued by Jerome at 2.35; rather it implies that in Porphyry's view the man-like figure symbolized the Jews triumphant and receiving the kingdom at some time in the past. The force of the objection, which is similar to that brought against the corporate view by Aphrahat, is that if they at some time past received the kingdom and the obedience of all nations for ever they should still have them—and they manifestly had not. The only past event that Porphyry could reasonably have thought to be symbolized by the triumph of the man-like figure is the Maccabean victory over the Seleucids in 164 B.C. This harmonizes perfectly with his exegesis of Dan. 11.21–12, and it is confirmed by his exegesis of the rest of Dan. 7, in that he saw in both passages the story of the persecution by Antiochus Epiphanes followed by the Maccabean victory.

Porphyry's view has however been obscured by Jerome's polemic at Dan. 7.14b, which has led scholars to think that Porphyry interpreted the man-like figure as Judas Maccabaeus. Jerome was completely certain of his own interpretation of the man-like figure as an individual, Jesus his risen Lord and Master, and for this reason he believed that Porphyry should have interpreted the figure as an individual. Hence his comment, 'Let Porphyry reply by telling us which man this can refer to, or who is that man who is powerful enough to break and crush the little horn, which he interprets as Antiochus'. Why 'let Porphyry reply'? Because Porphyry never had. Porphyry did not think it referred to any man at all—Porphyry held that it was a symbol of a corporate entity, the Saints of the Most High, the Jews. Jerome continues, 'If he replies that Antiochus' generals were defeated by Judas Maccabaeus, he must show how he comes with the clouds of heaven like a son of man, and is presented to the Ancient of Days, and power and kingship is given to him, and all peoples and tribes serve him, and his power be eternal and unending.' Note the beginning, '*If* he replies'. As Jerome knew full well, Porphyry had not said anything like this. Porphyry held that the Saints of the Most High were the Maccabees, and the man-like figure a symbol of them. Hence Jerome, looking for an individual whom Porphyry might have put forward as an interpretation of the man-like figure, hit upon the leader of the Maccabean triumph, Judas Maccabaeus. This interpretation he was then able to ridicule.

Thus the earliest adherent of the Syrian tradition held the corporate interpretation of the man-like figure, and the next witness, Aphrahat, provides evidence that other exegetes held it too. It will have been held also by R. Hayyim Galipapa, a late witness chiefly of interest because he is the only Jewish adherent of the tradition whom I have found. Galipapa clearly adhered to the outline structure of the Syrian tradition, the corporate interpretation is the only known interpretation of the man-like figure which fits the rest of his interpretation of Dan. 7, and any very unusual interpretation would have drawn comment from Albo. As it is, the identification of the Saints of the Most High as the Hasmoneans is sufficient for Albo's discussion.

In addition to the exegetes who held the corporate interpretation in a simple way, some adherents of the Syrian tradition preserved it in a more complex fashion. Ephraem comments on 7.13, 'While the significance of this was prefigured in the sons of the People in that they subdued the Greeks and all the surrounding kingdoms, its consummation was perfected in Our Lord'. Here the man-like figure is interpreted on two levels. At one level, that of the type, it symbolizes 'the sons of the people', that is, the Jews. They are more precisely defined in the comment on 7.22, as 'the saints of the house of the

Maccabees'. At this level Ephraem offers a clear interpretation of the coming of the man-like figure as a symbol of the victory of the Jews over the Seleucids and others, and thus the man-like figure may be seen to have been interpreted also as a symbol of the Saints of the Most High. At the second level, the type is fulfilled in Jesus. The theological pressures which caused the disappearance of the corporate interpretation in the Christian West were absorbed by Ephraem by means of his exegetical method, which allowed him to hold it at the same time as the view that the man-like figure is Jesus. In this form, the original corporate interpretation could then continue to be preserved by Syrian Christians. It is attested by Theodore bar Koni, who comments: 'In their historical context these words are to be interpreted of the Maccabees, but their essential quality is fulfilled in Our Lord the Christ'. Isho'dad of Merw comments similarly at 7.13: 'This refers to the Maccabees; but in truth it refers to the Christ'. The connection between the man-like figure and the Maccabees is held firmly in the tradition, so there is no need to mention the intermediate and logically necessary stage of the deduction, that the man-like figure was a symbol of the Saints of the Most High.

Of these two levels of interpretation, it is clearly the corporate one which is original to the Syrian tradition. Not only is this the author's own interpretation, it is also the one attested by the earliest witness of this tradition, at a time when the complete exegetical method used by Ephraem and others cannot be shown to have existed. This interpretation on two levels cannot have been handed down from the earliest period, because the exegetical method was unknown to the Jews who first transmitted the tradition. Moreover, the corporate interpretation according to which, as understood by the Syrian tradition, the man-like figure symbolized the Maccabees, fits straight into the complete structure of the whole chapter. The individual interpretation of this figure as Jesus does not, and any conjecture that a Jewish messianic interpretation might lie behind this Christian view would suffer from the same defect. It is therefore to be concluded that the level of interpretation of the man-like figure as Jesus is a later Western Christian accretion to the Syrian tradition. The flexible and atomistic nature of ancient exegesis made such accretions easy for their adherents to produce and accept, but they still appear as lying outside the main lines of the structure of the tradition's interpretation.

Ephraem's exegetical method allowed both the preservation of the corporate interpretation of the man-like figure and the view that it represented Jesus, but this method was not used by two later adherents of the tradition, Polychronius and Cosmas Indicopleustes. Both were Westernised enough to write in Greek, and both succumbed to Christian theological pressures enough to expound the view that the man-like figure was simply Jesus. Polychronius' fundamental comment is given at 7.28: 'As far as this, he says, the angel interpreted for me, but he was not willing to say the things concerning the Son of man, who appeared coming on the clouds'. The use of the Gospel term ὁ υἱὸς τοῦ ἀνθρώπου shows that the expression 'one like a son of man' has been interpreted of Jesus.

The comments at 7.13–14 presuppose this and amplify the picture without repeating the identification. Moreover it is clear that Polychronius did not hold the corporate interpretation of this figure, since he says that the angelic interpretation of Daniel's vision does not contain any interpretation of the man-like figure. His rejection of the double interpretation of this figure found in Ephraem and the later Syrians will not be due solely to Western influence but must owe something to his dis-satisfaction with the exegetical method which they used. Since he did not accommodate the corporate interpretation in this way, the theological pressures in favour of interpreting it as Jesus, pressures which did affect all extant Syrian Christian witnesses, drove him, like Aphrahat before him, to abandon it altogether. This is not a simple or dramatic change of tradition on the part of Polychronius (or his unknown Greek pre-decessors). The Syrian Christian interpretation of the man-like figure was already a mixed tradition, holding the original interpretation together with the Western Christian view by means of a particular exegetical device. Polychronius' unhappi-ness about this device left him with one half of the mixture, and it is not surprising that a Christian took the specifically Christian half.

Polychronius' view that the angel's interpretation omits to provide for the man-like figure is interesting in itself. It is a fatal consequence of any exegesis which regards that figure as an individual. Polychronius is the only surviving ancient exegete incisive enough to observe it, but the remark with which he leaves it illustrates well enough that, though incisive by patristic standards, he belongs to the pre-critical era. He does not have to explain why the author of the Book of Daniel wrote a vision and an interpretation, and yet oddly just left out one of the most striking features of the vision from that interpretation. He can take refuge in the attribution of mysterious and unexplained motives to a supernatural figure: 'The angel . . . was not willing to say'. It is not a refuge that is open to the critical scholar.

Having thus failed to adhere consistently to one exegetical tradition of the vision, Polychronius was led to a mixed interpretation of the Saints of the Most High. If, as he held, the fourth kingdom was the Macedonian, and the little horn was Antiochus Epiphanes, it follows that the Saints were the Jews whom Antiochus persecuted. He says this explicitly in a comment found in Mai's edition at 7.8, on the words 'and he made war against the Saints' interpolated here from 7.21, and he repeats it more elaborately at 7.25. The same view is implicit in comments at 7.25 and 7.28.

However, in the vision Polychronius had seen not only past history, but also eschatological triumph, and this second factor recurs, in his view of the angel's words, as a second interpretation of the Saints of the Most High. The comment on 7.18 'Saints of the Most High' begins with a simple definition: 'that is those who believe in Christ'. The same interpretation is implicit in the comment at 7.27, which stresses the universality and eternity of God's rule. That it is no aberration is confirmed by the comments on 2.44, the last of which concludes with the citation of Matt. 16.18. In this factor only, the interpretation of the Saints of the Most High, Polychronius puts forward the same two interpretations as we found laid side by side in Aphrahat. In the verses which are clearly tied to the little horn, 7.21 and 7.25, they are the Jews whom Antiochus persecuted: in the general summaries of their triumph, 7.27 and 7.18, they are Christians triumphing at the End. Polychronius' mixed interpretation of the vision has been carried through consistently in the division of the statements about the Saints of the Most High into two sets, each of which has then been applied to a different group. One belongs to the original Syrian tradition;

the other is a result of the same pressures as led him to adopt the Western Christian interpretation of the man-like figure.

The other adherent of this tradition who holds only an individual interpretation of the man-like figure is Cosmas Indicopleustes. Cosmas deals with Dan. 7 in a prolonged discussion at II, 66–73. He notes with great care the identity of interpretation of Nebuchadnezzar's dream in Dan. 2 and Daniel's vision in Dan. 7; then he interprets the four kingdoms as Babylon, Media, Persia, and Macedonia, and the little horn as Antiochus Epiphanes. At II, 69, Dan. 7.13 is interpreted of Jesus' first coming, and the careful parallelism with Dan. 2 reaches its climax in a unique feat of exegesis. In the West, the stone of Dan. 2 had been interpreted of Jesus, and this interpretation had spread to the Syrian Church. Many Christian exegetes interpreted the fact that the stone was cut without hands as a symbol of the virgin birth, and this view is found in both Ephraem and Isho'dad of Merw. Cosmas alone takes the clouds in the same way. 'For in the one passage (sc. Dan. 2.34) he said "without hands" meaning without the seed of a man, and in the other "on the clouds of heaven", which, without human hands, bear and bring forth the rains as from a womb.' His careful note of detailed parallelism between Dan. 2 and Dan. 7, and the fact that the virgin birth was already found in Dan. 2, made Cosmas look hard for it in Dan. 7. The second factor in his production of this exegesis is the interpretation of Dan. 7.13–14 of Jesus' first coming. His reference of Dan. 7.14 to the period immediately after the Ascension is the view of Cyprian, and V, 132 makes it clear that Cosmas knew it when he produced the exegesis found in II, 69. It enabled him to produce a consistent and coherent exegesis of Dan. 7 which is in some aspects unique in the material under review. He found the beginning of Jesus' earthly life at the beginning of vs. 13, and with perfect logical sequence he found an event immediately after the Ascension in vs. 14 (no doubt at the end of vs. 13 too, but he does not actually say so). Consistently with this interpretation of vss. 13–14 entirely of the first coming of Jesus, he found at vss. 11–12 the destruction of the four kingdoms 'at the time of Christ' (II, 70). The kingdom of Christ is taken to be eternal and dating from the time of Jesus' earthly life.

This concludes our study of the adherents of this tradition. The three who held the individual interpretation of the man-like figure, Aphrahat, Polychronius, and Cosmas Indicopleustes, have all been shown to have been particularly susceptible to Western influence. Aphrahat and Polychronius evidently adhered to a mixture of the two traditions, and Cosmas propounded an obviously unique and late view. None of them provides a coherent structure of the interpretation of the whole of Dan. 7 which could be understood as the Christian version of an ancient Jewish tradition which interpreted the man-like figure messianically. In the case of the group of interpreters who interpreted the man-like figure on two levels, Ephraem, Theodore bar Koni, and Isho'dad of Merw, it was possible to show that the corporate interpretation of the man-like figure was the original one, while the identification of this figure as Jesus was a late Christian accretion. This corporate interpretation was attested by this tradition's oldest witnesses, Porphyry, and unnamed exegetes known to Aphrahat as well as by the Jewish witness, R. Hayyim ben Galipapa. It must be concluded that the corporate interpretation of the man-like figure as symbol of the Saints of the Most High was the interpretation original to the Syrian tradition.

This is important because the Syrian tradition contains an outline of the author's own interpretation of this chapter handed down from Maccabean times. Moreover, there is nothing about an individual interpretation of the man-like figure which is logically so alien to this tradition that it could not have taken it over. The corporate interpretation cannot have originated in the shift of interpretation which identified the Saints as the Maccabees. Had the originators of the pure form of the Syrian tradition inherited a messianic interpretation of the man-like figure, they would surely have identified him as Judas Maccabaeus. The existence of the corporate interpretation in the Syrian tradition is therefore a powerful additional argument for the conclusion already established in ch. 2, that the corporate interpretation was the interpretation of the original author of Dan. 7. Scholars who wish to maintain an individual interpretation must now give an alternative account of the origin of the corporate interpretation in the Syrian exegetical tradition. Moreover, none of the remarks of any of the exegetes of this tradition suggest any real original connection between Dan. 7 and the Son of man problem. In particular, this tradition has preserved no trace of any idea that the man-like figure is a suffering one. As the remaining material is surveyed, it will become clear that all these conclusions fit perfectly with the rest of the evidence.

NOTES

1   A. Mai, *Scriptorum Veterum Nova Collectio*, vol. i., p. 203.
2   The exegetes are abbreviated for tabulation: Anon = Anonymous, Aphr. = Aphrahat, CI = Cosmas Indicopleustes, Eph. = Ephraem, Gal. = Galipapa, Ish. = Isho'dad of Merw, Pesh. = Peshitta version, Pol. = Polychronius, Por. = Porphyry, TK = Theodore bar Koni.
3   Cf. supra pp. 40–6.
4   For detailed discussion, P. M. Casey, 'Porphyry and the Origin of the Book of Daniel', *JThS* NS XXVII (1976), 15–33.
5   Infra, ch. 4.

4

The Western Tradition

In the West the original author's interpretation was altered by actualizing exegesis. The author expected the end of normal human history with the destruction of Antiochus Epiphanes; his successors continually reinterpreted the four kingdoms and the fourth beast's horns so that they would lead up to the End in Dan. 7.9ff. This exegetical tradition is just as coherent, logical, and consistent as the Syrian: the four beasts symbolize the course of world history down to its end at the time of the little horn, and judgement follows with the triumph of the Saints, with or without the Messiah. This outline is found in rabbinical and patristic exegesis alike, and in exegetical method and substance their interpretations are largely identical.

Throughout the rabbinical and patristic period the dominant power in the Mediterranean world was the Roman. From the perspective of important world powers in this area, it had in fact succeeded the Macedonian, and in secular writers the ancient sequence of kingdoms is duly found with the Romans in last place, a development which can be traced back to Aemilius Sura in the second-century B.C.: his comments, interpolated into Velleius Paterculus I, vi, 6, list the dominant world powers as Assyrians, Medes, Persians, Macedonians, and Romans.[1] Thus the last of Daniel's kingdoms came to be interpreted as the Roman, often mentioned in rabbinical literature under the ciphers of Edom and Esau. 'The fourth is the empire of the Romans, which now rules over the world' (Jerome, *On Daniel*, ad loc.). 'Some say that "dread" (Gen. 15.12) is Edom, because of the scripture "terrible and dreadful" (Dan. 7.7)' (*Lev. R.* 13, 5).

This identification of the fourth kingdom as Rome necessitated some change in the identification of the other kingdoms. Jews had long ago altered the primitive sequence by making the first kingdom the Babylonian instead of the Assyrian. The book of Daniel offered encouragement to anyone who wanted to take

71

the next step of identifying the kingdoms of the Medes and the Persians, and this is what was done. The result was so common that it could be expressed with reference to the one or the other, as well as to both. ' "And a bear met him" (Amos 5.19): this is Media, because the Scripture says "And behold another beast, a second, like a bear" (Dan. 7.5)' (*Esth. R.*, Proem 5). 'R. Joseph learnt: These are the Persians, who eat and drink like bears, and are coated with flesh like bears, and are hairy like bears, and never keep still like bears' (bT *Meg* 11a, ‖bT *Qid* 72a, bT *AZ* 2b, referring to Dan. 7.5). The third kingdom was then identified as the Macedonian. 'In naming it a leopard, he indicated the kingdom of the Greeks, which Alexander of Macedon ruled' (Hippolytus, *On Daniel* IV, iii, 6).

These changes should have caused trouble with the details of the beasts, but this was mitigated by the genuine obscurity of the interpretation of these pieces, and by the flexibility of ancient exegetical method. The result is that some of the new interpretations do not look at first sight less plausible than the old, so that until recently it was easier to misidentify the four heads of the third beast as the Diadochi than to identify the three horns cast down at all. Moreover the general tendency to overinterpret symbolic detail produces similar results when applied to different beasts whether the identification of a particular beast is right or wrong. Thus the Western tradition obtained a logical consistency of its own, and contained no problems serious enough to worry its adherents unduly until the critical era. In rabbinical literature, the identification of the four kingdoms as Babylon, Medo-Persia, Greece, and Rome became so obvious that they are regularly referred to as 'the kingdoms' or 'the four kingdoms' without being identified.

An alteration for a different reason was the identification of the first beast as the Assyrian kingdom. The first extant writer to do this is Eusebius, in a catena quotation from *Dem. Ev.* XV. His interpretation is evidently the result of his knowledge of the pre-Danielic four kingdom sequence as it was handed down by pagan writers, independently of the Book of Daniel. Later Western writers identified the Babylonian and Assyrian kingdoms in their interpretations of the first beast. In this way the correct tradition that the first beast is the Babylonian kingdom was reconciled with the older tradition which thought that the

first of the four kingdom sequence is the Assyrian. This is a
further example of the phenomenon better known through the
identification of the Medes and Persians. In each case two
empires have been identified with each other in order to accommodate existing dogmatic ideas. Theodoret sought to justify the
view that Assyrians and Babylonians formed a single kingdom
in his discussion at 2.31–3, alleging support from Scripture,
secular authors, and Persian custom. When he reached 7.4, he
explained everything that happened to the first beast of the
overthrow and humiliation of this composite empire, his use of
Isa. 10.12 being particularly noteworthy as a development
which could take place only after the identification of the first
beast with the Assyrian kingdom.

After the fall of Rome in the West, the tradition was reinterpreted in the same actualizing manner. One way of dealing
with the identity of the kingdoms was to stretch the Roman
empire. This was a simple matter in the eastern half of it,
because this had not fallen, and it was done in the West too,
Edom becoming virtually a Jewish cipher for the Christian
West. Secondly, the fourth kingdom could be stretched to
include the Arabs as well, much as Aphrahat had stretched the
Greek kingdom to include the Roman, and this was done by
Jephet (c. A.D. 1000), who in commenting on 2.40 expounded
at some length his view that the fourth kingdom was first the
Romans, then both the Romans and the Arabs. Ibn Ezra, in the
middle of the twelfth century, believed that the fourth beast
symbolized the Arab kingdom only, and included both Greeks
and Romans in the third; his view that the Roman kingdom
was still in existence in his own time led him to hold the
remarkable opinion that the Redeemer would come at the time
of both the third and the fourth kingdoms. Among the comments
collected in the medieval compilation known as 'pseudo-
Saadia', those on the vision identify the third kingdom as the
Greeks and the Romans, and the fourth as the Arabs, stretched
back long before the Arab conquest. All these variations illustrate the essential nature of the Western tradition. The eschatological interpretation of Dan. 7.9ff. was uniformly retained, and
the kingdoms reinterpreted so as to obtain the result that the
End will come without a further change of kingdom.

This gave the Western tradition the potential of being used to declare that the End was at hand. For this purpose the horns of the fourth kingdom could be interpreted in terms of contemporary events. This was evidently done by the author of the Epistle of Barnabas, IV, 4–5, though he does not specify the events to which he refers. A similar attitude is manifest in a piece of exegesis recorded at *Gen. R.* 76, 6, where the little horn is identified as Ben Netzer, that is, Odenathus, a Palmyrene vassal of Rome (A.D. 258–67), and the three horns cast down are identified as three of his contemporaries. Against this background, the interpretation of Rashi (A.D. 1040–1105), that the horns were figures of past history, the ten being Roman emperors from Caesar to Vespasian and the little horn Titus, should probably be regarded as the survival of a very ancient piece of actualizing exegesis, possibly lying behind R. Johanan's identification of the ten horns as descendants of Esau (*Gen. R.* 76, 6). This kind of use of Dan. 7 is also implied at bT *San* 97b, especially in sayings attributed to R. Nathan (*c.* A.D. 160) and Rab (died A.D. 247), both of whom refer to the unsuccessful calculations of their predecessors. Hippolytus knew of people whose expectations of the End had been disappointed, and he thought this relevant to his discussion of Daniel's times (Hippolytus, *On Daniel* IV, xv-xxiv).

These identifications and calculations from periods of eschatological excitement are indicative of the actualizing nature of the Western tradition, but the period during which it was held was not one of permanent or universal eschatological fervour. In calmer times the fact that another empire was not expected did not mean that the End was to be expected soon, and the best thing to do with the horns was to put them in the future. Most Christian interpreters did this, identifying the little horn as Antichrist.

But Daniel, contemplating the end of the last kingdom, that is the last ten kings among whom is divided the kingdom of those on whom the son of perdition will come, says that ten horns arise from the beast, and another little horn arises in the middle of them. . . . John, the disciple of the Lord, gave an even clearer revelation in the Apocalypse concerning the last time and these ten kings which belong to it, among whom the kingdom which now reigns will be divided, explaining the identity of the ten horns which were seen by Daniel (Irenaeus, *Against Heresies*, V, 25, 3 . . . 26, 1).

'This concerns Antichrist, that is, the little horn which spoke great things, for his kingdom is to be destroyed for ever' (Jerome, *On Daniel*, at 7.26). Rabbinical interpreters did not develop so useful a concept of Antichrist, and did not have the Book of Revelation. Hence their literature has little to say about the horns, which were not midrashically very useful save in an occasional atomistic manner.

All these approaches to the interpretation of the horns place them between the beginning of the last kingdom and the eschatological events portrayed in vss. 9ff. Eschatological use of these verses is not always clear in rabbinical literature, because vss. 9–10 were a major source of scriptural information about the heavenly world.

> One scripture says, 'Thousand thousands serve him, and myriads of myriads stand before him' (Dan. 7.10), and another scripture says, 'Can his divisions be numbered?' (Job 25.3). There is no contradiction. The second passage refers to the time when the Temple was still standing, while the first speaks of the time when the Temple was no longer standing and, as it were, the Family of Heaven was reduced in number. It was taught, Rabbi said in the name of Abba Jose son of Dosai, 'thousand thousands serve him' (Dan. 7.10) indicates the number of one division, but there are innumerable divisions. R. Jeremiah son of Abba said, 'Thousand thousands serve him' (Dan. 7.10) at the river of fire, as it says, 'A river of fire flowing forth from before him: thousand thousands serve him and myriads of myriads stand before him' (Dan. 7.10). Where does it come from? From the sweat of the Creatures. And where does it pour out? R. Zutra son of Tobiah said in the name of Rab, On the heads of the wicked in Hell . . . (bT *Hag* 13b).

Atomistic midrashic use of these verses is very common in rabbinical literature, simply because they were a major source of information about the heavenly world. Other passages could be used, such as Isa. 6 and Ezek. 1, but their number is quite limited, and Dan. 7.9–10 is unique for some items. Patristic commentators occasionally used these verses in a similar way. For example, Dan. 7.10 is quoted at 1 Clem. 34 to show that there really are innumerable angels always around the Creator, while Clement of Alexandria used Daniel's portrait of God as an old man with white hair to show that old men ought not to conceal their age by dying their hair (*Paedagogus*, III, 16, 4).

This kind of atomistic use of these verses in no way undermines the basic structure of the Western tradition. It merely illustrates the fact that ancient exegetes could appropriate any passage of Scripture and use it atomistically in support of any article of religious belief. The eschatological structure was clearly retained by all those exegetes who sought to comment on the text for its own sake, and hence it is explicitly adhered to by every commentator who belongs to the Western stream of tradition, as well as being retained for many midrashic passages.

'He shall subdue peoples under us, and nations under our feet' (Ps. 47.4). When? When 'he shall choose our inheritance for us, the pride of Jacob' (Ps. 47.5). Another comment. When will he 'choose our inheritance for us' and give it to us? When 'he shall sit on the throne of his holiness' (Ps. 47.9), and so it says 'and I will overthrow the throne of kingdoms' (Hag. 2.22), and so Daniel says, 'I was watching until thrones were cast down and an Ancient of Days took his seat' (Dan. 7.9). And when will he sit? When 'saviours arise on Mount Zion . . . and the kingdom shall be the Lord's' (Obad. 1.21) (Midr. *Ps.* 47, 2).

He thought it appropriate to mention the day of judgement after the termination of the four kingdoms, to show that at the close of their sovereignty they must expect judgement, punishment and condemnation, and that their works are taken count of against them (Jephet, ad loc.).

So the reckoning of the whole and complete life is made by what is called the kingdom of heaven, which is likened to a king, when 'we must all stand before the judgement-seat of Christ, so that each one may receive his due for what he did in his body' (2 Cor. 5.10): and then when the reckoning is being made, there shall also be brought into the reckoning 'every idle word that men speak' (Matt. 12.36) and 'a mere cup of cold water' which anyone has 'given someone to drink because he was a disciple' (Matt. 10.42). And this will take place whenever that which is written in Daniel occurs, 'The books were opened and the court sat' (Dan. 7.10); for a record is made, as it were, of all things that have been spoken, done and thought, and by divine power every hidden thing of ours shall be revealed . . . (Origen, *Commentary on Matthew*, XIV, 8–9, on Matt. 18.23ff.).

If the last judgement is seen to begin at vss. 9–10, one of its events must be the destruction of the final kingdom at vs. 11.

'The burnt-offering (הָעוֹלָה) shall be on the hearth' (Lev. 6.2). This is the wicked kingdom which has exalted (עִילְתָה) itself, as it is written, 'Though you soar as high as an eagle and your nest be set among the stars' (Obad. 1.4). It will be judged with fire, as it is written, 'I was looking until the beast was slain and its body was destroyed and given over to be burned with fire' (Dan. 7.11) (Tanch. *Ts.* 4).

In the one Roman empire all the kingdoms will be destroyed at once because of the blasphemy of Antichrist, and there will not be an earthly empire at all but the society of the Saints and the advent of the Son of God in triumph, of which it is said, 'behold! on the clouds of heaven one like a son of man was coming' (Dan. 7.13) (Jerome, ad loc.).

As in this comment by Jerome, the destruction of the fourth kingdom in vs. 11 should be followed by the coming of the man-like figure in vss. 13–14, and at that point in the eschatological events it is normally placed by adherents of the Western tradition. In Jewish sources, this position is universal, whenever any position is clear, for Jews, unlike Christians, expected a single coming of the Messiah at the End. The connected commentaries of the medieval period assume that the order of the final events will be that of the Danielic text. Most patristic writers follow the same outline by interpreting vss. 13–14 of the second coming of Jesus. For example Theodoret comments on these verses, 'What could be clearer than these words?' He quotes Matt. 24.30 and 1 Thess. 4.16–17, and continues, 'The blessed Daniel taught us this clearly, foretelling the second coming of the Saviour' (Theodoret, *On Daniel*, ad loc.).

The interpretation of the vision was easily fitted into the same pattern. Most commentators necessarily made most of their opinions clear in commenting on the vision, and it remained for them to add in some details and integrate the triumph of the Saints of the Most High into their picture of the events of the End. Of course, no Jewish interpreter failed to realize that the Saints were Jews!

> Because Israel observes the Torah among the nations, the Holy One, blessed be He, will make them inherit a throne of glory, as Scripture says, 'and he will make them inherit a throne of glory' (1 Sam. 2.8). This indicates that the Holy One, blessed be He, will restore the kingdom to Israel, as Scripture says, 'And the kingdom and the dominion and the greatness of the kingdoms under the whole heaven, shall be given to the people of the Saints of the Most High' (Dan. 7.27) (*Num. R.* 11, 1).

Few midrashic comments have however survived in rabbinical literature, for the vision was the main part of the revelation, and it provided the two themes for which Dan. 7 was a unique source—the four kingdoms and the heavenly world. When medieval Jews wrote commentaries, their comments fitted the orthodox pattern, leading up to the triumph of the Jews at the End. At vs. 22, this tradition believed that judgement was given in favour of the Saints.

In the hands of Christian interpreters, the actualizing universal among adherents of this tradition necessarily led to a result that differs in detail from the Jewish view, though it retains the same overall structure. The triumph of the Saints at the End meant that they must fundamentally be Christians, though the Jewish patriarchs of old were not to be excluded. This view was combined with the identification of the little horn as Antichrist to produce a standard interpretation which placed all the events of the interpretative section of Dan. 7 at the End.

> For 'the time has come' means that the whole of time was fulfilled, 'and the Saints will receive the kingdom', when the Judge of judges and King of kings shall come from heaven, remove all the dominion and power of the Adversary and punish all the wicked by burning them up with eternal fire,

but to his servants, prophets, martyrs, and all those who fear him, he will give eternal sovereignty (Hippolytus, IV, 14.3).

The clearest brief exposition of the whole Western structure is provided by Eusebius. In a catena comment on Dan. 7.18 he says,

> Clearly they too will reign together with God. And who can they be but the heirs of God, and fellow heirs of Christ? To them also the kingdom of heaven has been promised, a kingdom which will come into being after the four kingdoms which the prophet saw, concerning which we have just briefly commented. I think the holy apostle Paul had this passage in mind when he wrote as follows concerning the second coming of Christ: 'for at the command, at the sound of the archangel and at the trumpet of God, the Lord himself will come down from heaven . . .' (1 Thess. 4.16). And the same apostle describes also the final appearance and destruction of Antichrist and in addition to this the glorious appearance of our Saviour, in accordance with the prophecy: 'Let no one deceive you in any way. For that day cannot come unless the apostasy comes first and the man of lawlessness is revealed, the son of destruction, the opponent who exalts himself over every being called god and every object of worship, so that he sits in the Temple of God, proclaiming that he himself is God. Do you not remember that I told you this while I was still with you . . .?' (2 Thess. 2.3–5). The wonderful apostle gave an account of such important events in his words concerning the end of life, for he believed what was foretold through the prophet Daniel concerning Antichrist and the glorious kingdom of our Saviour.

Here we have it all, and Eusebius saw it all in Dan. 7—successively from the fourth kingdom contemporary with him, in the future the little horn Antichrist, to be destroyed at the last judgement in vss. 9ff., the coming of the kingdom of God at the second advent of Jesus in vs. 13, after which the fellow-heirs of Christ would reign with him for ever. This is a clear expression of a logical outline which is to be found throughout this tradition. To get it, no more was required than a consistent actualizing exegesis, and a consistent actualizing exegesis was

79

predictable among both Jews and Christians. When this consistent exegesis does occur in a straightforward way in the vast majority of witnesses to the tradition, divergent interpretations must be seen as such.

It is against this general structural background that this tradition's interpretation of the man-like figure must be seen. I have found ten passages of rabbinical literature in which there is a quotation from Dan. 7.13–14; bT *San* 98a; *Gen. R.* 13, 11; *Gen. R.* 13, 12; *Num. R.* 13, 14; Midr. *Ps.* 2, 9; Midr. *Ps.* 21, 5; Tanch. *Tol.* 20; Agg. *Ber.* 14, 3; Agg. *Ber.* 23, 1; Midr. Haggadol Gen. 49.10.

Four of these passages, bT *San* 98a; *Num. R.* 13, 14; Agg. *Ber.* 14, 3; and Agg. *Ber.* 23, 1 are straightforward examples of the messianic interpretation of the man-like figure, and this identification is also to be found at Midr. Haggadol Gen. 49.10. Few other details of the interpretation of Dan. 7.13–14 can be gleaned from them. The purpose of the quotation in *Num. R.* 13, 14 is to show that the Messiah will rule over the land, and it is thus clear that vs. 14 has been interpreted of the rule of the Messiah over the earth. Midr. Haggadol Gen. 49.10 contains a quotation of Dan. 7.27, and in view of the messianic interpretation in the context it should probably be deduced that the suffix of לֹה has been interpreted as a reference to the Messiah, a view found in the commentaries of Ps-Saadia and Samuel ben Nissim. This opinion has the advantage of getting the Messiah into the interpretative section of the vision. Finally it is to be noted that all examples of messianic interpretation of the man-like figure in Jewish sources necessarily involve an eschatological setting for Dan. 7.13–14, because the Jewish messianic hope was purely future.

At Midr. *Ps.* 2, 9 the interpretation of the man-like figure which is presupposed is altogether uncertain. It is evident from the other scriptural quotations that the author of this midrash regards texts which support the sonship of either the Messiah or Israel in the most general sense as coming satisfactorily within his purview, so the interpretation of Ps. 110.1, the other text from the Hagiographa, cannot be held to control that of Dan. 7.13. Thus either interpretation of the man-like figure will suit this passage adequately, and no deduction can be made about other aspects of its interpretation of Dan. 7.13–14.

Two passages, *Gen. R.* 13, 11 and *Gen. R.* 13, 12, contain atomistic midrashic uses of Dan. 7.13 for purposes foreign to this investigation. One point can however be deduced from R. Johanan's use of this passage at *Gen. R.* 13, 11. His opinion that the clouds come from above can be illustrated by Dan. 7.13 only if the original direction of movement of the man-like figure, from heaven downwards, has been preserved.

In the two remaining passages, Midr. *Ps.* 21, 5 and Tanch. *Tol.* 20, the original corporate interpretation of the man-like figure has been preserved. However, this is not obvious in either case, so we must discuss both passages in some detail.[2]

Midr. *Ps.* 21, 5 is a standard kind of passage from the formal point of view, consisting in the reconciliation of two apparently contradictory OT quotations. The quotations are from Dan. 7.13 and Jer. 30.21, and the latter has been an important factor in the usual messianic interpretation of this whole passage. The part quoted runs

והקרבתיו ונגש אלי

'And I will bring him near and he will approach me'. The suffix of והקרבתיו refers to the ruler of Israel, who is the subject of this verse. But there is evidence that a different interpretation was current in ancient times: both LXX and Targum took the suffix to refer to the people of Israel, who were thus assumed to be the subject of ונגש.[3] Is this the interpretation which was assumed by the author of Midr. *Ps.* 21, 5? The repeated אותן shows that it was. The author of this midrash says explicitly that he thinks both these scriptural passages are dealing with a plural entity, and since both passages are known to have been interpreted elsewhere of the people of Israel, that is how he must have interpreted them too. In the case of Dan. 7.13, that means he thought that the man-like figure was to be interpreted of the people of Israel.

The passage may therefore be translated as follows: like the LXX and Targum, I have had to use the plural in translating Jer. 30.21, in order to prevent the meaning from becoming unnecessarily obscured.

Rabbi Berekiah said in the name of Rabbi Samuel: One scripture says 'And he came to the Ancient of Days and they brought him before him' (Dan. 7.13), and another scripture says 'And I will bring them near and they will approach me' (Jer. 30.21). How can both these scriptures be right? The angels will bring them to their region and the Holy One, blessed be he, will stretch forth his hand and bring them near to him. Hence it is said 'And I will bring them near'.

The problem posed by the apparently contradictory OT texts is that in Dan. 7.13 the angels (assumed as the subject of 'they brought') are said to bring the man-like figure, the symbol of the people of Israel, before God; whereas in Jer. 30.21 God says that he himself will bring them near. The problem is solved by supposing that the angels bring them most of the way, as far as the place where the angels dwell; God then stretches out his hand and brings them the rest of the way. Thus this passage has preserved the original corporate interpretation of the man-like figure as a symbol of the people of Israel, and the eschatological setting. The direction of movement has however been altered. This is the kind of alteration which midrashic interpretation of Scripture everywhere allows; the direct cause may well have been Jer. 30.21.

In Tanch. *Tol.* 20, Dan. 7.13 is quoted as scriptural support for the interpretation of 'Anani in 1 Chron. 3.24 as the Messiah. The reason for the quotation of 1 Chron. 3.10ff. in this midrash is that this passage of Scripture contains a family tree of the Davidic line. It was natural that Jewish interpreters should conclude that the Messiah was to be found at the end of the Davidic line. The midrash in Tanch. *Tol* 20 was developed by interpreters who found him in the last word of the list, שבעה, but the person who added the quotation of Dan. 7.13 found him in the last proper name, ענני. It is normally supposed that he must have followed a messianic interpretation of Dan. 7.13, but this opinion has been misleading. If Dan. 7.13 is to provide exegetical support for the identification of 'Anani as the Messiah, the Messiah must be found in the word ענני and not in the man-like figure. The verse may then be translated '... and behold! with 'Anani of heaven one like a son of man was coming'. The man-like figure is then a symbol of Israel in accordance with one of the standard interpretations of this verse, and the verse is held to contain what so many people would have liked it to contain—both the people of Israel and their Messiah. The slight vowel change required to see here the name of the Messiah is paralleled in several other rabbinical texts. For example, one of four such sayings at bT *San* 98b runs, 'And there are some who say, His (sc. the Messiah's) name is Menahem the son of Hezekiah, as it is written, "for Menahem, the restorer of my soul, is far away" (Lam. 1.16).' Dan. 7.13 is the only OT text capable of accommodating 'Anani in this way, and it is this which explains the choice of Dan. 7.13 by the midrashist of Tanch. *Tol.* 20. This passage is therefore further evidence of the corporate interpretation of the man-like figure. The setting remains eschatological.

Later Jewish literature provides further evidence of both messianic and corporate interpretations of the man-like figure. In those sources which I have read, the messianic is the more common, being found for example in the Mysteries of R. Simeon ben Jochai and Midrash Wayosha'.[4] These two sources are of particular interest in that they quote Zech. 12.10 for the death of the Messiah son of Joseph. However there is no organic connection between the quotations of Dan. 7.13 and Zech. 12.10, which in the first of these passages are separated by a considerable section of midrash, so that their use does not provide helpful Jewish background for the application of both these texts to Jesus. The comments of Ps-Saadia are also of particular interest. He identifies the clouds of heaven as 'the angels of the Host, the great multitude which the Creator has given to Messiah', and stresses the figurative nature of the language of this passage. In the final comment on Dan. 7.13, the words 'and they brought him to an Ancient of Days' are supported with a quotation from Ps. 110.1 The only previous Jewish passage we have noted using both these texts is Midr. *Ps.* 2, 9, where they are not associated in this clear and explicit way. Messianic interpretation of Ps. 110.1 as of Dan. 7.13 is very old, and their eventual combination no surprise. It will very probably have been quite independent of Christian influence. The result of this process is remarkable because it is in some ways similar to what Glasson, Perrin, and others have supposed took place behind Mark 14.62.[5] Here Ps. 110.1 really is used to illustrate the results of the Messiah being brought to the Ancient of Days, and here the understanding of Dan. 7.13 is explicitly said to be figurative.

In view of this it is important to note some of the differences. Mark does not say that his interpretation is figurative, and he does not tie it to 'and they brought him to an Ancient of Days'. On the contrary, he follows Ps. 110.1 with the Son of man (the term does not occur in Ps-Saadia) coming with the clouds of heaven, using the first part of Dan. 7.13. Thus, while Ps-Saadia has the coming before the sitting, Mark notoriously has the Son of man sitting before he comes. Further, Ps-Saadia's interpretation of the clouds is unique. He wrote more than 1,000 years later than Mark, and that his particular figurative interpretation of the clouds goes back to the New Testament period is virtually out of the question because it does not occur earlier, and has an entirely satisfactory *Sitz im Leben* in the environment in which it does occur. Ps-Saadia demonstrates, what we already knew, that Ps. 110.1 and Dan. 7.13 might have been combined by the early Christians in the way that Glasson and others have suggested. It still has to be demonstrated that they were so combined, and it is at this point, in his interpretation of the Marcan evidence, that Glasson's argument really fails.

The stress on the figurative nature of Daniel's language is a remarkable feature of Ps-Saadia's commentary. We have noted it at vs. 13, where he in fact applied it also to a quotation from vs. 9, and he had already made the same point at some length in his comments on vs. 10. These comments are not unparalleled among commentators, but they are unusual in the material under review, so that other writers of different periods cannot simply be assumed to have followed an equally figurative interpretation.

Further evidence of Jewish exegetes who followed the messianic interpretation of the man-like figure is provided by patristic writers. Justin, Lactantius, Eusebius, and Jerome all knew Jews who adhered to the Western tradition of interpretation as they did themselves, and the first three knew Jews who interpreted the man-like figure as the Messiah coming at the End (Justin, *Dial.* 32; Lactantius, *Div. Inst.* IV, 12, 12; Eusebius, *Dem. Ev.* IX, 17, 4–7: cf. Jerome, *on Daniel, passim*).

The corporate interpretation of the man-like figure was preserved by Rashi and by Ibn Ezra. At vs. 13 Rashi comments 'This is the Anointed King', and on this basis his interpretation has been said to be messianic. However, after adding on vs. 13

that the Ancient of Days 'was sitting in judgement, judging the nations', a comment which should be interpreted as indicating the eschatological setting of the scene, Rashi proceeds at vs. 14, on the words 'and to him was given sovereignty' to comment, 'And to the son of man he gave sovereignty. He has compared the nations to beasts, and Israel he has compared to a son of man, because they are meek and faultless'. This is an explicit statement of the corporate interpretation of the man-like figure as a symbol of Israel. Moreover the reason given for the choice of this symbol is on the right lines. They are meek and faultless in obedience to God, and hence suitably symbolized by a man, for to be man-like is to be properly obedient to God. It is not clear how this should be reconciled with the messianic view expressed at vs. 13. The state of Rashi's text is so unsatisfactory that the possibility that the messianic comment is a later gloss may not be ruled out; alternatively he will have inherited both traditions, and he may have concluded that the man-like figure was a symbol of Israel and of her leader at the redemption, the Messiah.

Ibn Ezra espoused the messianic interpretation of the man-like figure in the shorter recension of his commentary on Daniel (c. A.D. 1142), but when he wrote the longer recension (c. A.D. 1153) he had come round to the corporate view. He had always been prepared to depart from opinions expressed in Talmud and Midrash, especially where legislative matters were not involved, and in some other cases also, for example Num. 24.17 and Zech. 9.9, he did not accept widespread messianic interpretations. He does this explicitly in his comment on Dan. 7.13: 'Rabbi Joshua says that this "man-like figure" is the Messiah (bT *San* 98a). This is a well-established opinion, but in fact this figure represents the holy people, that is to say, Israel.' The corporate interpretation is repeated in comments on vss. 14 and 18. It is to be noted that Ibn Ezra continued to express his belief in the Messiah.

Rabbinical literature thus provides evidence of both messianic and corporate interpretation of the man-like figure. It does not however help with the date. The traditional way of dating rabbinical sayings is by their authors, but the reliability of this method has not been established by critical investigation, and most of the sayings which interpret Dan. 7.13 are anonymous.

Of those that have a messianic interpretation, only bT *San* 98a
has any attribution. Its author is Joshua ben Levi, who is
regarded as one of the most outstanding Palestinian *amoraim* in
the first half of the third century. His associates included
Johanan and Samuel bar Nachman, the only other two rabbis
who have sayings which quote Dan. 7.13 attributed to them. He
was especially renowned as a haggadist, and several other
sayings are attributed to him in which he resolves apparent
contradictions between passages of Scripture. Of the two
rabbinical sayings which preserve the corporate interpretation
of the man-like figure, Tanch. *Tol.* 20 is anonymous but
certainly late, while the saying in Midr. *Ps.* 21, 5 is attributed
to R. Samuel. He is identified as R. Samuel bar Nachman, a
Palestinian *amora* of the third and fourth centuries, and one of
the most renowned haggadists of his time. He transmits sayings
both of his teacher Joshua ben Levi and of Johanan. Other
sayings attributed to him contain interpretations of Dan. 7.4
(*Lev. R.* 13, 5); 7.9 (*Esth. R.* 1, 6); and 7.19 (*Esth. R.* 4, 12),
which gives him a consistent basic outline of the chapter.

Minimal consistency is however insufficient, and third century
dates are not early enough for New Testament criticism. Help
with dating the messianic exegesis of Dan. 7.13 has often been
sought from another rabbinical passage, bT *Hag* 14a (‖bT *San*
38b).

One scripture says, 'His throne was flames of fire' (Dan. 7.9)
and another scripture says 'until thrones were placed and an
Ancient of Days took his seat' (Dan. 7.9). There is no
contradiction: one for him and one for David. As it was
taught, one for him and one for David, according to R.
Akiba. Rabbi Jose the Galilean said to him, 'Akiba, for how
long will you profane the Presence? Rather, one is for
Judgement and one for Vindication'. Did he accept this
opinion from him or not? Come and hear! 'One for Judgement and one for Vindication', this is the opinion of R.
Akiba! Rabbi Eleazar son of Azariah said to him, 'Akiba,
what have you to do with Haggadah? Get back to your discussions of spots and tents. Rather, one serves as his throne
and one as his stool—the throne for him to sit on and the
stool as a footstool for his feet, as it is written, "The heaven

is my throne, and the earth the footstool of my feet" (Isa. 66.1)'.

It is often supposed that in R. Akiba's original opinion, 'David' means the Messiah and that Akiba would not have found him here if he had not interpreted the man-like figure as the Messiah.[6] While the substantial authenticity of the saying is probable enough, this interpretation of it cannot be established. Firstly, the passage makes excellent sense if it is supposed that 'David' actually means 'David'. R. Akiba is then saying that the real historical David will rise from the dead and take part in the final judgement, sitting on one of the thrones. Secondly, there is nothing inconsistent in holding that there were two thrones, that David or the Messiah sat on one of them, but that vs. 13 actually symbolizes the arrival of the people of Israel. The lack of precise parallel to this combination of views may be due simply to the small quantity of extant evidence, and it is noteworthy that Ibn Ezra, who preserved only the corporate interpretation of the man-like figure in the longer recession of his commentary, nevertheless believed in the coming of the Messiah. Belief in the Messiah's participation in the judgement, like belief that he will come, cannot be regarded as sufficient evidence that an interpreter actually interpreted the man-like figure as the Messiah.

A sufficient reason for the choice of David or the Messiah in this context is to be found in the combination of two factors, namely current beliefs in the important role to be played in the last days by intermediary figures and the seriousness of the problem which the rabbis felt was constituted by the plurality of the thrones. Both Christian and heretical Jewish beliefs were held to find threatening support in Dan. 7.9, and it is this which explains the virulence of the rejection of R. Akiba's original opinion in bT *Hag* 14a‖bT *San* 38b, and of Jose the Galilean's opinion which he then took over, and the suppression of Akiba's original view altogether in the parallel passage Tanch. *Qed.* 1. The background of controversy with Christians is clear in bT *San* 38b and Mekh. *Shir.* IV, 23ff. (Exod. 15.3)‖Mekh. *Bah.* V, 24ff. (Exod. 20.2), while relevant Jewish material occurs not only in the enthronement of Enoch, where it is uncertain whether he has his own throne or not, but more dramatically, if later, in the case of Metatron: in 3 Enoch 15 Metatron is punished because Acher thought there must be two powers, and according to Odeberg the Bodleian Ms. MICH 9 fol. 67b explains the plural thrones in Dan. 7.9 of the thrones of God and of Metatron.[7] The rabbis were so worried by this problem that several discussions of it have been preserved, some partial parallels to others, providing no less than eight distinct, if largely related, solutions (cf. bT *Hag* 14a; bT *San* 38b; *Ex. R.* 30, 18; Tanch. *Qed.* 1; Tanch. *Mis.* 4; Midr. *Ps.* 4, 4; Midr. *Ps.* 47, 2). The problem was already there for Akiba, and his solution is perfectly comprehensible as the work of an interpreter who had not thought of a messianic interpretation of the man-like figure. Therefore his saying cannot be regarded as testimony to the messianic interpretation or as evidence of its date.

In view of the difficulties in the traditional way of dating sayings and their application to this particular case, it is fortunate that external criteria are useful. Here the general consistency of Western Jewish exegesis is important, because this enables it to be treated broadly as a single entity dateable by means of external criteria. The Western Jewish tradition will be shown in ch. 5 to have been in existence as early as the earliest group of rabbis to whom sayings belonging to it are attributed, and medieval commentators provide evidence that it continued to flourish in the medieval period. Rabbinical sayings show that this coherent exegetical tradition was the dominant tradition in Western Jewry throughout this period, and this result is both significant and independent of the reliability of the attribution of these sayings. These external criteria enable us to say that the corporate interpretation of the man-like figure was alive in the Western tradition throughout our period. It was the author's interpretation, so that comparatively late evidence of it within the Western tradition shows that it did not die out. External criteria are also helpful with the messianic interpretation, but they are not a complete answer to the problem. Other evidence shows that an individual interpretation of the figure as Enoch was known before the rabbinical period, IV Ezra 13 shows a messianic interpretation probably held in the first half of the second-century A.D.[8] and this is confirmed by the evidence of Justin (*Dial.* 32). This does not enable us to date the messianic interpretation as early as the time of Jesus, but it does allow us to say that the messianic interpretation of the man-like figure was known throughout most of the rabbinical period.

In the rabbinical passages just surveyed, the corporate view is outnumbered by the messianic, but this does not enable us to deduce the relative prevalence of these two opinions, because the corporate interpretation of the man-like figure renders it generally unsuitable for midrashic use. It is significant that the one straightforward use of Dan. 7.13 in this sense, Midr. *Ps.* 21, 5, is not an example of its use as exegetical support for a statement of Jewish triumph, and has been misunderstood. In Tanch. *Tol.* 20, the only other rabbinical passage in which it is found, it was the only text that could provide the kind of exegetical support required, and again it has been misunderstood. The corporate interpretation of the man-like figure may be clear enough in its context, but the context is removed when it is cited in the course of a midrashic exposition, whereas there are many passages, such as Isa. 45.17 and Obad. 1.21, which could be used with greater clarity for the eventual triumph of Israel.

It is customary to think that there are remarkably few quotations of Dan. 7.13 in rabbinic literature, but the standard of judgement in accordance with which the number of quotations that there are is regarded as a small number is not normally made evident. Christian use of this text is not a good reason for thinking that the rabbis should have made greater use of it,[9] for they were not Christians and were not concerned to argue that the clouds were a particularly good place for their Messiah to come. Hence other messianic texts were just as useful for them as this one, and we have seen that some of them did not interpret it messianically and that when corporately interpreted it is not midrashically useful. This also helps to explain why they should not have quoted these verses as often as they used parts of Dan. 7 for their four kingdom theory and for information about the heavenly world, as Dan. 7 is the best OT source for the four kingdom theory and one of the best sources of information about the heavenly world. Other OT texts are not used so often by the rabbis that their use of Dan. 7.13–14 appears unduly meagre by this standard of judgement. There is therefore no good reason to suppose that Dan. 7.13–14 should have been used by the rabbis more or less than it was, and attempts to explain why it occurs so little in rabbinic literature have been based on a false premise.

Finally it should be noted that these passages provide no evidence of the existence of a Son of man concept in Judaism. Evidence of this concept has been sought in other passages of rabbinical literature, and the question is of such importance to this investigation that we must discuss briefly four of the most important passages: Tg *Exod.* 12.42; Tg *Ps.* 80.18; pT *Ta'anith* 2, 65, 69; and bT *San* 96b.

The Targums to Exod. 12.42 have been discussed in detail by le Déaut.[10] They agree that on the fourth night, when the world comes to an end, Moses will come forth from the wilderness, but it is uncertain whether the Messiah will come forth from Rome or from on high, and whether Moses and the Messiah will come at the head of the flock or on top of a cloud. In either case, there is no question of a quotation of Dan. 7.13, and the possibility of an allusion is surely most doubtful. Sources which read 'cloud' for the Messiah, a reading which le Déaut rejects, read it for Moses too. The influence of imagery from the Exodus tradition is very clear, and renders appeal to Dan. 7.13 unnecessary. Even if the Messiah is said to have come from on high, reference to Dan. 7.13 is by no means clear. It was sometimes thought that Israel would be redeemed by a person who came down from heaven, whether the anonymous Messiah, Michael, Enoch, or Melchizedek, and this may be all that is involved here. In any case, there is certainly no mention of 'the Son of man'.

At Tg *Ps.* 80.18 בן־אדם is translated בר נש by the Targum because this is the most straightforward and simple Aramaic equivalent of it. Except in the book of Ezekiel, where the use of בר אדם is clearly exceptional, it is the normal Targumic rendering of בן אדם and should be regarded as natural and predictable. The LXX of vs. 18 (LXX Ps. 79.18) has υἱὸν ἀνθρώπου, the normal LXX rendering of בן אדם. The LXX of vs. 16 (LXX Ps. 79.16) has υἱὸν ἀνθρώπου simply by assimilation to vs. 18. Similarly the Peshitta has *bar nasha* predictably for בן־אדם is vs. 18b, and by assimilation in vs. 16b. In vs. 16 the Targum has מלכא משיחא for the MT בן. This is clear and straightforward evidence of messianic interpretation on the part of the Targum, but it does not show that בר נש was thought by its author or anyone else to be a synonym for מלכא משיחא. Since the Messiah was expected to be a man, a normal Aramaic term for 'man' could be used to refer to him as to any other man, so that the translator's messianic interpretation gave him no reason to diverge from the natural rendering of בן אדם as בר נש. This passage is therefore an example of the normal use of בר נש as an Aramaic expression for 'man', and does not provide any evidence of a Jewish Son of man concept.

The starting-point of R. Abbahu's saying at pT *Ta'anith* 2, 65b, 69 is Num. 23.19, a fact which must be borne in mind, because it explains so much of the form of the saying. It does not make sense except as the piece of anti-Christian polemic which it is universally recognized to be. Rabbi Abbahu said, 'If a man says to you "I am God", he is lying; "I am Son of man (בן אדם)", he will regret it in the end; if he says "I am going up to heaven", he has said it but he will not fulfil it.' The context ensures that 'Son of man' is correctly understood as a Christian title, and it follows that this passage is not evidence of the existence of a Son of man concept in Judaism. It is to be noted that there is no trace here of Dan. 7.13.

Finally, we must consider R. Nachman's saying at bT *San* 96b. 'R. Nachman said to R. Isaac, "Have you heard when the son of a fallen one (בר נפלי) will come?" "Who is בר נפלי?", he asked. "Messiah", he replied. "Do you call Messiah בר נפלי?" "Yes, is not this what the Scripture says, 'On that day I will raise up the tabernacle of David which is fallen (הנפלת) (Amos 9.11)' "'.' The problem lies in the expression בר נפלי. It has been suggested that נפלי = νεφέλη,[11] but this is unlikely. The uniqueness of the title makes it relatively probable that the author of the saying at least would know what he was talking about, and if the title meant 'son of the cloud' a different explanation would be expected. Moreover it is difficult to see why the Greek νεφέλη should be used instead of the Hebrew or Aramaic ענן. If however the title is derived from Amos 9.11 which is quoted, its uniqueness is not difficult to explain, because it is simply exegesis of a single scriptural text and it is not a particularly suitable messianic title when it is removed from this context. R. Isaac's ignorance is not difficult to explain

91

either. There is no quotation of Dan. 7.13. The assumption of a
connection is based on the Greek νεφέλη together with the fact
that this is the standard text that connects the Messiah with the
clouds. But if this were correct we would expect בר ענני or the
like to occur, and the more accurate בר ענן would be equally
intelligible as a reference to the Exodus cloud typologically
interpreted (cf Tg *Exod.* 12.42). It is therefore to be concluded
that this saying does not provide satisfactory evidence of the use
of Dan. 7.13 nor any evidence of a Son of man concept in
Judaism.

When the rest of the evidence has been surveyed in ch. 5, it
will clearly be seen that there was no Son of man concept in
Judaism, and this explains why none of the rabbinical passages
in which the man-like figure appears shows the slightest awareness that בר אנש was ever a title. Nor can Dan. 7.13 be shown
to have produced any other title. Conversely, the only rabbinical passage which shows awareness of the Christian use of 'Son
of man' as a title carries no trace of Dan. 7.13. The rabbis did
not connect the two. The connection was first made in Christian
circles. As for the interpretation of Dan. 7.13–14 itself, this has
been shown to fit beautifully into the overall structure of the
Western tradition. Apart from the occasional atomistic use of
these verses in the manner characteristic of ancient exegesis, the
placement of these verses is uniformly eschatological, whether
the man-like figure is interpreted messianically or as a symbol
of the Saints.

Patristic interpretation fits into the same pattern. The corporate interpretation was not preserved, and the Messiah was
of course identified as Jesus, but the important factor is that the
eschatological setting implied by the logic of the Western
tradition is almost universal. In a search through patristic
literature down to Eusebius, I found quotations of, or clear
references to, Dan. 7.13–14 in the following passages:

Justin
 Apology I, 51, 9.
 Dialogue 14, 8; 31–32; 76, 1–2; 79, 2; 126, 1.
Irenaeus
 Against Heresies III, 19, 2; IV, 20, 11; IV, 33, 1 and 11.
Acts of Peter xxiv

Hippolytus
  On Daniel IV, x-xi.
  On Christ and Antichrist XXII; XXVI; XLIV.
  Syntagma (ed. Nautin) p. 243.
Tertullian
  Against Marcion III, 7, 4; III, 24, 11; IV, 10, 9–14; IV, 39, 11;
  IV, 41, 4.
  Against the Jews XIV.
  On the Flesh of Christ XV.
Cyprian
  To Quirinus, Testimonia II, 26.
Anonymous
  The Dialogue on the Orthodox Faith XXV.
Lactantius
  Divine Institutes IV, 12–21.
  Epitome 42, 4.
Eusebius
  Prophetic Extracts III, 44.
  Ecclesiastical History I, 2.
  Demonstration of the Gospel IX, 17, 4–7; XV.
  Against Marcellus II, 1, 4–5.
  On the Theology of the Church III, 17.
  Commentary on the Psalms 96.1.
  Commentary on Luke 9.26; 19.12; 21.28.
  Catena comments on Dan. 7.13; 7.14; 7.18.

The occasional vague or uncertain references to Dan. 7.13–14
in passages such as Tertullian, *On the Resurrection of the Flesh*
XXII (cf. Justin, *Dialogue* 120, 4; Eusebius, *On the Lives of the
Prophets* s.v. Daniel, etc.) do not add anything to our knowledge
of patristic use and interpretation of these verses. There are
however three possible references in other documents which are
worthy of mention because of their comparatively early date:
Didache 16.8; *Apocalypse of Peter* 1, and 6. However, all three
passages appear to contain free expressions of Christian belief in
terms reminiscent of New Testament passages, especially Matt.
24.30, so that none of them may safely be used as evidence of
patristic interpretation of Dan. 7.13–14. The earliest patristic
passage in which a definite citation of Dan. 7.13 is found is
Justin, *Apology* I, 51, 9: 'That he (sc. Jesus) will arrive from
heaven with glory, listen also to what was said about this
through Jeremiah the prophet. It is this: "Behold, as a son of

93

man he comes upon the clouds of heaven, and his angels with him" '. It is evident that in this passage Dan. 7.13 has been interpreted of the second coming of Jesus. The attribution to Jeremiah is remarkable, and may be due to the use of a collection of testimonia; Justin got the right prophet in his *Dialogue*. In this work Justin expressed clearly his belief in two parousias of Jesus, the first being his earthly life, the second his future appearance in glory, and here again Dan. 7.13 is very obviously applied to the second. Irenaeus evidently took the same view, and Hippolytus is as straightforward as Justin: '. . . and his second parousia in glory was announced, that he will come from heaven with a force of angels and the glory of his Father, as the prophet says, "You shall see a king with glory" (Isa. 33.17), and "I was seeing on the clouds of heaven one like a son of man coming . . ." Dan. 7.13)' (Hippolytus, *On Christ and Antichrist* XLIV). Tertullian also expounded the idea of two advents of Christ: for the second he cited Dan. 2.34 and continued, 'Concerning this advent the prophet also said, "And behold! with the clouds of heaven one like a son of man was coming . . ." (Dan. 7.13)' (Tertullian, *Against Marcion* III, 7, 4).

The first patristic writer to diverge in any serious way from this view is Cyprian. His quotation of Dan. 7.13–14 at *Test.* II, 26 follows the Western Christian identification of the man-like figure as Jesus, but the scene is not considered to be his second coming to carry out the final judgement; the events of these verses are placed immediately after the Resurrection. The quotation is introduced by the heading, 'That when he had risen, he received all power from the Father and his power is eternal'. Not until heading 28 do we reach the eschatological judgement, which is followed by his eternal kingdom at II, 29.

If the normal Western tradition is otherwise adhered to, Cyprian's view causes a break at Dan. 7.13, when we suddenly go back from the End to the immediate sequel of Jesus' Resurrection and Ascension (*c.* A.D. 30). The enormous flexibility of ancient exegetical method made this possible. It is simplest when, as here, the exegesis of the rest of the chapter is not under consideration. When a text is required to support an item of religious belief, it may be interpreted in isolation. The new interpretation may, but need not, be grafted onto an existing interpretative tradition. In this case it was, for the identification of the man-like figure as Jesus was already well established. Separated from the rest of the chapter, vss. 13 and 14 fit Cyprian's interpretation perfectly well, given only the religious belief which they are required to support. The change in the direction of movement caused no problem because the events in vss. 9–14 could in themselves easily be thought of as taking place in heaven, and because Cyprian's exegesis is atomistic. The adaptability of the exegetical method which allowed the emergence of this by-form appears most beautifully in Lactantius, who having inherited both interpretations cheerfully adhered to them both (*Div. Inst.* IV, 12–21).

Yet because this requires the atomistic interpretation of these verses, and because there were no overriding religious reasons for allowing an atomistic isolation of these two verses to become dominant, Cyprian's view did not overcome the earlier tradition. The views of its subsequent adherents can be traced directly back to him. It is a view that he may have originated himself, for in his work the midrashic motivation for it is extremely obvious—texts are sought to support the view that Jesus received eternal power from the Father straight after the Resurrection. On analytical grounds, this must be regarded as precisely the kind of situation required for this exegesis to be originated.

By the beginning of the fourth century, only Lactantius has given Cyprian any support, so that the attestation of this view in the whole of the first three centuries is very weak. It is to be concluded that it was unknown in the earliest period of Christianity.[12] Many scholars have held a contrary view, and Gaston is distinguished from them only by his clarity: 'Cyprian's understanding is not only typical of the early church in general when they read Dan. 7.13f. for itself and not in connection with Mark 13.26, but it is also the natural and correct understanding'.[13] There are three things wrong with this. In the first place, as a statement about patristic exegesis, it is on empirical grounds simply false. Cyprian's interpretation is rare, late, contrary to the logic of the normal Western tradition, and unmentioned by Hippolytus, Jerome, and Theodoret, commentators who were reading Dan. 7.13f. for itself. Secondly, that Cyprian's view is natural is true enough, but the same can be said of the other ancient interpretations of this verse too, for the relevant criteria

95

for the naturalness of an interpretation are those prevalent in the ancient world, and by these standards most ancient exegesis is perfectly natural. Thus the naturalness of Cyprian's interpretation is of marginal relevance and does not lead to any useful conclusion. Thirdly, Cyprian's understanding should not be called 'correct' when his identification of the man-like figure is quite wrong. In short, Gaston's whole procedure is inappropriate for determining what exegesis of this verse is likely to have been in vogue in the earliest period. The same goes for all modern attempts to build on Cyprian's view.

One other development in the interpretation of the man-like figure must be noted. Once the expression 'Son of man' was divorced from its semitic environment, it could no longer function as an expression for 'man', and it was ripe for Western Christian interpreters to read into it as much as they could. One of the earliest works to utilize Dan. 7 has one of the oddest passages: 'Behold again Jesus, not son of man, but son of God . . .' (Barnabas 12.9). It appears from this that Barnabas was not aware of the Gospel title 'the Son of man'—indeed it is probable that he did not know any of the canonical Gospels. Here 'son of man' is contrasted with 'son of God', and the sense appears to be that the virgin-born Jesus was son of God and not a son of a man. This use however suggests that Barnabas did not have the identification of Daniel's man-like figure as Jesus in mind. He may not have thought much about Dan. 7.13 at all, perhaps having read Daniel's prophecies only in the works which he cites in IV, 4–5. The next extant interpreter of Dan. 7 adds in what was to become the classical Western interpretation of the expression: 'For when Daniel says "like a son of man" is he not hinting at the same thing? For to say "like a son of man" means that he appeared to be and became man, but shows that he was not of human seed' (Justin, *Dialogue* 76, 1–2). Subsequent interpreters continue to refer to the virgin birth and the human nature of Christ.

Once established, this interpretation was not removed by interpreters who might be thought to have known better. Theodoret, who explains the 'son of' idiom when commenting on Dan. 11.9–10, nevertheless comments at 7.13–14, 'clearly calling him "son of man", because of the nature which he took on.' Ignorance of the semitic idiom was useful in a measure, but not essential to the expression of the religious dogma of the Natures of Christ. To ancient exegetes the Word of God did not do things by chance, but by the will of God, so that significance could be felt in the parallelism of 'son of man' with 'son of God', and in the usual meaning of 'son of', even when an exegete knew intellectually that בר אנש was a normal term for 'man'. Ignorance is essential only to a theory which requires Jesus to have had Dan. 7.13 especially in mind when he used the term 'son of man' on the ground that this is the only suitable place where the term occurs.

Such a theory was provided by Tertullian. Writing in Latin, he did not even have the problem of the articles to deal with. 'What now, if Christ is celebrated in Daniel with the very title "son of man" (filii hominis)' (*Against Marcion* IV, 10). With the translation of the OT into Latin, 'filius hominis', the Gospel title, actually occurred in the Danielic text. Divorced from the semitic culture in which Jesus lived, Tertullian moreover supposed that at Luke 5.24 the historical Jesus was making a claim to forgive sins as the unique Judge of Daniel's prophecy.[14] It is an appropriate beginning for the theory that the Gospel 'title' is derived from Dan. 7.13, for the theory has never really come to terms with the articles, the Aramaic or the Jewish evidence as a whole.

If 'filius hominis' made it easier to believe that the Gospel title was found in the Danielic text, it is notable that patristic writers in Greek were also struck by the similarity between ὁ υἱὸς τοῦ ἀνθρώπου and ὡς υἱὸς ἀνθρώπου, rather than by the difference. Eusebius provided a good example. 'Daniel the prophet foretells this more clearly when he distinctly calls the Christ of God "son of man", just as therefore the Scripture of the Holy Gospels was accustomed to call him' (*On the Theology of the Church* III, 17, where a quotation of Dan. 7.13–14 follows immediately). When the normality of 'son of man' as a term for 'man' was unknown or unappreciated, and the Christian Bible had been put together as a complete sacred book, this similarity of the Danielic and Gospel terms could not be explained or be passed off by an ancient exegete as coincidence, but was seen as theologically significant.

The study of the Western tradition has led to two significant results. Firstly, the tradition, as found in both Jewish and

97

Christian interpreters, is a logical and coherent whole, developed from the author's original interpretation in a logical and predictable way in accordance with exegetical principles known to have been widespread throughout this period. This coherent exegetical tradition provides a pattern into which the earlier material can be fitted. The Jewish version of the tradition preserved the original corporate interpretation of the man-like figure within this overall structure. Secondly, certain details of Western interpretation which have been important in scholarly discussion of the Gospel term 'Son of man', particularly Cyprian's interpretation of Dan. 7.13, have been shown to be late developments.

NOTES

1 See further C. P. Swain, *CP* XXXV (1940), 1–20; D. Flusser, *Isr Or St* 2 (1972), 148–75.

2 For a much more detailed treatment of the original sources, P. M. Casey, *NT* XVIII (1976), 167–80.

3 P. M. Casey, op. cit., 169–73.

4 A. Jellinek, *Beth Ha-Midrash* (6 vols, ²1938) III, 80 and I, 56.

5 Infra, 179–82.

6 E.g. E. Dhanis, *Gregorianum* 45 (1964), 36; G. Vermes, *Jesus the Jew* (1973), 171.

7 For Enoch, cf. infra, 110; for MICH 9, H. Odeberg, 3 *Enoch, or The Hebrew Book of Enoch* (1978), 106, cf. 35.

8 Infra, 88–107 on Enoch; 124–9 on IV Ezra.

9 Cf. especially M. J. Lagrange, *Le Messianisme chez les Juifs* (1909), 228.

10 R. le Déaut, *La Nuit Pascale* (1963), especially 263ff, 359ff.

11 Cf. J. Levy, *Neuhebräisches und chaldäisches Wörterbuch über die Talmudim und Midrashim* (1876–9), I, 259a.

12 On the New Testament evidence, infra 158–201.

13 L. Gaston, *No Stone on Another* (1970), 385.

14 Cf. infra, 159–61, on the Marcan parallel, Mark 2.10.

5
Apocrypha and Pseudepigrapha

The most important section of the evidence outside the New Testament consists of the Jewish Apocrypha and Pseudepigrapha. Here we must establish the extent of the use of Dan. 7 as well as its interpretation, and see whether it can be fitted into the exegetical traditions discussed in chapters 3 and 4. Moreover, this is the crucial material for deciding whether the Jews at the time of Jesus already possessed a 'Son of man concept'. I have therefore systematically re-read all the published literature which can reasonably be dated within two or three centuries of the time of Jesus, excepting only Philo and Josephus. This clearly showed that previous workers have combed all this literature thoroughly and catalogued all possible references to Dan. 7. Evidence of the interpretation of Dan. 7 was found in the Similitudes of Enoch, the Dead Sea Scrolls, the Sibylline Oracles, Josephus, 4 Ezra, 2 Baruch, 3 Enoch, and the Hebrew Apocalypse of Elijah.

The Similitudes of Enoch

The Similitudes of Enoch is a difficult work whose interpretation and dating have not been facilitated by the fact that it is extant only in late Ethiopic manuscripts, but it is a central piece of evidence for the widespread scholarly belief in the existence of a Son of man concept in the Judaism of the time of Jesus.[1] It should probably be dated c. 100 B.C.–A.D. 70, since its ideas can be made intelligible against the background of this period. The crucial use of Dan. 7 made by its author[2] consists in his employment of the vision of Dan. 7.9f., beginning at 1 Enoch 46.1, with the first occurrence of the term 'son of man' at 46.2. In these verses Daniel's Ancient of Days has become 'one who had a head of days'. The alteration might be felt to indicate more clearly the eternal pre-existence of the deity rather than his age, and this may be the reason for it. The remainder of the description of him is virtually lifted from Dan. 7.9. The description of the man-like figure is more elaborate than in Dan. 7.13, but the likeness to a man is clear enough, and in 46.2 Enoch's question contains the phrase 'that son of man'. If, like this author, you ignore the interpretation of the son of man figure in Dan. 7 itself, or at least do not recognize that the Saints of the Most High constitute that interpretation, the figure is in fact mysterious, and the questions in 46.2 arise naturally out of the OT text as this author understood it.

This leads straight to the problem of the use and meaning of the term 'son of man' in the Similitudes. The attempts to prove that he is really a corporate entity have not been successful.[3] Final proof that he is an individual will come with his identification, but first it must be shown that throughout the Similitudes the term 'son of man' is not a title. Charles argued that the demonstrative represents the definite article of the Greek *Vorlage*, and Sjöberg accepted this as being at least possible.[4] It is true that the Ethiopic demonstrative could be used as a translation of the Greek article and that it is so used in those parts of 1 Enoch where the Greek text has survived; moreover, it is possible that it was so used by the translator of the Similitudes. Charles quotes three examples (62.10; 71.13; 52.5). But the data which he uses to establish that the demonstrative represents the Greek definite article are quite uncontrolled; for all we know the Greek *Vorlage*, assuming for the moment that there was one, may have had the article with the title Lord of Spirits all 104 times; in which case Charles' examples would show that the translator of the Similitudes could use the Ethiopic demonstrative to translate the Greek article, but usually did not. The one piece of evidence that we can really control is the title 'the Elect One'. In the twelve relevant examples (39.6; 40.5; 49.2, 4; 51.3, 5; 52.6, 9; 61.5, 8, 10; 62.1) the demonstrative does not occur once. Therefore its occurrence twelve times with the expression 'son of man' cannot be the result of a random process whereby the translator sometimes did, but sometimes did not, represent the Greek article by means of the Ethiopic demonstrative. This argument is all the stronger for the fact that the remaining four occurrences of the term 'son of man' can be explained as not needing a demonstrative.

So far a Greek *Vorlage* has been assumed, but Ullendorf has again canvassed the possibility of direct translation from Aramaic into Ge'ez without the interposition of a Greek version.[5] The argument is plausible but not decisive. He expounds the general situation like this:

> . . . direct translation from an Aramaic language would scarcely have presented any serious difficulty for the Syrian monophysite monks who had settled in Ethiopia in the fourth and fifth centuries. . . . These Syriac-speaking monks were among the translators of the Bible into Ethiopic and the unmistakable imprint of Syriac on ecclesiastical Ge'ez is too well known to warrant repetition here.[6]

A further general observation is necessary. The Enoch material from Qumran, with the notable absence of any recognized fragments of the Similitudes, has demonstrated the existence of quantities of the material found in 1 Enoch quite separate from the Similitudes. It is therefore possible that the Similitudes were translated into Ge'ez quite separately from the rest of 1 Enoch, and the present 1 Enoch put together first in Ethiopic, so we cannot assume that the Similitudes were translated from the same language as other parts of 1 Enoch. If they were translated directly from Aramaic, a simple explanation of the absence of Greek fragments is obtained, but neither this nor the detailed arguments so far put forward may be regarded as decisive. We must therefore provide some assessment of the effect of the hypothesis of direct translation from Aramaic on the above discussion of the use of the demonstrative with the term 'son of man'. If the Similitudes were translated directly from Aramaic (or Hebrew), the general tenor of the above argument is strengthened. The rarity of the demonstrative with the titles of God is now relevant, for this supports the absence of the demonstrative with the title 'the Elect One' and constitutes further evidence that the demonstrative with the terms for 'son of man' represents a genuine demonstrative in the original text. This weight of evidence cannot be overthrown by the difficulties of 1 Enoch 62.10; 71.13; 52.5, and in all these examples one may suspect a failure to perceive the precise force of the Aramaic or Hebrew הדין.

A further problem is the fact that there are three different Ethiopic expressions for 'son of man' in the Similitudes: *walda sab'e* 46.2, 3, 4; 48.2; and the Noachic passage 60.10; *walda be'esi* 62.5; 69.29 (*bis*); 71.14; *walda 'eguala 'emmaheiaw* 62.7, 9, 14; 63.11; 69.26, 27; 70.1; 71.17. These should all be regarded as translation variants[7] for בר אנשא or, if the original language of the Similitudes was Hebrew, בן אדם.

It is now evident that this term required definition, normally supplied by means of a demonstrative. Clearly it is not a title. But in that case, which man does this author keep referring to? The answer to this question is given at the climax of the Similitudes where God says to Enoch, 'You are the man who is born unto righteousness . . .' (71.14). Overliterally, 'You are the son of man . . .', but 'son of man' means 'man'. When it is realized that ch. 71 provides the identification of the mysterious figure seen in the preceding visions, the structure of the Similitudes becomes clearer.[8] The term 'son of man' first occurs in the second parable, in which Enoch sees 'that son of man' in heaven; his name is named, and he is revealed to the righteous and elect. Thus the identification with the Elect One is made known in heaven and passed on to the righteous and elect. In the third parable, the Elect One is actually enthroned, and the revelation is made to the kings and the mighty and the exalted and those who dwell on the earth (1 Enoch 62.1). Here Enoch sees the time of the general unveiling, the Day of the Elect One, when those brought to judgement find out who he is. Ch. 71 then provides the real name of this figure—Enoch himself. This is the secret already known to the elect and being made known by the author of the Similitudes.

With this structure in mind, we must discuss some of the son of man sayings. The term first occurs at 46.2, as we have seen, and the description of the figure of whom it is used has caused several scholars to assume that a heavenly being is described. But this is not what the author says. The key is given to us by ch. 71—this is the description of an exalted man. In 46.3 the relative clauses define the term 'son of man'; they tell us which son of man the author means. This makes good sense of the fact that Enoch rather than the angel is the first to use the term. A new translation is a straightforward way of making the point.

2 Then I asked one of the angels, one who went with me and showed me all secrets, concerning that man, who he was,

where he was from, and why he went with the Head of
Days.

3 He replied, 'This is the man who has righteousness;
righteousness dwells with him, and he reveals all the
treasures of that which is hidden, because the Lord of
Spirits has chosen him, and his lot is pre-eminent before the
Lord of Spirits in uprightness for ever.'

Why then is the term for man *walda sab'e*? The term in the
Vorlage will have been בר אנשא (or בן אדם). The use of this
rather than any other expression or word for 'man' is to be
explained by the influence of Dan. 7.13 at this point. In considering his identification, we must recall the circles from which
this work emanates. As early as Gen. 5.24 we find the exaltation
of Enoch; in the literature of our period we find ample evidence
of the development of speculation about him resulting in the
attribution of a remarkably high position to him. To some
people Enoch was a figure of primary importance and incomparable distinction. Such a person wrote 1 Enoch 46.3, in which
he first of all identifies the mysterious visionary figure of 46.1 as
a man, and then says four things about him.

1 Righteousness is his outstanding characteristic: cf. 1 Enoch
1.2; 12.4; 15.1; 13.10; 14.1; Wisd. 4; T. Levi 10.5; T. Dan 5.6;
Jub. 10.17, and above all 1 Enoch 71.14. In the intertestamental
period as a whole other people were designated as outstandingly
righteous as well, and this quality is predicated of the whole
group of the elect in the Similitudes, but to a member of the
Enoch circles the simple description of a single, otherwise
unidentified, man as 'the man who has righteousness, with
whom righteousness dwells' could hardly mean anyone but
Enoch himself.

2 He reveals all the treasures of that which is hidden. But who,
in the view of the Enoch literature, is the great revealer? Enoch.

3 God chose him. This time we do not have a recognizable
exclusive description, but this does more than just fit the
picture, it identifies him as the Elect One.

4 'His lot is pre-eminent before the Lord of Spirits in uprightness for ever.' This appears to make him the most distinguished

103

human being ever, and thus further identifies him as Enoch.

All this is seen from the point of view of people familiar with current speculations about Enoch. The extent to which it would be clear to any outsider is another matter. But the Enoch speculations were quite widely known, and if the term 'son of man' is not a title, it would naturally be read as the equivalent of 'man'. Given that a man is being described here, and that the description of 46.1 suggests that this was a man exalted to heaven, the identification might have been clearer than is usually supposed. Thus the final and explicit answer to the first question in 46.2, which comes in 71.14, makes explicit what many readers would already know.

Walda sab'e also occurs in the Noachic passage, 60.10. Here it is especially reminiscent of the way 'son of man' is used in the book of Ezekiel, but it is more interesting that this passage is like all the other occurrences of 'son of man' in the Similitudes in that its use falls within the normal range of the Hebrew and Aramaic expressions for 'man'.

In the third parable, the term 'son of man' recurs at 62.5. Enoch has been seated on the throne of his glory and revealed to the kings and the mighty and the exalted who recognize him and are duly distressed 'when they see that son of man sitting on the throne of his glory'. There should be no doubt which son of man is involved—this is the Elect One on his throne of glory, that is, to the initiated, Enoch. The whole passage is linked with the vision that began in ch. 46 in that the same figure is involved, but if 'son of man' is a fixed expression, it is reasonable to see it as a further means of linking the visions together prior to the explicit revelation at 71.14. The next occurrence of the term at 62.7 has been the subject of comment because it is one of the four examples without the demonstrative. But here the demonstrative is not necessary because of the context. The figure of whom the term 'son of man' is used has been under discussion since the beginning of the chapter, and the term has just been used of him at 62.5. This context supplies the reference usually indicated by the demonstrative—the son of man referred to is the son of man the author has just been talking about. The same applies to 69.27, where the demonstrative is not necessary immediately after the occurrence of the term in 69.26 (though the possibility of a demonstrative in the *Vorlage* of 69.27 may not be excluded).

70.1 is more difficult, because of the problems involved in establishing the correct text. The text of the Similitudes is in such a state that considerations of intrinsic probability must carry great weight in an example like this, and for this reason it is best to follow the reading of U.[9] By standards which prevail in the manuscript tradition of this work U is a good manuscript, possibly as early as the fifteenth century, and it is supported by two further manuscripts. It reads, 'Now it came to pass after this that the name of that son of man was raised aloft while he was still alive to the Lord of Spirits'. This makes excellent and straightforward sense: 'that son of man' is Enoch, and the verse begins the narrative of Enoch's translation. The absence of 'the son of man' in 71.1–13 is no longer a difficulty. The third similitude ends at 69.29, and 70–71 does not tell us more of Enoch's visions, but recounts the story of his translation. Thus we no longer have to deal with two figures, Enoch in the past having a vision, and Enoch in the future in the vision. We have only Enoch in the past being translated, and of him the term 'son of man' is used at 70.1 and again in 71.14, 17 as it was used of him before. The whole passage 70–71 now appears as a more unified narrative.[10]

The final passage 71.14–17 contains some further points of difficulty. 71.14 is the fourth passage where the term 'son of man' is alleged to occur without a demonstrative (excluding the Noachic 60.10). Twice, at 62.7 and 69.27, we have found it unnecessary because of the context (though in the second of these passages it might have stood in the *Vorlage*). Here, as at 46.3, there is a relative clause instead to tell us which son of man the author means. This deals with all four occurrences of the term 'son of man' without a demonstrative; all of them are readily explicable on the assumption that where the demonstrative does occur it is a genuine demonstrative. Here as elsewhere the term 'son of man' means simply 'man'.

> You are the man who is born of righteousness;
> Righteousness dwells in you
> And the righteousness of the Head of Days will not leave you.

There is a clear reference back to 46.3, not because both verses

contain a title, but because of the context. 71.14 identifies Enoch
as the visionary figure of 46.3, whose description begins: 'This
is the man who has righteousness; righteousness dwells in
him . . .'. The use of the same term 'son of man' is helpful; but
the keynote is righteousness. The speaker is apparently God, the
subject (the Head of Days) being taken over naturally from vs.
13 to vs. 14. The speech which begins in vs. 15 ends at the end
of vs. 16, and vs. 17 is to be regarded as a concluding passage
by the author. The term 'son of man' again refers to Enoch, and
the whole verse forms a straightforward summary conclusion.

And so there will be length of days with that man
And the righteous shall have peace and an honest way of life
In the name of the Lord of Spirits for ever and ever.

What more could the Enoch circle ask for?

This author's picture of the Enoch story may now be summarized as follows. Enoch was pre-existent, like other righteous
people (1 Enoch 70.4; cf. 39.4f.). He was born, and lived his life
on earth. During this life he saw visions, including visions of
himself as the eschatological judge. He did not die, but was
exalted to heaven, where he was greeted by God. There he is
now, shortly to reappear at the end as the eschatological judge.
In that capacity he would deliver and vindicate the group of
which the author was a member, condemning their oppressors.
This picture may not be entirely familiar, but it should not on
that account be regarded as beyond belief. The brief report of
Gen. 5.21–4 is sufficient on its own to provide an early date for
the presence of Enoch speculation in Israel. Already in 1 Enoch 13
we find Enoch occupying the role of an intermediary figure who
conveys the news of the judgement of God to the wicked angels,
and the whole Enoch literature testifies to the extraordinarily
high position which the Enoch circle accorded to him. By the
time the Similitudes were written, theological and other
pressures had produced the variety of intermediary figures who
lie at the centre of the multiform messianic expectation of this
period. When these pressures hit the Enoch circle, it was Enoch
whom they elevated to the position of eschatological judge and
redeemer. Then the author of the Similitudes, or the group of
which he was a member, read the book of Daniel, and found
their man in Dan. 7.13. This finding, though unique in extant

literature, is perfectly comprehensible and fully in accord with the exegetical methods universal in contemporary Judaism. The author then proceeded to make creative use of his discovery; it is this use which explains why he chose to use the term 'son of man' rather than any other word for man in his descriptions of his heavenly hero. He used it, not as a title, but as an ordinary expression for 'man'.

We must now return to this author's use of Dan. 7 as a whole. Table 1 provides a list of passages which may be considered worthy of examination for possible use of this chapter.

TABLE 1

1 Enoch	Dan. 7	1 Enoch	Dan. 7
40.1	10	52.4	14
41.9	22	53.6	13
45.3	9	55.1	9, 13
46.1–2	9, 13, 16	55.4	9
46.3–5	13–14, 25–6	60.1–2	9–10
46.6	25	60.10	13
46.7	19, 23	61.8–9	9–10
46.8	25	62.1	7f.
47.2	10, 22	62.2–16	13–14
47.3	9–10	63.11	13
48.2	13, 9	65.12	18, 22, 27, 14
48.5	14	69.26–9	9–10, 13–14
48.7–8	13	70.1	13
48.8–10	11–12, 17–27	71.1	9
49.2	14	71.2	10
51.3	9	71.6–17	9–10, 13–14

It does not seem possible to demonstrate that the author had made use of any of the Danielic interpretation of the vision of Dan. 7.9f.: the whole section Dan. 7.15–28 has left no definite trace in this work. In considering the possibility that Dan. 7.22 might have been interpreted to mean that the Saints became the judges, the most interesting passage is 1 Enoch 69.27, 'and the sum of the judgement was given to the son of man'. If the son of man figure of Dan. 7.13 was interpreted as the leader of the Saints of the Most High, Dan. 7.22 thus interpreted might conceivably lead to the conception of their leader as the man who did the judging. But this procedure is very hypothetical; the similarity of expression is not of itself sufficient to imply literary dependence; and the thought of the two passages is not really the same. Therefore the origin of the entrusting of judgement to the son of man is to be found elsewhere, and the similarity of the two passages, such as it is, must be coincidental. It follows that Danielic influence should not be found in 41.9. 47.2 is a little different: 'that judgement may be done unto them'. But here, while the passages have in common the thought of the vindication of the righteous, the sense of 'judgement' in 47.2 is different from that of Dan. 7.22. 1 Enoch 65.12 comes from a Noachic interpolation, so that dependence on the interpretation of the vision of Dan. 7 in this passage would not demonstrate such dependence on the part of the author of the main part of the Similitudes. Here Enoch says to Noah, 'The Lord of Spirits . . . has destined thy righteous seed both for kingship and great honours'. The kingship of the whole group of the righteous is a particularly interesting contact of thought, but it must remain doubtful whether this is due to direct dependence. Finally, the righteous and elect in the Similitudes are also called holy (1 Enoch 38.4, 5; 39.4; 43.4; 48.7, 9, etc.). But the Danielic expression 'holy ones of the Most High' is conspicuous by its absence, and the use of the term 'holy' of human beings in this period is less remarkable than is sometimes thought.[11]

If the last paragraph has seemed at times a little far-fetched, the need for it is shown by the work of Hartman.[12] His suggestions are the source of all the remaining comparisons for 1 Enoch 46.1–8 in Table 1. His discussion of the Similitudes is confined to 46.1–8. He arranges the OT material in five columns. Col. 1 contains 'passages of which I am certain that they and no others influenced that text *and* that in this connection the wording of the text was considerably influenced by the passage (it becomes almost a quotation)'. In col. 1 he has placed Dan. 7.9, 13: that may be granted. Col. 2 contains 'passages which I am still certain have influenced the text (these passages and no others), without the text being so "quoting" as in the first case'. For 1 Enoch 46.2–3 col. 2 has Dan. 7.16.[13] Hartman's certainty is unwarranted, though the logic of a case like this is such that the scope for unprofitable debate is almost infinite. What the two passages have in common is a seer asking an angel about the interpretation of what he has seen. Since the Danielic vision was used by the author, the possibility that Dan. 7.16 was in his mind cannot be ruled out, but since the situation was part of the common coin of apocalyptic, it cannot be confidently assumed. Also in col. 2 Hartman has 1 Enoch 46.7 influenced by Dan. 7.19, 23.[14] The text of 1 Enoch 46.7 is unfortunately doubtful, but it may be right and the stars of heaven may symbolize the righteous as they may in Dan. 8.10 (cf. 1 Enoch 43.4). If this is so, a reasonable case can be made out for literary dependence on Dan. 8.10, a passage which Hartman puts in col. 4. But the case for Dan. 7.19, 23 is weak. Here verbal connection is minimal. Hartman in fact puts his citation of Dan. 7.19, 23 opposite the only part of the verse that sounds like an echo, 'and tread upon the earth', and we lack any other indication that our author was attempting any interpretation of the fourth beast. The current experience of the Enoch group and the common stock of apocalyptic expressions are sufficient to explain the use of this language here, and reference to Dan. 7 is hardly helpful in terms of literary dependence and interpretation. The remaining allusions for 46.1–8 in Table 1 belong to Hartman's col. 4, which 'includes passages in which motifs which resemble those in the texts are to be found'. Thus no more than a most general context of thought is really indicated.

I can find no trace of the earlier part of Dan. 7 in the Similitudes. For 1 Enoch 61.1, Ps. 75.4 is much more relevant than Dan. 7.7f. Likewise there is no trace of Dan. 7.11–12. One significant item does emerge from consideration of the remaining possible allusions in Table 1. The vision of Dan. 7.9f. is used elsewhere in the Similitudes, outside the son of man passages. One such example is 1 Enoch 47.3. Once we have established the use of this vision by the author, we cannot deny its place as a source in such passages as this. Of especial interest is the earlier part of 1 Enoch 71, where the imagery of these verses is used, as in 1 Enoch 14; cf. also Ezek. 1. Whether anything else of significance can be extracted in the way of literary contact is doubtful. Reminiscences of other parts of the book of Daniel may be sought. Thus for Dan. 12.1–3 cf. 1 Enoch 38.4; 39.7; 43.4; 47.2–3; 50.1; 56.5f.; 56.8; 61.6; 62.10–16; 71.1. In none of these passages can literary dependence be demonstrated; there is however the same context of thought, and that is in itself worth noting.

We can now begin to draw together the information collected and consider Dan. 7 from this author's point of view. He was familiar with the book of Daniel; he drew upon the vision of Dan. 7.9–14, and it is not surprising that possible reminiscences of other parts of Daniel can be found in his work. The Similitudes belong to the same context of thought as Dan. 7. The group which the author represents is oppressed; but the time will come shortly when they will be vindicated by their God; as part of this process the dead, or some of them, will rise: those accepted by the group for vindication, but their oppressors for condemnation and punishment; the criterion whereby membership of the group is delineated is that of relationship to the deity whom they worship. It is precisely in the interpretation of the vision that differences appear.

In Dan. 7.9, thrones were placed, one Ancient of Days took his seat, and the description of him and his throne goes on into vs. 10. In the Similitudes, there is no mention of the placing of thrones, but the description of God and his throne is used, apart from statements that Enoch or God sat on a throne, in 46.1 and 71, and the term 'Ancient of Days' appears to be a source of the divine title 'Head of Days'. As far as the thrones are concerned, it is possible, but it cannot be established with certainty, that Enoch, like Enoch/Metatron in 3 Enoch, has a separate throne to sit on.[15] In that case our author may have thought that these two thrones were the thrones of Dan. 7.9. In the rest of Dan. 7.9–10, we have the myriads who stand before the Ancient of Days and serve him, the sitting of the heavenly court and the opening of the books. These features recur in the Similitudes, except for the sitting of the court. This was the reason for the plurality of thrones in Dan. 7.9, but in the Similitudes, the beings who stand before God always stand; this is specifically stated in 1 Enoch 40.1; 47.3; 60.2, and later became a rabbinical doctrine. In 71 there is a similar conception, but the scene is less static. The absence of the court may be related to the fact

110

that Enoch, the man-like figure, has taken over the function of judging, though the opening of the books still takes place in front of the Head of Days in 1 Enoch 47.3. Dan. 7.13 deals with the arrival of the man-like figure before the Ancient of Days. The author of the Similitudes interpreted this figure as his hero Enoch. He appears to have taken the כ in כבר אנש as an indication of the difference between an ordinary man, and a man who has been exalted to heaven as Enoch is in 1 Enoch 70–71. The coming before God takes place in 1 Enoch 71, which is chronologically prior to the material which Enoch foresaw in visionary form during his lifetime. That might be thought to produce a chronological problem, in that the coming to God then takes place before the judgement, whereas in Daniel it is the other way round. But there is no sign that our author was aware of any problem of this kind. He was a creative writer who wrote a new work, not a critical commentator, and he has reused the imagery of his source material with complete freedom.

The absence of the clouds in 1 Enoch 71 is a minor point. They are there in 1 Enoch 14.8, though this may not be connected with Dan. 7.13. Here as there Enoch goes up into heaven, and it is difficult to see why every detail of Dan. 7 should be retained for explicit mention. In the course of the Similitudes Enoch appears to have been given everything that the man-like figure receives in Dan. 7.14, including the reverence of all peoples and nations of every language (1 Enoch 47.5; cf. 62.6). The apparent exception is kingship. Terms such as 'king', 'kingship', 'kingdom', 'reign', seem to have been alien to the author of the Similitudes as a means of expressing the position of the exalted Enoch (contrast only the Noachic passage 1 Enoch 65.12). Enoch was not a king in the older Jewish material about him, and deliberate rejection of the expectation of a king from David's line may have played a part here (though the two occurrences of the term 'anointed', 48.10 and 52.4, are quite unselfconscious). But Enoch could be said to have been given the reality of kingship—he is enthroned and clearly is the leader of the community of the righteous and elect, and on his act in vindicating the elect and righteous by condemning the kings and mighty depends their salvation.

The absence of vss. 11 and 12 coheres well with the absence

of traces of the rest of the chapter. This author was not concerned with the four kingdom theory, nor with a particular mythological form of expressing it. Whereas Dan. 7 contains a symbolic vision and then, necessarily, its interpretation, the visions of the Similitudes are intended to convey reality, mostly future reality. But if their author was not concerned with past kingdoms, and probably not with Antiochus Epiphanes either, he was very concerned about the people who were oppressing the righteous and elect at the time when he wrote; it is of their overthrow and the vindication of this group that he writes. Enoch was, he believed, the redeemer of that group, and the deduction that he was to be found in the man-like figure of Dan. 7.13 is fully in accord with the exegetical methods universal in contemporary Judaism.[16] Against this background his use of Dan. 7.9–14 is not in any way difficult to comprehend. It implies that these verses have been given an eschatological setting, and this places the author of the Similitudes in general within the Western traditions of interpretation of these verses. Against the background of this actualizing tradition, his application of the prophecy of the man-like figure to his own hero Enoch is another example of the way in which this tradition, unlike the Syrian, was always capable of reinterpretation in the light of current belief.

The most important result of the investigation of this author's use of Dan. 7 is not, however, the way he interpreted it, but the demonstration that he does not witness to the existence of a 'Son of man concept' in Judaism. He used the term 'son of man' as an expression for 'man', choosing it rather than any other term for 'man' because he was inspired by the vision of Dan. 7.9f. with its use of 'son of man' at Dan. 7.13. But the Similitudes have always been the mainstay of the widespread scholarly belief in the existence of this 'Son of man concept', so that its absence here will enable us to demonstrate that there never was any such concept in Judaism at all. This demonstration will be completed in dealing with the other documents discussed in this chapter.

The Dead Sea Scrolls

Since the majority of these scrolls emanate from the same community, all are generally homogeneous, and the quantity of

material relevant to this investigation is limited, it is convenient
to follow the common practice of dealing with them all together.
Fragments of seven copies of the book of Daniel itself have been
found at Qumran, including two unpublished ones, 4QDn[a] and
4QDn[b], which apparently preserve the transition from Aramaic
to Hebrew in Dan. 7.28–8.1.[17]

Of primary importance is 4Q174, where quotations from
Daniel 11 and 12 are introduced by the rubric 'it is written in
the book of Daniel the prophet', one of the standard introductory formulae for the citation of Scripture. There is no
longer any doubt that the book of Daniel was regarded as holy
Scripture by the Qumran sect, and the position of biblical
interpretation at Qumran entails the conclusion that Dan. 7
was interpreted there. The task of recovering that interpretation
is complicated, because there are no quotations of this chapter
in the surviving published literature. Reminiscences have however been suggested. Milik quotes the beginning of a dream
from 4Q Giants (Starcky's lot) and declares that it is followed
by 'the description of the Judgement, which is drawn from Dan.
7.9–10'.[18] Milik's claim cannot be tested until the remainder of
the passage is published. If true it would be very interesting; a
judgement is in fact to be found in these verses, so that up to a
point the interpretation would be accurate, including the
preservation of the original author's conception of the descent
of the Ancient of Days in order to carry out the judgement.
Moreover such use of these verses in a work other than a commentary would prefigure some of the rabbinic exegesis of these
verses.

Strugnell believes that the influence of vs. 10 is to be found in
4Q Šerek Sirôt 'Ôlat Haššabāt, but the part which he has
published points with certainty only to Ezek. 1.[19] The part
which comes closest to Dan. is 40, 24, 5: 'round about them is
an appearance of rivers of fire (שבולי אש) in the likeness of
electrum'. Strugnell believes that שבולי אש is derived from the
river of fire (נהר די נור) of Dan. 7.10, but the derivation is by
no means obvious. The context of these references points very
clearly to Ezek. 1, and Strugnell rightly describes Ezekiel as
'the fountain head of all this literature'. For 40, 24, 5 Ezek. 1.4,
27; 8.2 provide as good a parallel as does Dan. 7.10. Similarly
the throne is more likely to be drawn from Ezek. 1.26 than from

Isa. 6.1 or Dan. 7.10. Yet these matters will be more happily discussed when the whole of the Qumran material is made available. Dan. 7.9–10 was as obvious a passage for them to use for information about the heavenly world as it was for the rabbis; decisive evidence that they did so use it at an early date may yet be forthcoming.

At CD XX, 8 occurs the expression קדושי עליון. The possibility has been suggested that this is intended to pick up the Danielic Saints of the Most High.[20] But there is nothing in the context to suggest this, and it is noteworthy that the phrase does not recur in the Qumran material so far published. It should rather be regarded as one of the many pieces of evidence of general affinity between the Qumran community and those pious Jews from whom the book of Daniel had appeared many years before.[21]

Thus no certain reminiscences of Dan. 7 are to be found in surviving published literature from Qumran. The outline of its interpretation there must be deduced in a more complex manner. In the first place evidence of a living Danielic tradition at Qumran is provided by 4QOrNab and 4Qps-Dan. The latter is especially significant: here it appears that Daniel gives a prophecy of world history which includes the four kingdoms and goes down beyond the date of the canonical book of Daniel. So far, however, there is no clear sign of the interpretation of the four kingdoms, nor of reminiscences of the canonical book. There is evidence that the last kingdom will be terrible, in a manner generally reminiscent of the fourth kingdom in Dan. 7, and there will be a time of distress before the End. It is moreover noteworthy that the summary of the End announces the rise of the people of God without any mention of the Messiah: 'until the people of God arise and everyone rests from the sword'. This is the same context of thought as Dan. 7, but it is not evidence of literary dependence, so that pending publication of the full text, the significance of 4Qps-Dan is simply that it does provide evidence of a living Danielic tradition.[22]

There is further relevant evidence from an Aramaic work which is still unpublished, though Milik gave a preliminary account of it twenty years ago.[23] In it a visionary encounters four talking trees, of which the first is Babylon and the second

114

Persia. The third and fourth ought therefore to be Greece and
Rome. It appears therefore, though one must be cautious until
the actual text of this work is published, that the Qumran sect
knew the four kingdom sequence with Rome as the fourth
kingdom. If they held this view, they can hardly have failed to
apply it to the interpretation of Dan. 7. That they did so is
suggested also by 4Q174, where the quotations from Dan. 11
and 12 are given an eschatological setting, which is characteristic of the Western tradition. There is further, but uncertain,
support from 11QMelch 3, line 18, where דנ[י]אל should
probably be read. The context demands an eschatological setting for the quotation, which again therefore belongs to the
Western tradition, no doubt of Dan. 9.24–6. It is reasonable to
deduce that the same tradition of actualizing exegesis, which is
in general characteristic of biblical interpretation at Qumran,
was followed for Dan. 7 also. It follows therefore that the
Qumran sect interpreted the four kingdoms of Dan. 7 as
Babylon, Persia, Greece, and Rome. Their interpretation of the
man-like figure cannot be deduced, as the Jewish version of the
Western tradition preserved both corporate and messianic
interpretations of it. The Saints of the Most High will have been
interpreted as the pious of Israel, with or without the angels of
God. For this stream of interpretation 4Q174 gives a *terminus a
quo*, certainly not later than the beginning of the first-century
A.D., a date at the end of the first-century B.C. being more
probable on palaeographical grounds. This clearly shows the
Western tradition in existence at the time of Jesus. It is however
unfortunate that its interpretation of the man-like figure at
Qumran remains unknown. Finally, it should be remarked that
the lack of certain trace of Dan. 7 in so many Qumran documents, while not really surprising, does appear to show that this
chapter was not of especially fundamental importance to the
sect.

What of the Son of man problem? 'Plainly, what Qumran
has done for us is to illuminate the OT phrase as belonging
quite certainly to Messianic ideas in the century before the
ministry of Jesus.' 'The Qumran community probably thought
of itself as fulfilling the propitiatory ministry of the 'Ebed
Yahweh (1QS 5.6–7; 9.3–5; 1QSa 1.1–3) and the judicial
ministry of the Son of man (1QpHab 5.3–6).'[24] Such opinions

are widespread, but unconvincing. בן אדם occurs three times in the published scrolls. At 1QH IV, 30 it is in synonymous parallelism with אנוש and clearly refers to mankind in general. At 1QS XI, 20 בן אדם occurs similarly in a collective sense, parallel to יליד אשה. This example is of especial interest because a scribe has inserted ה over אדם, thus giving us our only extant example of בן האדם. Again the reference is clearly to mankind in general. The third example is 4Q184, frag. 4, line 4, which is too fragmentary to interpret. In Aramaic בר אנוש occurs in its normal generic sense at 1QApGen XXI, 13, where it represents איש from Gen. 13.16. בר אנש occurs with reference to mankind in general at 11QTgJob IX, 9 and XXVI, 3, where it is a straightforward literal rendering of the Hebrew בן אדם at Job 25.6; 35.8.

Thus there are no examples at all of the use of the term 'son of man' as a messianic title at Qumran. Therefore the evidence of these documents does not illuminate it 'as belonging quite certainly to Messianic ideas'. However, the absence of the actual title 'Son of man' at Qumran is generally recognized, and a fundamental fault in attempts to find a 'Son of man concept' in these documents lies in the supposition that there is evidence from outside Qumran that there was such a concept. Thus when Bruce cites 1QpHab V, 3–6 as evidence that the community expected to execute judgement at the end of the age he hardly misinterprets this passage of 1QpHab. The main fault in his treatment lies in his view that there was in Judaism the concept of a 'Son of man' who had a judicial ministry to fulfil. If there were ample evidence of such a concept, it would be natural and methodologically not unsound to cite such a passage as evidence of contact with it, but the evidence surveyed in this chapter (and in ch. 2 above) shows that there was no such concept. Therefore a passage such as 1QpHab V, 3–6, which does not contain the term 'son of man', cannot be held to provide evidence of a 'Son of man concept'. Thus the Qumran documents, which contain no examples of the use of the term 'son of man' as a messianic title, do not provide any evidence that there was a 'Son of man concept' in Judaism. They do provide a large quantity of very interesting evidence about intermediary figures and the function of the community, but this evidence must be fitted into other theoretical categories.

116

The Sibylline Oracles

This is a collection of very disparate material, some of it clearly Jewish in origin, some of it equally clearly owing its present form to Christian influence. The main passage where the influence of Dan. 7 is very probably to be found is III, 397–400. It is a difficult passage to interpret, perhaps at least partly because the text has not been accurately transmitted. The particular references to ten horns and an additional horn in lines 397 and 400, combined with the suitability of the general context, are sufficient to warrant the universal view that Dan. 7 is in mind here. It is generally held also that, at least in the present form of the text, the terrible figure of lines 388ff. is Antiochus IV Epiphanes, and that the passage refers to subsequent events after his death. This too can hardly be denied. The passage therefore constitutes evidence of the correct identification of the fourth kingdom as the Macedonian; the details have, however, been brought up to date at some time later in the second century to conform them to later history. The motivation is that of actualizing exegesis, and the passage does not belong to the Syrian tradition. It is an example of the kind of exegesis characteristic of the Western tradition, but it comes from a period prior to the rise of the Roman power in Palestine, and hence the fourth kingdom is still the Macedonian.

The detailed events referred to may be identified with reasonable probability. Lines 394–5 make the general prediction that his line, that is, the line of Antiochus IV Epiphanes, will be destroyed by the members of the family he wishes to destroy. The family which Antiochus IV Epiphanes wanted to destroy was that of his brother Seleucus IV Philopator, and the prophecy refers to the murder of Seleucus IV, an action which was attributed to Antiochus IV Epiphanes, and the murder of Seleucus' son, Antiochus. The prediction is that the descendants of Seleucus IV Philopator will destroy those of Antiochus IV Epiphanes. Lines 396–7 continue

Putting forth one root, which a destroyer of mortals shall cut off,
From ten horns indeed he will in addition beget another creature.

The subject is Antiochus IV Epiphanes. The 'one root' is Antiochus V Eupator, the only real son of Antiochus IV

117

Epiphanes. The destroyer of mortals is Demetrius I Soter, who cut off the one root by having Antiochus V Eupator assassinated. The ten horns are mentioned to make reference to the prophecy of Dan. 7, and 'another creature' is Alexander Balas, who made a spurious claim to be a son of Antiochus IV. He is then the subject of line 398,

He shall cut down the warrior parent of a purple race.

The warrior parent is Demetrius I Soter, who died in battle against Alexander Balas. Line 399 is the most difficult on any hypothesis, and it seems impossible to avoid the conclusion that the text must be emended. I propose to read

καὐτὸς ἀφ' υἱῶν ὢν ἐς ὁμόφρονα ἀΐσσων ἀρὴν
φθεῖται.

This may be translated 'And he, since he is one of the sons, plunging to a similar ruin shall perish'. The subject is still Alexander Balas. ἀφ' υἱῶν ὢν includes him among the sons of Antiochus IV Epiphanes and therefore under the general rule of line 395 that he will be destroyed by the descendants of Seleucus IV Philopator. In fact, he was killed after a battle against Demetrius II Nicator; his death could reasonably be brought under this general head by an apocalyptist because it was a result of the struggle against Demetrius II. It is to be noted that this part of my reconstruction of line 399 follows the reading of the manuscripts. The second half of the line is more difficult, and its reconstruction entails a greater amount of guesswork. The phrase I have used is both close to the manuscript reading and accurately points out that Alexander Balas suffered a fate similar to that of Antiochus V Eupator, son of Antiochus IV. Line 400 concludes, 'and then indeed an additional horn shall rule'. The mention of the additional horn (παραφυόμενον κέρας) fixes the reference to the Danielic text, and it is to be identified as Trypho. The connection 'and then indeed' requires a short interval, and Trypho is well described like this because he did not belong to the Macedonian royal family.

The ten horns were probably Seleucus IV Philopator, Antiochus IV Epiphanes, Antiochus son of Seleucus, Ptolemy VI Philometor, Antiochus V Eupator, Demetrius I Soter, Alexander Balas, Ptolemy VII Euergetes, Demetrius II

Nicator, and Antiochus VI Epiphanes. This list neatly covers all the events referred to in this passage. The prophecy will date from *c.* 140 B.C., when Trypho, the additional horn, had put down Antiochus VI by murder and might be thought to have put down Demetrius II Nicator. The author perhaps expected him to put down a third horn, Ptolemy VII Euergetes, before the End came, but such is the flexibility of actualizing exegesis that he may have seen the putting down of a third horn in the death of Alexander Balas.

A handful of other passages in the Sibylline Oracles have been suggested as reminiscences of Dan. 7, but in no case can this be demonstrated. The main ones are II, 241–4; III, 49–50; IV, 47f.; V, 414. With II, 241–4, we may compare Dan. 7.9, 13. Geffcken, however, more appropriately compared Matt. 19.28; 25.31, Chrys. *Hom. de Res.* 1.[25] There is certainly Christian influence in Sib.Or.II, and it is no more than reasonable to see it here, too; any influence of Dan. 7 is but indirectly mediated.

At III, 49–50, direct borrowing from Dan. 7.13–14, 18 was suggested by Nikiprowetzky, but he barely attempted to justify this judgement.[26] Genuinely distinctive features of Dan. 7.13–14 are lacking, the long rule of the Messiah being too widespread to serve as such, even on the assumption that it has been read into the text of Daniel.

At IV, 47f., Nikiprowetzky saw the four empires of the book of Daniel and further suggested that the Sibylline author may have expected the rule of the Son of man after the renewal of the Age.[27] But there is no sign of Daniel in the text. There is a succession of worldly kingdoms, five in number. The first four are the original four of the four kingdom theory, Assyria, Media, Persia, and Greece; the fifth is Rome. Thus the four kingdom theory has been modified to take account of the Roman empire by turning it into a five-kingdom theory, and it is notable that it is the original sequence which has been modified, with Assyria in first place, not the Danielic sequence, which began with Babylon. Divine judgement is threatened on the fifth kingdom, to be followed by the resurrection of the godly to a new life, but there is not the slightest trace of the man-like figure of Dan. 7.13. It is therefore to be concluded that the author was making use not of Dan. 7 but of another version of the four-kingdom theory.

V, 414 has also been thought to be dependent on Dan. 7.13.[28] The passage belongs to the general category of Jewish messianic belief, and the term 'son of man' does not occur in it, so that it should not be used as evidence of the existence of a Son of man concept in Judaism. The messianic figure is probably one of the heroic figures of the past returning, though the possibility that this is a rather overwrought description of a pre-existent man cannot be ruled out. In either case he is called a man because that is what he was expected to be. In the Judaism of this period this should cause no great surprise, and once that is granted there is no especial connecting link with Dan. 7.13.

The Sibylline Oracles therefore provide no evidence of the existence of a Son of man concept in Judaism. There is one passage, III, 397–400, which is demonstrably dependent on Dan. 7, and it is the only example I have found of the actualizing Western tradition at work before the advent of the Romans caused this tradition to identify the fourth kingdom as the Roman instead of the Greek.

Josephus

Josephus provides clear evidence that he did interpret Dan. 7, but he does not tell us clearly what his interpretation was. The main passage is *A.J.* X, 188–281, which contains a lengthy summary of the book of Daniel. Josephus regarded it as holy Scripture and at X, 267 he ranks Daniel himself with the prophets, among whom he is indeed especially distinguished because he not only foretold the future, but also specified the time at which future events would occur.[29] Unfortunately, the summary omits ch. 7 altogether. Josephus' whole account is biased towards stories rather than visions and he had already summarized Dan. 2, interpreting as much of the scheme of the four kingdoms and the subsequent Jewish triumph as he dared. We must therefore turn to his outline of the interpretation of Nebuchadnezzar's dream in Dan. 2 in order to deduce from it an outline of his interpretation of Dan. 7. *A.J.* X, 208 tells us that the first kingdom is the Babylonian. The succeeding kingdoms are not named, but it is clear that they are interpreted according to the standard Western schema as the Medo-Persian, the Greek, and the Roman.[30] The stone belongs to future events, but Josephus explicitly refuses to say what it means. Clearly he thought, as the Western tradition did, that this prophecy symbolized the destruction of the Roman empire by the hand of God. That was not, however, a sensible, practical thing for a Jew to say. This interpretation of Dan. 2 may be applied straight to Dan. 7. The same sequence of kingdoms will have been seen here. As at Qumran, however, the interpretation of the man-like figure cannot be deduced precisely, and for the same reasons. There is no explicit statement, and both individual and corporate interpretations of it were preserved in the Western tradition among the Jews. That Josephus held it to symbolize the destruction of the Roman empire is clear enough. He must surely have interpreted the Saints of the Most High as Jews, possibly with angels. The rest of his interpretation of the chapter is, however, a matter of guesswork, and unprofitable beyond the point we have now reached.

One trace of the original interpretation of Dan. 7 may possibly be found at *B.J.* I., 19; I, 32, where Montgomery sees a reminiscence of Dan. 7.25 in the $3\frac{1}{2}$ years,[31] but if this is its ultimate origin at least the reference is not direct. Neither passage mentions the Book of Daniel, and Josephus followed the normal interpretation of Dan. 8 as an account of the Greek kingdom ending with Antiochus Epiphanes (*A.J.* X, 269–76), specifying the period of the desolation of the Temple as 1,296 days (*A.J.* X, 271). This is the $3\frac{1}{2}$ years of *B.J.* I, 19 and I, 32. Josephus will probably have followed the later Western tradition of interpretation of Dan. 8.14 as 2,300 days, and seen the 1,296 days as included here. The origin of the figure of 1,296 is more problematical, but it may be simply an attempt to render $3\frac{1}{2}$ years precisely, in the manner of other Danielic predictions. While it is not impossible that this dating goes back to the Syrian tradition correctly interpreting Dan. 7.25, the inconsistent and sometimes confused chronology of Josephus in this matter suggests that simple confusion with other time indications in Daniel may have taken place. Certainly this does not constitute evidence that Josephus himself interpreted Dan. 7.25 of the events which took place under Antiochus Epiphanes.

It is therefore to be concluded that Josephus is another early Jewish witness to the Western tradition of interpretation of Dan. 7.

4 Ezra

There is no doubt that 4 Ezra 11–12 is dependent on Daniel, and ch. 13 is also rightly recognized by most scholars to be dependent on Dan. 7. It is convenient to begin with a brief discussion of the remainder of the work. The closest passages concern the narrative framework of visionary experiences: 4 Ezra 3.1–2, cf. Dan. 7.1, 15; 4 Ezra 5.14–15, cf. Dan. 7.28. In both cases we are dealing with the visionary terminology of Jewish apocalyptic, and while the author may have had Danielic examples of this terminology in mind, such passages cannot constitute definite evidence of such use. Other examples of visionary terminology which has some Danielic parallel are to be found at 4 Ezra 4.21; 9.38; 10.25, 30. Similarly 6.20 might be accounted a reminiscence of Dan. 7.10, but the opening of the books is too common an apocalyptic motif for this to be regarded as a certain deduction. We must therefore conclude from this evidence that the author of 4 Ezra 1–10, 14 belonged to the same general thought-world as Daniel, but literary dependence cannot be demonstrated. Finally, that this differs from the positive results obtained for 11–12 and 13 is not to be accounted as evidence of diversity of authorship; in these two visions the author had especial reasons for having recourse to Dan. 7.

We turn next to the fifth vision (4 Ezra 11–12), which provides such straightforward evidence of dependence on Dan. 7. 'The eagle which you saw coming up from the sea is the fourth kingdom which your brother Daniel saw in a vision' (12.11). That Dan. 7 (not Dan. 2) is in mind is shown by other references: the clear and unambiguous ones are listed in Table 2.

However, if it is clear that this author used Dan. 7, it is equally clear that, like the author of the Similitudes of Enoch, he was a creative writer who reused the Danielic material for

TABLE 2

4 Ezra	Daniel 7	4 Ezra	Daniel 7
11.1	3	11.40–42	7, 23
11.2	2	12.3	11
11.39	2–8	12.13	7, 23

his own purposes. From it he has taken the four kingdoms, of which the fourth is contemporaneous with him and to be followed by the triumphant fifth. Secondly, he has taken imagery as he wanted it. As a result of this procedure, it is difficult to recover much of his interpretation of Dan. 7 itself, but the main lines can be laid down.

It is obvious, and undisputed, that the eagle represents Rome. At 12.11 this is clearly identified as the fourth kingdom in Dan. 7. It should follow that the author of 4 Ezra believed that the fourth beast in Dan. 7 symbolized the Roman kingdom, and this is how his remarks should in fact be interpreted. 'The eagle which you saw coming up from the sea is the fourth kingdom which your brother Daniel saw in a vision. But it was not interpreted for him as I am now interpreting it, or have interpreted it, for you' (12.11–12). This first of all clearly identifies Daniel's fourth kingdom as the Roman. It then says that this kingdom (the subject of the next sentence is the fourth kingdom, already identified as Rome) was not interpreted for Daniel in the same way as it is now to be interpreted for Ezra. Comparison of the two interpretations shows at once that this is the case. Instead of Daniel's ten kings, followed by another king who puts down three kings, 4 Ezra has 12 + 3 kings in the main sequence of Roman emperors and eight lesser ones. Once this kind of difference is looked for it emerges that while the general picture of Rome is the same in 4 Ezra as in Daniel the details are different, and this is reflected in the fact that Dan. 7.23 is the only verse of the angelic interpretation of Daniel's vision to find a place in Table 2. This makes perfect sense of 4 Ezra 12.12. If the author believed, as he says, that Daniel's fourth kingdom was as a matter of fact the Roman, he is not likely to have believed that Daniel's angelic interpreter thought otherwise.

Thus the author of 4 Ezra is one of the earlier examples of the Western tradition. It may safely be supposed (cf. especially 11.39) that he identified the previous kingdoms as Babylon, Medo-Persia, and Greece; at Dan. 7.11 he saw the destruction of Rome (4 Ezra 12.3). The Danielic vision was to him a series of symbols, and he felt quite free to use it for his own symbolism. The sequence of empires was however a reality, as was the divine overthrow of Rome shortly to be accomplished by God through his Messiah. The man-like figure is not used in this vision, however. The symbolism of 4 Ezra 11–12 is kept within the animal world, the Messiah being symbolized by the Lion of Judah. The symbolism of the man-like figure is reserved for the climactic vision of 4 Ezra 13.

In ch. 13 clear reminiscences of Dan. 7 are confined to vss. 2 and 13 which are repeatedly recalled, at 13.2, 3, 4, 25, 32. It is this use of Dan. 7 which explains why the man comes from the sea and then flies with the clouds of heaven. If the man-like figure of Dan. 7 is interpreted as an individual it is natural to ask where he came from (as in 1 Enoch 46), and the reply that, like the beasts, he came from the sea, is logical enough. The Danielic winds also reappear at 4 Ezra 13.2, and it is the wind that takes the man from the sea flying along with the clouds of heaven (4 Ezra 13.3).

It is not difficult to deduce this author's interpretation of the Danielic figure—he thought it was a symbol of the Messiah. Thus he was able to use it in his own symbolic vision. This free use of symbolism as such is the same as is to be found in the fifth vision (4 Ezra 11–12). The author really did believe in the vindication of Israel by God through his Messiah. He had a very clear appreciation of the difference between visionary symbolism and actual reality, not in any way inconsistent with his great love of the former, and it is unfortunate that this clear appreciation has been largely obscured by scholars who have not shared his ideas about the reality shortly to be accomplished.

The actual word used for 'man' in the original Hebrew or Aramaic *Vorlage* is difficult to determine. It has been widely assumed that it was בֶּן אָדָם or בַּר אֱנָשׁ, and the chapter has been used as evidence of the existence of a Son of man concept in Judaism.[32] In the first place, it is unlikely that this was the term used for 'man' in the *Vorlage*. The Latin version uses *homo* consistently in the vision (13.3, 5, 12), and *vir* in the interpretation (13.25, 32, 51). The Syriac version supports the distinction, with *bar nasha* in the vision and *gabra* in the interpretation. In all cases the reference is to the figure which first appears in 13.3 where there is a lacuna in the Latin and the Syriac reads '*ayk dmutha dbarnasha*. The Latin must surely have read *homo* here too. This leads us back to the Greek which must

124

have read ἄνθρωπος in the vision and ἀνήρ in the interpretation. If, as appears probable, the original language of 4 Ezra was Hebrew, this means that אדם will have been used in the vision. The expressions used at the first occurrence may then be compared with Ezek. 1.5 דמות אדם; 1.26 דמות כמראה אדם; Dan. 10.18 כמראה אדם. Having been used like this in the opening phrase, אדם was retained in the rest of the account of the vision. In the interpretation, however, the author used איש as a natural word to refer back to a particular man.[33] Should the original language of this work have been Aramaic, one may for the same reasons conjecture אנש in the vision and גבר in the interpretation.

If the original had read בן אדם or בר אנש, the Greek should have read υἱὸς ἀνθρώπου and hence the Latin *filius hominis*. Absolute certainty on this matter is not obtainable, since it really is true that ἄνθρωπος would be an accurate translation of בן אדם or בר אנש, but the consistency of the LXX and Vulgate of the OT in rendering בן אדם with υἱὸς ἀνθρώπου and *filius hominis* respectively makes it more probable that the term was אדם (or possibly אנש). The Syriac *bar nasha* was such a common word for man as to be a regular translation of ἄνθρωπος; the Latin *homo* is therefore the decisive evidence with the Syriac supporting the evidence of the Latin that separate words were used in the vision and the interpretation and supporting also the kind of distinction that must be made between the words so used.

If, as is therefore probable, the term 'son of man' did not occur in 4 Ezra 13, this chapter cannot be used to demonstrate that there was a Son of man concept in Judaism. But the possibility that it did so occur remains, and it is therefore important to establish the way in which the term 'man' is used in this chapter. Is it a title? The first occurrence is clearly not a title, *'ayk dmutha dbarnasha*, 'one like the resemblance of a man' in 13.3. Here the term 'man' is part of the description of the visionary figure, not a title of this being. In the vision, the remaining occurrences of *homo* (*barnasha*) are all accompanied by some defining term making clear a reference back to this visionary figure: a demonstrative at vss. 3 and 12, and a relative clause at 13.5. This is necessary because the term 'man' is not a title; some defining item is needed to make it clear that the reference is to the visionary man of 13.3. The evidence of the interpretation is similar: each time 'man' (*vir, gabra*) occurs it is accompanied by 'going up' and in the first and last of these examples the phrase 'from the heart of the sea' completes the picture. Here too, then, the word 'man' is not a title. Thus throughout this chapter the words for 'man' are used as the semitic words for 'man' (including בן אדם and בר אנש) normally are used. Each instance is carefully defined to refer back to the figure 'like the resemblance of a man' in the vision, 13.3. It is clear from the interpretation that this visionary figure is a symbol of the Messiah, though in the interpretation of this vision the term itself does not occur—God refers to him as 'my servant'. It is therefore to be concluded that the term 'man' is not a title in 4 Ezra 13 and that 4 Ezra does not provide evidence that there was a Son of man concept in Judaism.

But did the author of 4 Ezra write this vision and its interpretation? It is almost universally held that he did not. The earlier scholarship, which saw 4 Ezra as a collection of disparate fragments, has in general been corrected by Stone and Breech,[34] whose approach and criticisms of earlier work are assumed here, but in this instance even Stone has joined the general view. His argument[35] requires refutation, for it implies that the exegesis of Dan. 7 in this vision was found in an earlier source, and the son of man aspect of the problem becomes that much more complex if a definite written source is presupposed.

Stone's first argument concerns the visionary man: the interpretation of the man is given in 13.25ff., whereas the interpretation of his rising from the sea is added only at the end of the interpretative section, at 13.51ff. But we must not require of an author that he expound his interpretation only in the order most obvious to us. The source of this piece of symbolism is Dan. 7.2. The separation of its interpretation has the function of giving it emphasis. It should be concluded that the problem with which it deals was of especial concern to the author and his group. They were in the utmost distress; God would shortly deliver them through his Messiah. But was the Messiah not a man? Where then was he to be found? 'Just as no one can examine or know what is in the depth of the sea, so no one can see my Servant or those who are with him on the earth except at the time of his Day.' This is the reply of a desperate apocalyptist rather than a learned don, but its position makes perfect sense as a device of the author himself.

The next argument is that vss. 27f. state that the weaponlessness of the man and his fiery breath are to be interpreted. But seven verses intervene, wherein is included 'a reference to the man's voice which was mentioned in vs.4 and is not interpreted elsewhere', and an explanation of the mountain. Here a main source of confusion is the assumption that the voice of the Messiah in 13.33 is an interpretation of the symbolic voice of 13.4. This assumption should be rejected. The symbolic voice of 13.4, like the symbolic look of 13.3, is not interpreted at all. They belong to the symbolism, and were intended to produce an awesome picture from traditional imagery; that they have not had this effect on modern observers is a function of the observers. The voice of 13.33 is nothing to do with this; it is the voice of the real Messiah. Once this is seen, the order and logic of this section of the interpretation can be straightened out. Verses 29–33 give the setting in real life necessary to explain how and when the events symbolized in the vision will take place. These then occur in their proper order: the gathering of the nations (vs. 5, interpreted in vs. 34), the mountain (vss. 6–7, interpreted in vss. 35–6), the weaponlessness of the man and his fiery breath (vss. 10–11, interpreted in vss. 37–8) culminating in the destruction of his enemies (vs. 11, interpreted in 38). The summary of 13.5–11 in 13.27–8 is indeed brief. But for literary reasons it had to be brief, and the author selected the most important item for it, namely the man destroying his enemies, which symbolized the forthcoming deliverance of the Jews by the Messiah.

Stone's third argument is that the ten tribes material seems to be an originally independent pericope. That it depends on older tradition is not in dispute, but it makes perfect sense as interpretation of the visionary material (13.12–3), and Stone has done nothing to show that this author could not have written it. His fourth argument points out that the companions of the Messiah introduced in 13.52 are mentioned nowhere else in either the vision or the interpretation. However, they are not mentioned in 11–2 and do not actually do anything in 7.29 and 14.29. It should be concluded that this author did believe in them but did not think they were important enough to symbolize or to mention repeatedly. Stone's next point is the 'seemingly double explanation' of the mountain, though Stone himself is not inclined to lay too much stress on this particular argument, on the grounds that Zion and Mt Zion are to be regarded as virtually identical. The author has indeed combined two items of tradition, the descent of the heavenly Jerusalem (cf. 7.26) and the condemnation or defeat of the nations at Jerusalem (cf. 2 Baruch 40). Given that this is what he has done, it seems quite plausible that he should symbolize it as in 13.6–7 by means of the mountain which he has partly drawn from Dan. 2, a source to which he returned for the 'without hands' of 13.36. It is to be concluded that the interpretation is not confused, and does not provide reason for believing that it was not written by the author of the vision.

Finally Stone argues, rightly enough, that the concept of the Messiah in the interpretation corresponds broadly to the ideas about him in the rest of 4 Ezra. However, he thinks that the notion of the Messiah in the vision is different and that this supports the view that the vision was originally an independent piece. But the author used imagery in the vision of 4 Ezra 13 which he did not use elsewhere in order to construct a piece of dramatic visionary symbolism. 4 Ezra is not full of three-headed eagles with umpteen wings either, but that does not constitute a reason for thinking that its author did not write the Eagle vision. It is in the whole nature of Jewish apocalyptic that unique visions may be constructed, largely, as here, from traditional materials. This argument represents the failure, so common in scholarship on this book, to appreciate the author's clear distinction between his visionary symbolism and his ideas of reality.

It is therefore to be concluded that, like his predecessors whom he so justly criticized, Stone has failed to demonstrate that this work had more than one author. We can now summarize the results of investigating this author's interpretation of Dan. 7. He believed that the vision of Dan. 7 was a piece of visionary symbolism. On this symbolic level he thought that the man-like figure, like the beasts, came from the sea. This symbolism he felt free to use for his own creative purposes. The reality which it represented included a series of four wordly kingdoms, Babylon, Medo-Persia, Greece, and Rome. The destruction of Rome was symbolized in vs. 11. The man-like figure was a symbol of the Messiah. Thus the author of 4 Ezra is one of the earlier extant examples of the Western tradition of exegesis. The second result is of greater general significance, though it is not new: this work does not provide evidence of the existence of a Son of man concept in Judaism.

2 Baruch

The main passage of this work where dependence on Dan. 7 is normally assumed is chs. 39–40. Here there is a sequence of four kingdoms as in Dan. 7: the fourth is the most awful and the most fully described, and it is to be succeeded by the rule of God's Messiah. Some caution is, however, appropriate. The idea of four kingdoms to be followed by a fifth existed before and independently of Daniel, in rabbinical literature it is often mentioned without reference to Daniel, and the survival of the original sequence has been noted in Sib.Or.IV, 47f.[36] Detailed examination of 2 Baruch 39–40 does not reveal the detailed agreement with Dan. 7 that would constitute proof of literary dependence. Perhaps the closest parallel is 40.3 'and his principate shall stand for ever', cf. Dan. 7.14, 27. Yet 4 Ezra 11–12 shows how different an account of the fourth kingdom can be from Dan. 7 even when the author is certainly dependent on it; lack of detailed contact with Dan. 7, even in 2 Baruch 39.5–7a, cannot therefore be held to constitute proof of literary independence. General considerations favour the usual view that this author was dependent on Dan. 7. They certainly have the basic four kingdoms and a fifth in common. A Jew of this period should have known the book of Daniel, and 2 Baruch has very strong affinities with 4 Ezra, whose author was certainly dependent on Dan. 7. On these general grounds it is to be concluded that the author of 2 Baruch was probably dependent on Dan. 7.

Two other passages should be mentioned where dependence on Dan. 7 has been suspected. At 24.1 'the books shall be opened', such dependence is not out of the question, but the motif is too common for this to be certain. At 53.8 Charles commented, 'The imagery is derived from Dan. 7.13'.[37] This is a surprising judgement. The two passages have very little in common; the main common item is cloud, which is very differently used in 2 Baruch 53 from Dan. 7.

If it is right to suppose that the author of 2 Baruch is dependent on Dan. 7, a bare outline of his interpretation of it is not difficult to deduce. The first kingdom is, predictably, Babylon (39.3), and it is equally clear that the fourth and last kingdom is Rome. It must follow that the second and third were Medo-Persia and Greece respectively. The fourth kingdom has a single final leader; this unnamed ruler was presumably seen as the little horn. The fourth kingdom is then followed by the reign of the Messiah, and the evidence of 4 Ezra supports the possibility that the man-like figure was interpreted as the Messiah.

Thus it is to be concluded that the author of 2 Baruch was probably dependent on Dan. 7, though the evidence is not strong enough for this conclusion to be regarded as certain. If it is right, his interpretation is one of the earlier examples of the Western tradition of interpretation to have survived.

3 Enoch

Dan. 7.9–10 has been used at 3 Enoch 18.19; 28.7; 30.2; 35.4; 36.1. The interpretation is consistent in these passages. The Ancient of Days has been identified as God. The scene is taken to be that of God sitting in judgement every day. The description of his clothing and hair (Dan. 7.9) has been utilized in 28.7. This work contains a good deal of speculation about the river of fire. It is interpreted literally, and taken as a permanent feature of the divine environment; so also are the angels of Dan. 7.10. 'The court sat' is interpreted of the heavenly Council sitting at the beginning of the daily judgement (30.1–2). The opening of the books takes place at the daily judgement; the books are further defined in 28.7 as 'books of the living and books of the dead'. The placing of the thrones is not dealt with; it is natural to conjecture that the heavenly Council sat on them. Finally, this work fills in the picture with many details not found in Dan. 7, but this may not be described as exegesis of these verses. There is no trace of any use of the rest of this chapter in 3 Enoch. In view of the results obtained from the Similitudes of Enoch, it is particularly noteworthy that there is no trace of any part of Dan. 7 in the Enoch-Metatron sections of 3 Enoch.

Though there are differences in detail, the general pattern of exegesis of Dan. 7.9–10 in this work corresponds to that of orthodox rabbinical literature, in that these verses are used to give information about the permanent state of the real heavenly world above. There is, however, no trace of the placing of these verses at the eschatological consummation of all things characteristic of the Western traditions.

The Hebrew Apocalypse of Elijah

This work, which is possibly to be dated as early as the third century A.D., provides the only Jewish evidence in the material surveyed for the identification of the little horn as a sort of Antichrist figure—the evil king who opposes God and his people in the last times. The description of him is clearly based on this Danielic figure and explicitly identified as 'the horn which Daniel saw', though it is amplified and developed beyond anything found in Daniel.[38] There are no other certain traces of the book of Daniel, but there is mention of the four kingdoms. The fourth is clearly Rome, so the standard rabbinical schema of Babylon, Medo-Persia, Greece, Rome is to be assumed. In view of the interpretation of the little horn it must be concluded that the author of this work interpreted the four kingdoms of Dan. 7 in this sequence too. There is no trace of his interpretation of the man-like figure; the author clearly believed in the coming of the Messiah, and could have used the man-like figure to portray him if he had wished to. However, this evidence is sufficient to classify this work as belonging to the Jewish version of the Western tradition.

In addition to these works, evidence of the interpretation of Dan. 7 has naturally been sought in the early versions. The LXX is probably as old as the second century B.C. In Dan. 7 it is not wildly different from the MT and Theodotion, as it is in Dan. 3–6, but it does have a number of variants, some of which bear witness to corruption of the text used by the translator. The most discussed variant is at vs. 13, where the LXX has ἐπί for עִם, and it is this variant which is often ascribed to messianic interpretation.[39]

This suggestion cannot be satisfactorily verified. No messianic interpreter, whether a commentator or a creative writer, shows signs of finding any difficulty in the Messiah coming with the

clouds, and conversely a heavenly figure employed as a pure
symbol could as well have come on the clouds as with them.
Mechanical error may reasonably be suspected, with עַל
instead of עִם, on the ground that the LXX shows ample
evidence of minor corruptions in this chapter, but either scribe
or translator may have slipped up because his imagination
naturally portrayed a heavenly figure coming on the clouds
rather than in them. Unfortunately there are other variants, of
which the most awkward is ὡς παλαιός. This variant has
seemed to add plausibility to the view that the translator interpreted the man-like figure messianically, but even if it were part
of the original LXX text, it would by no means follow that the
translator identified the man-like figure with the Ancient of
Days. A comparison between the two figures would more
probably have been intended, and this could be consistent with
a corporate interpretation of the man-like figure. However, this
reading should probably be treated as a corruption of the
original LXX ἕως παλαιοῦ, the ἐ having dropped out after
καί.[40] The change from παλαιοῦ to παλαιός will have been con-
sequent upon the loss of the ἐ, and the manuscript evidence is
so meagre that the unanimity of its witness to ὡς παλαιός cannot
be regarded as a strong argument in favour of its originality.
The insertion of οἱ παρεστηκότες correctly identifies the subject
of προσήγαγον; the bare αὐτῷ is surprising and again suggests
corruption (παρῆσαν probably owes its origin to dittography of
παρῆν). Vs. 14 also shows variants of a minor nature which
appear to owe their origin to a corrupt text. In short, the
translator appears to have done his best with a difficult and
somewhat corrupt text. His variants are hardly those of someone with definite interpretative ideas confidently imposed in his
translation, and they do not demand either the corporate or the
messianic interpretation of the man-like figure.

Two other variants are worthy of note. At the end of vs. 10,
κριτήριον must mean 'the court', so the translator knew that the
heavenly court sat down. At vs. 22, καὶ τὴν κρίσιν ἔδωκε τοῖς
ἁγίοις τοῦ ὑψίστου is a literal translation of the Aramaic,
assuming יְהַב for MT יְהִיב. This Greek, like the Aramaic,
could, if taken in isolation, mean that the Saints became the
judges, but in the LXX, as in the Aramaic text, the context
favours the interpretation 'he gave judgement for the Saints of

the Most High'. All exegetical traditions support this view, and the translator shows no sign of having to guard against misunderstanding.

Theodotion's translation also appears to be of Jewish origin, and it is of early but uncertain date. It is an accurate translation of Dan. 7 into Greek, and at that level the translator interpreted the chapter correctly. At the exegetical level, however, this translation is of very little value, because there are so few interpretative alterations. In particular, there is no indication as to whether the translator interpreted the man-like figure in a corporate or a messianic sense. At vs. 10, he has κριτήριον like the LXX, so it appears that he too knew that the heavenly court sat down. At vs. 22, ἔδωκε, again like the LXX, presupposes יְהַב with the Ancient of Days as the subject, and the whole clause represents the Aramaic accurately at a literal level. The context and known exegetical traditions suggest that the translator supposed that judgement was given in favour of the Saints.

A few other documents must be discussed because they have been thought to contain information about the interpretation of Dan. 7. Of these the most important are those which make up the remainder of the composite work now known as 1 Enoch. The publication of the Aramaic fragments from Qumran has made it clear that some parts of 1 Enoch are earlier than the book of Daniel,[41] and the evidence of literary dependence either way was never convincing in any case. For example, 1 Enoch 1.9 belongs to the same general background as Dan. 7.10, but its picture of the judgement differs in detail from that of Dan. 7 and the 'ten thousands' are not sufficient indication of literary dependence in either direction (cf. Deut. 33.2). At 1 Enoch 18.2f Enoch sees the four winds of heaven, and at vs. 5 they carry the clouds, but comparison with Dan. 7 does not indicate literary dependence because these notions were too widespread. The most interesting passage in the opening section of 1 Enoch is 14.8–25, where the suggestions of dependence on Dan. 7 are balanced by Glasson's view that the dependence of Dan. 7 on 1 Enoch 14 is obvious.[42] While there are clearly similarities between these two documents, literary dependence is not demonstrable. Glasson exaggerates their similarities by misinterpreting both documents, particularly in supposing that in Dan. 7 the man-like figure ascends to heaven, and that in 1

Enoch 71 (which he regards as relevant) 'the identification, Son of man = Enoch, reappears'. It is not found there, and had never appeared previously. Morever, some of his detailed correspondences involve items which are clearly too common to serve as evidence of literary dependence. This applies especially to the word 'behold', and the fact that one has 'in the night visions' and the other 'in the vision'; these correspondences are simply due to the fact that both passages are apocalyptic visions. Finally, Glasson's statement that 'Both accounts were originally written in Aramaic and the original resemblance was probably even closer' has not been justified either by work on the versions or by the discovery of the Aramaic fragments of part of this passage. It is clear that the items which the two passages have in common became part of the stock of apocalyptic imagery, and the evidence is too scanty to enable us to determine whether they had already done so. On the other hand, there is nothing improbable in the suggestion that one of the authors used the other's work. If this is right, it is overwhelmingly probable that it was the author of Dan. 7 who drew on 1 Enoch 14 for his stock of imagery of the heavenly world. In any case, it is clear that both creative authors revised their imagery, and the author of 1 Enoch 14 took the ascent of Enoch to heaven from Enoch traditions, not from Dan. 7.

Further evidence of dependence on Dan. 7 has been suggested for 1 Enoch 90. At 90.20 there is evident contact with the thought-world of Dan. 7, but there are differences between the two documents as well, and the opening of the books is too common a feature to serve as sufficient evidence of literary dependence. Glasson suggested that in this work God is assisted by the angel Michael, and he comments, 'evidently the writer thought that the phrase (sc. Son of man) in Dan. 7.13 stood for Michael'. But Glasson made no serious attempt to show that Dan. 7 is being used here at all.[43] At 90.37 Strack–Billerbeck found direct dependence on Dan. 7.13–14 and deduced that this was the earliest evidence for the individual interpretation of this figure.[44] But they had to admit that the man-like figure is not mentioned, and the simplest explanation of that is that he was not in mind. Again Jewish triumph provides some contact of thought, but no evidence of literary dependence. It is to be concluded that there is no sufficient evidence for supposing that the authors of any of these parts of 1 Enoch were dependent on Dan. 7. As far as we know, the first author in this group to be inspired by this chapter was the author of the Similitudes.

A reminiscence of Dan. 7 has been conjectured at Test. Jos. 19.12. Unfortunately the text of this passage is in an unsatisfactory condition, and Christian influence seems fairly clear at vs. 11, so that it cannot be excluded with any confidence here. However, even if Christian influence be excluded, the agreement with Dan. 7.14, 27 is not sufficient to allow of the assumption of literary dependence, in view of generally similar statements elsewhere; cf. Dan. 3.33; 4.31; 6.27; Ps. 145.13.

In the Apocalypse of Abraham 11, one phrase in the description of Jaoel recalls Dan. 7.9, 'and the hair of his head like snow'.[45] The reminiscence is not precise, and is not paralleled in the rest of the description of Jaoel. It indicates the dependence of this work on the traditions of Jewish apocalyptic, but it does not constitute sufficient evidence of literary dependence on the book of Daniel.

In this chapter I have assembled all the evidence of the use of Dan. 7 in Jewish documents of the earlier (mostly pre-rabbinical) period. The first result to note is that this use cannot be described as extensive. This is not especially surprising once this chapter is no longer connected with a Son of man concept in Judaism, but it is of some importance because of the contrary assumptions of so much scholarship. Secondly, all those documents which have yielded positive results belong to the Western, not the Syrian, tradition of interpretation; the one document which might appear to be an exception, Sib.Or.III, 388–400, is in fact an example of the kind of actualizing exegesis characteristic of the Western tradition dating from the period before the Roman conquest of this area, and hence interpreting the fourth kingdom not as the Roman, but as the Macedonian kingdom running down beyond Antiochus IV Epiphanes into the second half of the second century. An early date is thus provided for the Western tradition, which has been shown to antedate the teaching of Jesus. However, the Western Jewish tradition preserved the corporate interpretation of the man-like figure, and it is not clear that an individual interpretation had been produced as early as this. From this evidence, meagre and geographically not emanating from the main area where the

Syrian tradition is known to have flourished, firm conclusions cannot be drawn as to the relative strengths of the two interpretative traditions in this early period.

The origins of the Western tradition are clearly to be found in the actualizing nature of much biblical exegesis of this period. Given this attitude to Scripture, the fact that the eschatological events predicted in the Book of Daniel did not occur at the time of the death of Antiochus Epiphanes was bound to result in some interpretative readjustment. In the immediately succeeding period, a gap could be imagined between the little horn and the End, a view not found in the meagre evidence as long as the little horn is interpreted as Antiochus Epiphanes, though it is evidenced later as the Western tradition repeatedly came to terms with historical changes. Alternatively, actualizing exegetes of the earliest period, still with the fourth kingdom as the Macedonian, could bring the list of horns up to date; this is found in Sib. Or. III, 397–400. As the Seleucid power faded and the Romans trampled over the whole Mediterranean area, a more fundamental adjustment was called for. The last kingdom was evidently not the Macedonian, for the Romans had come to power. Their rule was not always kind, and the identification of them as the fourth kingdom was bound to be made by actualizing exegetes. The Macedonians would have to become the third kingdom, and the Medes and Persians had Danielic encouragement for becoming the second. It is a probable deduction, though unsupported by the meagre empirical evidence, that this adjustment was made before the latest date that palaeography will allow us to assign to 4Q 174, though the important factor for this investigation is that it must have taken place before the ministry of Jesus.

This actualizing approach to Scripture allows, but it by no means necessitates, an individual interpretation of the man-like figure. In rabbinical literature, in which the classical form of the messianic hope is to be found, the man-like figure is identified as King Messiah. Such an identification could hardly occur in this form in a group of documents written before the messianic hopes of the Jews had really crystallized into this classical form of expectation of 'the Messiah', but it was preceded by similar identifications with two of the redeemer figures characteristic of Judaism at the time of Jesus. One of them, 'my servant' in 4

Ezra 13, clearly anticipates the rabbinical identification of the man-like figure as the Messiah, though it differs in its assumption that Daniel's figure is a symbol, and hence suitable for creative reuse as a symbol. The other is Enoch, an identification to be found in a work whose date is uncertain, and cannot be confidently asserted to be earlier than the ministry of Jesus or even the writing of the Gospels. This makes it all the more important to observe the dynamic identity of the situation of early Christian exegetes and members of the Enoch circle. All were profoundly religious Jews, and as such they shared all fundamental Jewish beliefs, including an actualizing and flexible mode of biblical exegesis; both groups held allegiance to a single intermediary figure, whom they believed to have lived on earth as a man, to be now in Heaven, and to be going to carry out a judicial function which would vindicate them at the last day in the very near future. These factors explain the similarity in their use of Dan. 7.13, and they did not require an earlier identification with any other redeemer figure, be he termed 'the Messiah' or not. They provide moreover special reasons for the use of Dan. 7.13 which were absent from the more orthodox beliefs of later rabbinism, so it is a plausible guess that our meagre evidence correctly represents the position, that these two sectarian groups employed Dan. 7.13 at an earlier date than Pharisaic Jewry, as well as with the greater intensity that characterizes the Similitudes and the Gospels. Hence our inability to date the Similitudes of Enoch accurately matters little. The important factor is the similarity of the situation of the Enoch circle to that of the early Christians, such that independent application of Dan. 7.13 to their respective intermediary figures is readily comprehensible.

Another important, and related, result of this investigation is the demonstration that there was no Son of man concept in Judaism. Evidence that there was such a concept in Judaism has been found primarily in three passages, Dan. 7.13, 4 Ezra 13 and the Similitudes of Enoch, and this investigation of them has shown that this is not correct. In the case of Dan. 7.13, it was found that in the present form of the chapter the man-like figure is not a real entity at all, but simply a symbol of the Saints of the Most High. Attempts to find a source behind this chapter in which this man-like figure was something else were shown to be

137

uniformly unconvincing. At 4 Ezra 13, it was found very unlikely that the term 'son of man' had occurred, and if it did, it was not a title, but a normal semitic expression for 'man', used to describe a purely visionary figure who symbolizes the Messiah. A main source of this figure is in fact Dan. 7.13. In the Similitudes of Enoch, the foundation document for the view that there was a Son of man concept in Judaism, the term 'son of man' does occur but it was found to be the normal Aramaic expression for 'man'. The particular man referred to throughout this work is Enoch. The reason for the choice of this term is that this work is also dependent on Dan. 7. Thus the three passages are Dan. 7.13 and the only two passages of early Jewish apocalyptic which are dependent on it, and this dependence largely explains their common features.

On these few passages the notion that there was a Son of man concept in Judaism has been founded, so that even some of its confident supporters have had to confess that the evidence is meagre.[46] Others have denied its existence altogether, but the difficulties of giving a satisfactory account of the evidence, above all of the Similitudes, have prevented this view from gaining general acceptance. It is to be hoped that the above account may be regarded as more satisfactory. Once it has been shown that these three passages do not provide evidence of the existence of a Son of man concept, the logic of the argument must be altered to deal with other passages in which it has been found. It has not been suggested that the existence of a Son of man concept in Judaism may be founded on other passages; only that a Son of man concept, whose existence is supposed to be established on the basis of Dan. 7.13, 4 Ezra 13 and the Similitudes, has been influential elsewhere. Once it is shown that these three passages do not provide evidence that there was such a concept, allegations of its influence elsewhere necessarily collapse. In particular, once it is shown that Dan. 7.13 does not provide evidence of a Son of man concept, an argument that another passage is dependent on it may no longer be held to show that it too is influenced by the Son of man concept, but quite the reverse. Into this general absence of a Son of man concept the negative evidence of the rabbinic literature fits perfectly. It is well known that the rabbis had no Son of man concept; it is no longer necessary to argue either that they were exceptional, or that the concept was confined to ever-narrowing circles of early Jewish apocalypticists.

Thus the Son of man concept in Judaism is a product of modern scholarship. Most of the passages which have been brought together under this umbrella should really be classified under two heads, visionary symbolism, and messianic and intermediary figures. Visionary symbolism accounts for only two of them, but they are two of the central ones, Dan. 7.13 and 4 Ezra 13. Most of the others come under the heading of messianic and intermediary figures. Judaism at this time produced a rich abundance of these, and it is altogether natural that this abundant flowering in the imaginations of disparate groups was not governed by a fixed terminology. Most of them were men, raised up to an unusually high position, but there are exceptions: Michael, Jaoel, some people's views of Melchizedek, later Metatron; all these were heavenly beings at some time thought by some people to be especially active in some function between man and their transcendent God. That words for 'man' are occasionally used of individuals who belong to the former group is not surprising. Here belongs the Similitudes: that the figure seen in the vision is Enoch is not to be explicitly revealed until the end, so בר אנש was taken from Dan. 7.13 to serve as a description of him, repeated many times. Here, too, go Test. Abr. 7, with its use of ἄνθρωπος in a general statement with implicit reference to Abel; Sib. Or. V, 414 ἀνὴρ μακαρίτης; LXX Num. 24.7, 17 ἄνθρωπος. There was a kind of 'man' concept in Israel at this time, but we usually call him the Messiah. In neither case do we respect the variegated terminology of the primary evidence.

The Jewish evidence can now be seen clearly. The Jews had no Son of man concept, and their use of Dan. 7 did not turn בר אנש into a title. It follows that the origin of the Gospel term ὁ υἱὸς τοῦ ἀνθρώπου must be sought in developments for which Jesus or his followers were responsible.

NOTES

1 For more detailed discussion, P. M. Casey, *JSJ* VII (1976), 11–29.
2 For different views of literary dependence in this passage, Casey, op. cit., 20–2.

3 Ibid., 11–13.

4 R. H. Charles, *The Book of Enoch, or 1 Enoch, Translated from the Editor's Ethiopic Text* (²1912), 86–7; E. Sjöberg, *Der Menschensohn im Äthiopischen Henochbuch* (1946), 46.

5 E. Ullendorf, *Atti del Convegno Internazionale di Studi Etiopici, Accad. naz. dei Lincei, Problemi attuali di scienza e di Cultura*, quad. 48 (1960), 259–68.

6 Ibid., 262.

7 R. H. Charles, op. cit., 86; E. Sjöberg, op. cit., 42–4; for other suggestions P. M. Casey, op. cit., 17–18.

8 Cf. M. D. Hooker, *The Son of Man in Mark* (1967), 37–48.

9 For more detailed discussion of the textual problem, P. M. Casey, op. cit., 25–6.

10 On the unity of 1 Enoch 70–1, Sjöberg, op. cit., 159–67.

11 Cf. supra, 40–6; C. H. W. Brekelmans, *OTS* XIV (1965), 305–29; G. F. Hasel, *Bib* 56 (1975), 173–92.

12 L. Hartman, *Prophecy Interpreted* (1966).

13 Ibid., 112, 118, 119.

14 Ibid., 124.

15 E. Sjöberg, op. cit., 62ff; for the contrary view, J. Theisohn, *Der auserwählte Richter* (1975), 68–98.

16 For the Jewishness of the Similitudes in general, cf. Theisohn, op. cit.

17 F. M. Cross, *RB* 63 (1956), 58.

18 J. T. Milik, *The Books of Enoch* (1976), 305.

19 J. Strugnell, *VT.S* VII (1960), 318–45.

20 E.g. F. F. Bruce, in *Neotestamentica and Semitica*, Festschrift M. Black (1969), 228 n. 18.

21 Cf. in general A. Mertens, *Das Buch Daniel im Lichte der Texte vom Toten Meer* (1971).

22 On 4Qps-Dan, Mertens, op. cit., 42–50.

23 J. T. Milik, *RB* 63 (1956), 411.

24 Respectively Albright and Mann in M. Black, *The Scrolls and Christianity* (1969), 24; F. F. Bruce, op. cit., in Festschrift Black (1969), 228 n. 17.

25 J. Geffcken, *Die Oracula Sibyllina* (GCS 8, 1902), ad loc.

26 V. Nikiprowetzky, *La Troisième Sibylle* (1970), 136.

27 Ibid., 99.

28 E.g. J. Bowman, *Exp. T.* LIX (1947–8), 286; E. Sjöberg, *Der verborgene Menschensohn in der Evangelien* (1955), 53; D. S. Russell, *The Method and Message of Jewish Apocalyptic* (1964), 344–5.

29 For Josephus and the book of Daniel see further F. F. Bruce, *ASTI* 4 (1965), 148–65.

30 Ibid.

31 J. A. Montgomery, *A Critical and Exegetical Commentary on the Book of Daniel* (1927), 313.

32   E.g. J. Bowman, loc. cit.; U. B. Müller, *Messias und Menschensohn in jüdischen Apokalypsen* (1972), 107–55.

33   Cf. G. Dalman, *Die Worte Jesu* (²1930), 200.

34   M. Stone, *Features of the eschatology of 4 Ezra* (Diss., Harvard, 1965, unpublished); id., in *Religions in Antiquity*, Essays in memory of E. R. Goodenough (1968), 295–312; E. Breech, *JBL* 92 (1973), 267–74; cf. also J. Keulers, *Die eschatologische Lehre des vierter Esrabuches* (1922), Pt. I, ch. IV.

35   Stone, op. cit., in *Religions in Antiquity*, 303–10.

36   Cf. J. Swain, *CP* XXXV (1940), 1–20; supra, 119.

37   R. H. Charles, *The Apocalypse of Baruch* (1896), ad loc.

38   For the description, M. Buttenwieser, *Die hebräische Elias-Apokalypse* (1897), 16f, the identifications being at p. 18, lines 3f.

39   E.g. W. Bousset, *Die Religion des Judentums im späthellenistischen Zeitalter* (³1926), 264–5.

40   So e.g. J. Ziegler, *Septuaginta. Vetus Testamentum Graecum Auctoritate Societatis Litterarum Gottingensis*, vol. XVI, pt. 2; J. A. Montgomery, op. cit., ad loc.; for other interpretations, cf. F. F. Bruce, *OTS* XX (1977), 25–6.

41   J. T. Milik, *The Books of Enoch* (1976).

42   T. F. Glasson, *The Second Advent* (1945), 14–16; id., *NTS* 23 (1976–7), 82–90.

43   Glasson, *The Second Advent*, 28.

44   H. L. Strack and P. Billerbeck, *Kommentar zum Neuen Testament aus Talmud und Midrasch* I (1922), 486 and 956.

45   *The Apocalypse of Abraham*, ed. G. H. Box and J. I. Landsman, TED I, 10 (1918), 49.

46   E.g. U. B. Müller, *Messias und Menschensohn in jüdischen Apokalypsen und in der Offenbarung des Johannes* (1972), 145, 146.

6

The New Testament:
the Book of Revelation

John was steeped in the Old Testament. 'He had so profound a knowledge of the Old Testament that he constantly uses its phraseology not only consciously, but even unconsciously.' 'In proportion to its length the Book of Daniel yields by far the greatest number' of Old Testament reminiscences.[1] Of John's extensive use of Daniel there is indeed no doubt, despite the absence of explicit quotations. Nor is it any surprise to learn that a writer of such semitic Greek read the Old Testament in its original languages.[2] Table 3 lists passages where reminiscences of Dan. 7 may reasonably be sought.

TABLE 3

Revelation	Daniel 7	Revelation	Daniel 7
1.7	13	13.1–8	3–8, 11, 20–1, 25
1.13	13	14.14	13
1.14	9	17.3	7
5.11	10	17.7	7
7.1	2	17.8	11
11.2	25	17.12	20, 24
11.7	3, 7, 21	17.16	7
11.15	14, 27	20.4	9, 22, 26, 27
12.3	7	20.11	9
12.8	21	20.12	10
12.14	25	22.5	18, 27

At Rev. 1.7 'with the clouds' is a literal rendering from Dan. 7.13, and 'behold, he comes' recalls the same text. In an author demonstrably dependent on Daniel it can hardly be denied that this is the genuine reminiscence all scholars confess it to be. The man-like figure has been interpreted as Jesus. With Jesus already established as the subject of the previous verses, John's purpose would not have been well served by taking over the expression 'one like a son of man'. The reference is clearly to the parousia, and a descent from heaven is implied. It is therefore reasonable to suppose that John adhered to the normal view of the Western Christian tradition, that the parousia of Jesus was to be found at Dan. 7.13, though some caution is appropriate, since he may have taken his information directly from another source.

We must consider next the possible source. Rev. 1.7 also quotes from Zech. 12.10. Like Dan. 7.13, this text is quoted elsewhere in the New Testament on its own (John 19.37), and Dan. 7.13 and Zech. 12.10 are quoted together also at Matt. 24.30. These two OT texts are used adjacently in one Jewish source, Midrash Wayoša', where Zech. 12.10 is cited for the death of the Messiah son of Joseph, and this is immediately followed by the appearance of the Messiah son of David, for which Dan. 7.13 is quoted. They are both used in the Mysteries of R. Simeon son of Jochai as well, though in this case the two texts are separated by a considerable section of midrash.[3] However, the two texts are not organically connected in either Jewish source. More fundamentally, it is difficult to see how the Jews could have used Zech. 12.10 of a Messiah at the time when John wrote the Book of Revelation, as they do not appear to have held appropriate messianic beliefs as early as this. Therefore Jewish use of these texts together should be dated later than the time of the Book of Revelation. Therefore the combination of these two texts in two late Jewish sources is the result of independent work, and does not constitute satisfactory evidence that John was dependent on a Jewish source which combined them. Some scholars have argued that he was directly dependent on Matt. 24.30. This is especially true of the earlier scholarship, written at a time when any reasonable similarity was interpreted as evidence of literary dependence.[4] Torrey specifically argued 'Direct dependence of the one passage on the other is certain, for the clause "all the tribes of the earth shall mourn (for him)" is not found in the Old Testament, but is made up from two separate verses (10 and 12) in Zechariah.'[5] This argument is unsound, because such a combination could just as easily be made by the author of a testimonium which was then used independently by John and Matthew; indeed, this cannot even be regarded as proof that a definite exegetical tradition was not handed down orally. Lack of more definite literary contact between the two passages makes direct literary dependence very unlikely. Use of a common exegetical tradition is clear; the false ascription of this same combination of OT texts to Hosea by Justin (*Dial.* 14.8) suggests that this tradition was written.[6] Matthew, like John, applies Dan. 7.13 to the parousia.[7] It may therefore be supposed that the common exegetical tradition on which they depend did the same. Thus Rev. 1.7, together with Matt. 24.30, provides evidence of early Christian use of Dan. 7.13 with reference to the parousia. This use of Dan. 7.13 should almost certainly be dated earlier than the Book of Revelation.

At Rev. 1.13 dependence on Dan. 7.13 is almost universally assumed, but Dalman rightly dissented, referring to Dan. 10.5, 6 for the general picture and deriving the actual expression 'one like a son of man' from Dan. 10.16, 18.[8] The imagery of the verse is reminiscent also of Ezekiel (cf. e.g. Ezek. 1.26; 9.2). The factor which suggests dependence on Dan. 7.13 is the expression ὅμοιον υἱὸν ἀνθρώπου. But ὅμοιον is a standard component of visionary material, and in dealing with a writer of such semitic Greek it cannot be too strongly emphasized that בר אנש and בן אדם are normal terms for 'man' and for this reason the occurrence of 'son of man' cannot of itself point to a particular biblical text at all. For the same reason Dalman's reference to Dan. 10.16 also cannot be regarded as more than possible, though the contact with Dan. 10.5ff. makes it a better choice than Dan. 7.13. It should also be noted that ὅμοιον υἱὸν ἀνθρώπου is not the same as ὁ υἱὸς τοῦ ἀνθρώπου, a Gospel expression of which John shows no knowledge. Nor should this passage be connected with any Jewish Son of man concept, since it has been shown above that there was no such concept in Judaism, and it would be methodologically unsound to use Revelation, a Christian work, as evidence for the existence of such a concept in Judaism when it is absent from Jewish sources. However, the expression ὅμοιον υἱὸν ἀνθρώπου is genuinely difficult, as ὅμοιος should be expected to follow normal Greek usage and take the dative. It is natural to point straight to Rev. 14.14 where the

144

identical expression recurs, but we shall see that, whereas 1.13f is a description of the heavenly Jesus, 14.14 describes a different being; the explanation of the expression which John uses in two quite independent descriptions is to be found in careful study of his language.[9]

The expression ὅμοιον υἱὸν ἀνθρώπου contains two semitisms, which are susceptible of separate explanations. υἱὸν ἀνθρώπου rather than ἄνθρωπος is due to the semitic בר אנש or בן אדם (of which it is the normal translation in the Septuagint). It is normal in Jewish apocalyptic to compare supernatural beings to men: John did it again with part of a supernatural being at 4.7 where he is dependent upon Ezekiel (cf. Ezek. 1.10, 10.14). So John has υἱὸν ἀνθρώπου twice, in descriptions of two different heavenly beings, one description being possibly dependent on an occurrence of בן אדם in his text of Dan. 10.16. This should not be regarded as remarkable in an author of such semitic Greek.

John's use of ὅμοιος is normal in content, but his grammar here, as elsewhere, has a tendency to go astray. He uses it no less than eighteen times in his efforts to describe visionary phenomena (1.13, 15; 2.18; 4.3 (bis), 6, 7 (ter); 9.7 (bis), 10, 19; 13.2, 11; 14.14; 21.11, 18), together with three more mundane comparisons (11.1; 13.4; 18.8). Of the twenty-one examples, four show irregularities in the use of case (at 4.3 it is in the right case, but it is feminine). 1.13 and 14.14 have already been cited; the others are 9.10 (χ A 69 pc) καὶ ἔχουσιν οὐρὰς ὁμοίοις σκορπίοις: 13.11 (P 47) καὶ εἶχεν κέρατα δύο ὁμοίῳ ἀρνίῳ. Mussies has provided the basis of an explanation: 'These attractions may perhaps be explained from the fact that in Hebrew and Aramaic "like" formed one word with the following substantive'.[10] This has helped John to put ὅμοιος and its following substantive in the same case four times. The examples at 1.13 and 14.14 have one thing in common, indirectly related to the fact that both are comparisons of a complete supernatural being to a man; they are the only two of the twenty-one examples of ὅμοιος in Revelation in which a noun is not first established in a case so that ὅμοιος can agree with it. In both cases υἱόν is in the accusative after εἶδον, and ὅμοιον has been attracted into agreement with it.[11] A striking example of a similar phenomenon is found at 11.3, where there is no noun established in a case for περιβεβλημένους to agree with; the result is that σάκκους is correctly in the accusative and περιβεβλημένους has been attracted to agree with it!

At 1.14 it is universally and rightly recognized that John has drawn on the picture of the Ancient of Days at Dan. 7.9 for the imagery which he has used in his description of the risen Christ. It is not impossible that John identified the Ancient of Days as Jesus. Some Jewish exegetes saw an angelic figure here, Galipapa identified him as Mattathias, and the identification as Jesus was held by Ephraem. In that case John will have interpreted the man-like figure as a symbol of the Saints, and extracted 'he comes with the clouds' from a testimonium. However, this author's creative reuse of OT imagery is too original for these conclusions to be regarded as demonstrable on the basis of such slight evidence. At this time Jewish authors did reuse such imagery in their descriptions of the intermediary figures characteristic of their apocalyptic works, and it is consistent with John's use of the rest of the OT to suppose that he did the same. Moreover, his view of Jesus, for which he has supplied abundant evidence of a more straightforward kind, cannot be read off such use of the OT. It must therefore be concluded simply that John has used the imagery of Dan. 7.9 for his description of the risen Jesus; but further conclusions as to his interpretation of Dan. 7.9–14 cannot be extracted with any confidence from this passage.

At Rev. 5.11, the number of divine beings round the throne, 'myriads of myriads and thousands upon thousands', is probably derived from Dan. 7.10. This cannot always be affirmed with certainty, but in a writer steeped in the OT and demonstrably dependent on Daniel, it is the most probable source. Mussies notes the avoidance of χίλιαι and μύριαι, presumably to ensure that the number is indefinitely huge, an exegetical point observable in rabbinical use of this verse.[12]

The four winds of Rev. 7.1 are too common to be tied down to Dan. 7.2, though their occurrence here is of some interest because the four angels recur among the fathers as an interpretation of the four winds of Dan. 7.2.

At Rev. 11.2 the interval of forty-two months is that of Dan. 7.25; 12.7 (when correctly interpreted, as it was in both Syrian and Western traditions); it recurs at 13.5, as at 12.14, where it has been taken from Daniel more literally as 'a time and times and half a time': cf. also the 1,260 days of Rev. 11.3; 12.6. The Western tradition of interpretation is implied up to a point, in that this period now refers to a part of the eschatological events, not to past history at the time of Antiochus Epiphanes. However, free use of the phrase has been made in the creative formation of a new apocalypse. If this phrase stood on its own, one might have to conclude that interpretative deductions could not be made from such creative reuse. However, in the case of this author, consistent use has been made of so much of the material from Dan. 7 as to justify the deduction that John followed the outline of a Western tradition of interpretation. The next such passage is 11.7, where 'he will make war with them and conquer them' in such a context must go back to Dan. 7.21: the beast itself takes us to Rev. 13 and its source again in Dan. 7, 'the beast which comes up from the abyss' recalling especially Dan. 7.3, 7. With Dan. 7 clearly in the author's purview one cannot refrain from citing Dan. 7.14, 27 for the last clause of Rev. 11.15, though this sentiment is not distinctive enough to be tied down to this single OT passage.

Rev. 12 contains further possible examples of material from Dan. 7. At 12.3 the mythological beast has ten horns, the number of which may plausibly be derived from Dan. 7.7, 24. At vs. 8, the idea of direct dependence on Dan. 7.21 seems rather forced. The expression at Rev. 12.14 has already been noted as reminiscent of Dan. 7.25; 12.7.

At Rev. 13.1–8, the strange beast is clearly an amalgam which draws on all four beasts from Dan. 7. Charles notes that it

is clearly based on Dan. 7.2–7. It comes up from the sea, as the four beasts in Daniel did: the number of its heads may be directly derived from adding together the heads of the four beasts, though this characteristic has probably an older history; its ten horns are from the fourth beast, and its likeness to a leopard, its possession of the feet of a bear, and the mouth of a lion, are borrowed from the first three beasts.[13]

The 'mouth speaking big things', of which 'blasphemies' is an accurate interpretation, is from Dan. 7.8, 20 (cf. 7.11, 25). The forty-two months have already been noted as from Dan. 7.25; 12.7. At Rev. 13.7, 'to make war with the saints and to conquer them' is from Dan. 7.21. This mighty beast is clearly symbolic of Rome. It is reasonable to deduce again the Western tradition, with the fourth beast as Rome, the Saints of vs. 21 being Christians, and the setting eschatological. However, we should not go further than this in extracting the exegesis of so creative and allusive an author.

At 14.14, ὅμοιον υἱὸν ἀνθρώπου occurs for the second time. We have already seen that this term consists of two semitisms, and does not of itself constitute adequate reason for any specific identification of the being in question nor sufficient evidence of dependence on Dan. 7.13. The latter point may be dealt with first. Other features of Rev. 14.14 may be held to provide evidence of dependence on Dan. 7.13. εἶδον, καὶ ἰδού is too much part of the common coin of apocalyptic to be so regarded. The cloud is a point of general similarity, but it is too differently dealt with to constitute actual evidence of dependence.

> This is far too slight a circumstance to indicate the reaper's identity . . . there is every difference between the single motionless white cloud of John's vision, and the great surging mass of threatening storm-clouds, which were to chariot the Messiah. John has spoken before of cloud as an accompaniment of angelic appearance: the strong angel of ch. X was 'clad in a cloud'. Again, we must remember how the witnesses rise to heaven 'in a cloud'. The fact is that the reaper's position 'on a cloud' simply corresponds with the flight in mid-heaven of the angels who shout their messages to the world in verses 6–12. His static position is dictated by the metaphor of the sickle, sweeping with one final stroke through the ripe corn of wickedness.[14]

Swete talks of 'the white cloud . . . which was so familiar to dwellers by the Mediterranean and Aegean',[15] and because of general considerations such as these, one finds that Vergil provides a closer literary parallel than Daniel, when he has Apollo sitting on a cloud watching the battle and talking to Iulus (*Aen.* IX, 638–40). It is to be concluded that John is not dependent here on Dan. 7.13, and that the view that he is has derived its vital support from failure to understand the expression ὅμοιον υἱὸν ἀνθρώπου.

The understanding of this expression also removes the only plausible reason for identifying this figure as the heavenly

Christ. It is to be seen as an angelic figure, obeying the command of 'another angel' (14.15), and performing a function very precisely parallel to that of 'another angel' (14.17–19).

At Rev. 17 the ten horns mentioned repeatedly may reasonably be derived from Dan. 7; it is less reasonable to derive the destruction of this beast from Dan. 7.11. At vs. 12, the ten horns are identified in accordance with Dan. 7.24 as ten kings. Then we are told that they will rule simultaneously in the last times. This is the later Western tradition of Danielic interpretation. It is probable that John really did interpret Dan. 7 like this; it is one of the few points which enable us to go through John's creative reuse of Danielic material back to his interpretation of it.

Rev. 20.4 contains several possible reminiscences of Dan. 7. The thrones recall vs. 9: here the victorious martyrs sit on them. καὶ κρίμα ἐδόθη αὐτοῖς is reminiscent of Dan. 7.22, 26. In Dan. 7.22 the meaning is that judgement was given in their favour. At Rev. 20.4 it is generally supposed that they became the judges, but it should be noted that the Danielic meaning would not be unduly difficult. θρόνους are not necessarily more than 'seats': it would make good sense for the victorious martyrs to be sat on heavenly seats even if they were not going to judge; the judgement (its outcome for them a foregone conclusion) was then given in their favour 'and they lived and reigned with Christ'. This is parallel to the outcome in Dan. 7.22, 27. Furthermore, this creative author reuses his material so freely that it is in any case unsafe to deduce that he saw the Saints made judges in Dan. 7.22, especially when that exegesis is unexampled in the material under review.

The single throne of Rev. 20.11 is to be found at Isa. 6.1 as well as Dan. 7.9, and was by this time an established item of belief. At Rev. 20.12 the opening of the books is probably from Dan. 7.10. It had become a feature of Jewish apocalyptic, but in a writer who so clearly made use of Daniel an identical phrase should be accepted as coming from that source. Rev. 22.5, however, is more probably to be regarded as a parallel to the expression of victory for the Saints in Daniel.

The following conclusions may now be drawn. John was a creative apocalyptist who used Dan. 7, as he used other parts of the Old Testament, as a source of dramatic imagery. Con-

THE BOOK OF REVELATION

sequently, it is not always possible to tell when he really is
dependent on it, and the task of deducing his interpretation of
it is hazardous. The main lines of his interpretation can, however, be laid down. In general, he was an early adherent of the
Western tradition. In his view the fourth kingdom was Rome,
and in Dan. 7 eschatological events were predicted. The ten
horns were ten kings who would have a brief and simultaneous
reign in these last times. Rome, the fourth kingdom, would be
destroyed and the Saints, victorious Christians, would reign
with Christ. It is probable that he identified the man-like figure
of Dan. 7.13 as Jesus, and saw his parousia predicted there. If
John did not take this view himself, he used a source which did,
so that he constitutes in any case early Christian evidence of this
exegesis. Verses 9 and 10 he used as a source of imagery,
apparently placing the judgement there in the last times.

Finally, John shows no knowledge of the Gospel expression
ὁ υἱὸς τοῦ ἀνθρώπου. The expression ὅμοιον υἱὸν ἀνθρώπου, which
he does use twice, is a combination of semitisms. The two
occurrences of it are connected with each other only at this
linguistic level, and are not dependent on Dan. 7.13.

NOTES

1 R. H. Charles, *Revelation* (ICC, 1920), I, xxi; H. B. Swete, *The
   Apocalypse of St John* (1909), cxlviii.

2 Cf. L. P. Trudinger, *JThS* 17 (1966), 82–8; A. Vanhoye, *Bib* 43 (1962),
   436–76.

3 Supra, 83.

4 E.g. R. H. Charles, op. cit., ad loc.

5 C. C. Torrey, *The Apocalypse of John* (1958), 94.

6 B. Lindars, *New Testament Apologetic* (1961), 127 and n. 2.

7 Infra, 177.

8 G. H. Dalman, *Die Worte Jesu* (²1930), 206.

9 Cf. in general G. Mussies, *The Morphology of Koine Greek as Used in the
   Apocalypse of St John: A Study in Bilingualism* (1971).

10 Ibid., 139.

11 Cf. ibid., 100.

12 Ibid., 223: supra, 75.

13 R. H. Charles, op. cit., ad loc.

14 M. Kiddle, *The Revelation of St John* (1940), ad loc.

15 H. B. Swete, op. cit., ad loc.

7

The New Testament Epistles

It is convenient to begin with the letters attributed to St Paul. The book of Daniel has not been very influential in them. Ellis, finding 93 quotations from the OT, has none at all from this book.[1] Allusions have, however, been sought: above all Dan. 7.13 and the Son of man have been sought behind the major Pauline epistles, since they patently do not occur in them, and when both are held central to the historical Jesus and/or the Gospel writers, this is difficult to explain. We shall discuss the most important passages in the order of the Canon.

The first passage is 1 Cor. 6.2. The idea that this verse contains a reminiscence of Dan. 7.22 requires us to suppose that Paul interpreted Dan. 7.22 in a sense which is not impossible but is unexampled in the material covered in this investigation. While the author of Dan. 7 meant that judgement was given in favour of the Saints of the Most High, we have to believe that Paul took it to mean that they became the judges. The real difficulty with this view, however, is the lack of evidence that Paul had this passage in mind at all. Closer parallels are provided by Wisd. 3.8, which says of the righteous 'they shall judge the nations', and 1QpHab V, 4, 'by the hand of his elect God will carry out the judgement of all the nations'. Thus there is clear Jewish evidence for this belief, which was naturally taken over into Christianity. There is no evidence that requires us to associate it with misinterpretation of Dan. 7.22, which moreover certainly cannot be held responsible for the parallel remark at 1 Cor. 6.3, 'do you not know that we shall judge angels?' On these grounds it is best to conclude that Paul did not have Dan. 7.22 in mind.

At 1 Cor. 15.47, Paul declares that 'the second man is of heaven'. His argument did not require absolute precision in the definition of 'of heaven', but Goudge's comment gives the most probable sense:

The reference is still not to the Incarnation, but to the Lord as glorified. Our Lord is 'of heaven' from the Ascension onwards; it is thence that He acts, and thence that we look for Him to come (1 Thess. 4.16; 2 Thess. 1.7). The latter thought is already in St. Paul's mind. It is the Second Coming, that will be the signal for the transformation of the earthly bodies of his people. Cf. Phil. 3.20, 21 and Col. 3.4.[2]

The background to the description of Jesus as 'the second man' may lie in Jewish Adam speculation as well as the fact that Jesus was actually a man; but that he was a man was blindingly obvious, and that he was 'of heaven' in this sense was a commonplace of early Christian belief. There is no need of any other figure of a man from heaven to explain it, and there is no particular feature of the Pauline passage to link it to Dan. 7.13. The term 'second' is simply derived from comparison with Adam, and the selection of Jesus as the fundamentally important salvation figure; it, too, has no connection with Dan. 7.13.

1 Cor. 15.23–8 has been cited, not so much for Dan. 7.13, as to argue that Paul thought of Jesus as the Son of man. '. . . there can be little doubt that he (sc. Paul) thought of Jesus as the Son of Man. The *locus classicus* is 1 Cor. 15.27 (cf. 15.47). Paul's use of Ps. 8.6 is only explicable if Christ be identified with the Son of Man.'[3] This is misleading. Paul's argument does require the identification of Jesus as אנוש and/or בן אדם of Ps. 8.5 (LXX ἄνθρωπος and υἱὸς ἀνθρώπου), but it does not require any reference to, or knowledge of, the Gospel term ὁ υἱὸς τοῦ ἀνθρώπου, a term which Paul never uses. בן אדם, in standard Septuagint translationese υἱὸς ἀνθρώπου, means 'man'. If the Word of God said something about any unidentified man which was, in the view of an early Christian exegete, actually true of Jesus, it followed that God was speaking about Jesus. This basic presupposition of early Christian exegesis explains Paul's choice of Ps. 8 here. It is what the psalm says, not its use of the term υἱὸς ἀνθρώπου, which is the decisive factor. The same factor explains its combination here with a reminiscence of Ps. 110.1. It is noteworthy that Ps. 8 and Dan. 7.13 are not combined anywhere in the New Testament.

Phil. 2.7 is part of a passage genuinely difficult to interpret, and hence the subject of much learned conjecture. Lohmeyer argued that ὡς ἄνθρωπος is a representation of כבר אנש from Dan. 7.13, but his theory has been severely, and justly, criticized.[4] It depends on a misunderstanding of the man-like figure in the text of Daniel itself, and it presupposes a Jewish Son of man concept. Lohmeyer did not explain why Paul wrote ὡς ἄνθρωπος instead of ὡς υἱὸς ἀνθρώπου; this highlights the fact that there is no real relationship between the existing text of Phil. 2.7 and Dan. 7.13, necessitating the conjecture that it was more like Dan. 7.13 once than it is now. Lohmeyer's understanding of 'Son of man' in the Gospels is also unsatisfactory, and does not provide an adequate foundation for the concept which he found behind Phil. 2.7. His theory is therefore to be rejected. One factor in early Christian belief which should not be in need of very profound and complex explanation is the usual view that when Jesus was on earth he was 'as a man'.

1 Thess. 4.17 has reminded many scholars of Dan. 7.13. There is no sign here of the Son of man, and the clouds should not be regarded as sufficient evidence of the influence of Dan. 7.13. In the ancient world, clouds were normal vehicles for heavenly journeys.[5] In most stories, it is true, one person went in a cloud, but this is because, in most stories, only one person went. A lot of people go in Pes. R. I.3, where the children of Israel travel on clouds to Jerusalem at the End, Isa. 60.8 being quoted in support. The rarity of this kind of passage (at least in extant, published Jewish sources that I have seen) accounts for the absence of a more precise Jewish precedent for 1 Thess. 4.17. In Jewish thought of this period, the Jews do not go up to or towards heaven at the time of the End, or at any other time. Hence they do not normally go all together on clouds. Christians normally depicted the End by bringing Jesus down to earth at his parousia, but the author of 1 Thessalonians was different: he supposed that Jesus and faithful Christians would meet in the air. This is unusual, though given the presuppositions of his thought it is not illogical. Given that he had a heavenly journey for a lot of people, it is entirely natural that he should take them there on clouds. There is, however, no special contact with Dan. 7.13, which cannot be the origin of the whole idea because this idea is not to be found there, neither in the original interpretation of this text nor in the specifically Christian interpretations of it which gradually emerged. The usual Christian use of Dan.

7.13 would have applied it to the descent of Jesus rather than the ascent of the faithful. Nor should we deduce that Jesus must have been interpreted here as the man-like figure coming on the clouds to meet them. The author does not say this, and therefore we may not be sure that he had Dan. 7.13 in mind at all.

2 Thess. 2 has been less often associated with Dan. 7, but the attempt has been made, and the absence of this connection is in fact of some importance. The most definite attempt was made by Orchard, but even then he was not able to find definite traces of the language of Dan. 7, having to content himself with pointing out the general correspondence of Paul's picture of 'the man of lawlessness' with the Danielic description of Antiochus Epiphanes.[6] This is not enough. On the contrary, the lack of specific trace of Dan. 7 suggests very strongly that Paul did not have it particularly in mind. In itself that is not surprising; but together with other negative evidence it falsifies the theories of scholars who believe that 'this chapter was much in the mind of early Christian thinkers'.[7] If this were the case, 2 Thess. 2 was an obvious place to make use of it.

It is thus to be concluded that traces of Dan. 7 are absent from the Pauline and deutero-Pauline epistles. It is also to be noted, though it is well enough known, that the Gospel term ὁ υἱὸς τοῦ ἀνθρώπου does not occur in Paul. If this were because his Greek was too good for such a barbaric phrase it should have been removed by Luke for the same reason. In fact, however, its absence in Paul has helped its barbarity to be exaggerated.[8] The numerous attempts to find Dan. 7.13 and the Son of man behind some Pauline passages have been due to the erroneous belief in a Jewish Son of man concept and to the failure of New Testament scholars to solve the Son of man problem in the Gospels.

The Epistle to the Hebrews

There are no quotations of or allusions to Dan. 7 in this work. υἱὸς ἀνθρώπου occurs at 2.6 in a clear citation of Ps. 8.5 according to the LXX version, which is here rendered literally in its usual manner. The author's exposition of the psalm does not fasten on this term at all, and he shows no sign of knowing the Gospel term ὁ υἱὸς τοῦ ἀνθρώπου. Nevertheless, some scholars have

154

sought to show that Dan. 7.13 lies in the background and that the author used a Son of man Christology.[9] The decisive evidence against this view is the readily observable fact that the author does not use the title ὁ υἱὸς τοῦ ἀνθρώπου as he could so easily have done if he knew it and saw any sign of it in Ps. 8.[10] The frequency of the term in the Gospels cannot override the evidence of its absence in the text of Hebrews. Moreover, there is nothing in the context to point to Dan. 7. Ps. 8 is applied to Jesus in the normal manner of early Christian exegetes: ἄνθρωπος and υἱὸς ἀνθρώπου in accordance with the semitic parallelism of the psalm, he is seen as an ideal representative man, but not as 'the Son of man'.

The Catholic Epistles

None of these documents shows any sign of Dan. 7; the absence of any trace of it at 2 Pet. 3.10f.; Jas. 5.7–8; 1 John 2.18; 4.3; 2 John 7 is perhaps worthy of note, because it might be considered surprising if Dan. 7 had in fact been an exceptionally important part of Scripture to the early Church.

Thus this chapter is in effect a catalogue of negative results. That such a large part of the New Testament shows no definite trace of Dan. 7 is important because it falsifies the belief of many scholars that Dan. 7 was an especially important chapter to the early Christians. The well-known absence of ὁ υἱὸς τοῦ ἀνθρώπου is important too. The general failure to solve the problems of its use in the Gospels has prevented the straightforward consequence of its absence in the Epistles from being accepted: there is no Son of man concept in the Epistles, whose authors show no sign of knowing the Gospel term.

NOTES

1   E. E. Ellis, *Paul's Use of the Old Testament* (1957), App. I. A.

2   H. L. Goudge, *The First Epistle to the Corinthians* (1903), ad loc.

3   A. M. Hunter, *Paul and his Predecessors* ([2]1961), 86; likewise, e.g. A. E. Rawlinson, *The New Testament Doctrine of the Christ* (1926), 124–5; against them e.g. D. E. H. Whiteley, *The Theology of St Paul* (1964), 117.

4   E. Lohmeyer, *Kyrios Jesus, Eine Untersuchung zu Phil.* 2:5–11 (1928). For criticism, especially R. P. Martin, *Carmen Christi* (1967). Martin includes a reconstruction of a hypothetical original Aramaic text.

5   Cf. infra, 204.

6 J. B. Orchard, *Bib* 20 (1939), 172–9.
7 C. H. Dodd, *According to the Scriptures* (1952), 67.
8 Cf. infra, 239.
9 E.g. F. F. Bruce, *The Epistle to the Hebrews* (1964), ad loc.; P. Giles, *ExpT* LXXXVI (1974–5), 328–31.
10 For a full discussion, see E. Grässer in *Jesus und der Menschensohn. Für Anton Vögtle* (1976), 404–14.

156

8
The Gospels and Acts

The main purpose of the investigation which led to this book was to find out whether the Gospel term 'the Son of man' was derived from Dan. 7.13. We must now consider the interpretation of sayings which may reasonably be considered to show signs of the influence of Dan. 7. It might be thought that all Son of man sayings should be discussed, on the ground that the expression 'the Son of man' is itself a sign of the influence of Dan. 7.13. Manson's formulation is famous: 'We have no good reason to suppose that he (sc. Jesus) was aware of any other Son of Man than the Danielic'.[1] Here we have in a nutshell one main reason for persistent scholarly attempts to find the origin of 'the Son of man' in Dan. 7.13, but Manson's statement is misleading. Jesus had known another son of man ever since he was old enough to find human speech intelligible. His mother tongue was Aramaic, and it is rightly agreed by all competent scholars on the basis of sufficient evidence that בר אנש was a normal Aramaic term for 'man'.[2] Therefore Jesus must have heard and used this 'son of man' regularly, and the simple occurrence of the term ὁ υἱὸς τοῦ ἀνθρώπου cannot be regarded as sufficient evidence of the influence of Dan. 7.13.

This does not exclude the possibility that a result of the investigation might be that the term is in fact derived from Dan. 7.13; all Son of man sayings might theoretically have shown many different signs of Dan. 7.13. However, most of them in fact do not, and in arguing that they are not dependent on the influence of Dan. 7.13 I shall draw attention to this fact and discuss in detail only sufficient sayings of this kind to ensure that a fair presentation of other theories is provided; this discussion, and that of borderline cases where the influence of Dan. 7 is possible but not obvious, will ensure that all the necessary points are made without repeating them for each saying where the influence of Dan. 7.13 is not in my view to be found. Table 4 lists those sayings which will be discussed.

TABLE 4

New Testament Text	Daniel 7
Mark 1.15‖Matt. 4.17	22
Mark 2.10‖Matt. 9.6‖Luke 5.24	13–14
Mark 8.38‖Matt. 16.27‖Luke 9.26	13–14
Mark 9.12‖Matt. 17.12	21
Mark 10.45‖Matt. 20.28	14
Mark 13.26‖Matt. 24.30‖Luke 21.27	13–14
Mark 14.62‖Matt. 26.64‖Luke 22.69	13
Matt. 10.23	13
Matt. 13.41	13–14
Matt. 16.28	13–14
Matt. 19.28‖Luke 22.30	9, 10, 13, 22
Matt. 24.27‖Luke 17.24	13
Matt. 24.44‖Luke 12.40	13
Matt. 25.31	13–14
Matt. 28.3	9
Matt. 28.18	14
Luke 1.32–3	14
Luke 12.8	13
Luke 12.32	14, 18, 27
Luke 17.22	13
Luke 18.8	13
John 1.51	13
John 5.27	13
Acts 1.11	13
Acts 7.56	13

Mark 1.15‖Matt. 4.17

Mark 1.15 was suggested by Dodd.[3] He utilizes Theodotion's Greek version of Dan. 7.22, but relies on a hypothetical Aramaic original to conform Mark's ἤγγικεν to the quite differently used ἔφθασεν of Dan. 7.22 Theod. His opinion that מטא underlies the Marcan ἤγγικεν is very improbable, and is derived from a theory of 'realized eschatology' alien to the Gospel evidence.[4] ἤγγικεν makes excellent sense, and its natural equivalent is קרב. Mark 1.15 and Dan. 7.22 in fact have two things in common: the fulfilment of the time, and the concept of the kingdom of God. The latter is a fundamental Jewish concept writ large in the teaching of Jesus and the synoptic tradition. It is therefore not sufficient to tie down the reference to any single scriptural passage. The concept of the fulfilment of the time, somewhat differently expressed in the two passages, is too common an apocalyptic idea to be attached to a single text. It is moreover a different time which has come: in Mark 1.15 it is the ministry of Jesus, the decisive time when the kingdom is still at hand; in Dan. 7.22 the final time has really come and the kingdom is received by the Saints, the central group of Dan. 7 who are not mentioned here or anywhere else in the Gospel of Mark or the teaching of Jesus. Mark 1.15 does not claim or need direct dependence on an OT text. It is a summary statement of the centre of Jesus' teaching as Mark saw it. Dodd's argument should therefore be rejected.

Mark 2.10‖Matt. 9.6‖Luke 5.24

At Mark 2.10 the influence of Dan. 7 is found to be fundamental by Farrer, as it was by Tertullian.[5] He begins by misstating what he calls the 'lexicographical sense' of 'Son of man' which according to him means 'the coming bearer of Adamic rule'. This is philologically unsound, and it is one of several indications that he could not handle the philological evidence, a fatal weakness evident in the work of many researchers in this field. He supposes that anyone who was master of Galilean Aramaic must have been able to refer with sufficient clarity to 'Daniel's phrase', but the vital question which he obscures is whether a first-century Aramaic speaker could have done so in such a way that the sentences which he spoke could be translated into Greek in a normally comprehensible manner to produce Gospel sayings which we now possess. It will be argued that in order to refer with sufficient clarity to Dan. 7, an Aramaic speaker had to make it clear in the context that he was in fact intending such a reference, and that this might explain Mark 14.62 but cannot explain Mark 2.10.

In search of a 'deeper meaning' Farrer asserts the direct dependence of Mark 2.10 on Dan. 7. ' "The Son of Man hath authority upon earth" puts together the most important phrases of Daniel 7.' Why 'authority' should be regarded as more important than 'kingship' and 'Son of Man' more important than 'Saints of the Most High' Farrer does not explain; this indicates his unDanielic perspective. Verbal contact between the two passages is not sufficient to indicate literary dependence. ὁ υἱὸς τοῦ ἀνθρώπου is not obviously dependent on כבר אנש primarily because בר אנש is too common an Aramaic term for 'man'. The use of ἐξουσία in Mark is different from the use of שלטן in Dan. 7; in Dan. 7 the authority of God is only equated with the authority of the Saints (or, when 7.13 is messianically interpreted, the authority of the man-like figure) in the sense that the authority of the Saints to rule in their kingdom is the divinely given authority of God, not in the sense that the Saints are given other aspects of God's authority, such as forgiveness of sins. Farrer then proceeds with the improbable supposition that at this time Dan. 7.22 was held to mean that judgement was given to the Saints, and asserts, 'Putting Daniel's several statements together we get the result: the divine authority over the earth, and especially the divine authority in judgement, is given to the Son of Man'. We do not get anything of the kind; even if Dan. 7.22 were held to mean judgement was put in the hands of the Saints (which it does not), that would not make the man-like figure the judge. But the final blow is still to come. 'Now if the divine authority of judgement does not consist in the remitting and retaining of sins, in what does it consist? . . . Daniel says he confers it on the Son of Man.' This theological statement is not to be found in the Danielic text at all; in Dan. 7 the authority given to the Saints is that of exercising rule in their kingdom, and if anyone thought that in vs. 22 they were given the function of judgement (it has not been shown that they were or that Mark thought that they were), its purpose would be the annihilation of the fourth kingdom, not the forgiveness of sins.

However, the matter cannot be settled without the uncertain labour of reconstructing an Aramaic sentence that Jesus might have spoken and which might have given rise to Mark 2.10; one might suggest the following: ותנדעון די שליט בר אנשא למשבק חטאין על ארעא. Which son of man? There is nothing in the context of the sentence to supply the automatic answer 'the one in Dan. 7'. Moreover, the constant exegesis of the

Western tradition places the giving of this authority to the man-like figure after he has come on the clouds at the eschaton, not while Jesus was on earth. The variant of Cyprian gives it to him after the Resurrection. The Syrian tradition brought Jesus in at Dan. 7.13–14 only by means of an exegetical device altogether absent from the New Testament. Thus Farrer's view involves the invention of a unique exegesis of Dan. 7 which was fundamental to Jesus and then forgotten. That is not a point in his favour.

Farrer attempts to avoid it by digging out yet a third level of meaning. 'The enthronement of the Son of Man will impose the public recognition of an authority already spiritually actual, the authority to forgive sins; and it is this authority that Christ exercises here and now.' Mark did not say this; as so often, the attribution of profundity, of pattern, of another layer of meaning, is but an excuse for the abandonment of all reasonable criteria of assessment. It is all the more plausible and misleading for its general approximation to genuine Marcan Christology, so that one can almost forget that Mark is supposed not merely to believe this, but to believe it as exegesis of Dan. 7. Moreover, Mark normally ascribes authority to Jesus without the use of the term 'Son of man', and Matthew at least appears to have known that the authority to forgive sins could be exercised by other men too (Matt. 9.8).[6]

Finally, the phrase 'on the earth' defines the place where the person mentioned has power to forgive sins. It is the same place as Dan. 7 (though it does not occur in 7.13–14), the same place as most of the OT and the same place as the whole of daily life in the time of Jesus; in short, it does not point to Dan. 7 in particular.

It is therefore to be concluded that there was originally no reference to Dan. 7.13 in this saying; and that Mark has given no sign that he saw any such reference either. Moreover, it may be suggested that the Aramaic reconstruction which I have proposed makes excellent sense of a different kind.[7]

Mark 8.38‖Matt. 16.27‖Luke 9.26

Mark 8.38 is a more widely canvassed and more reasonable suggestion. It is normal, and right, to see this saying as a further development of Luke 12.9‖Matt. 10.33. $\epsilon\pi\alpha\iota\sigma\chi\upsilon\nu\theta\hat{\eta}$ and

ἐπαισχυνθήσεται go back to the Aramaic חפר, whereas
(ἀπ)αρνοῦμαι translates כפר, so that there has been bifurcation
in the Aramaic tradition.[8] The original Aramaic may be
reconstructed:

וכל די יחפר בי קדם אנשא
בר אנש יחפר בה קדם מלאכיא די אלהא·

The Marcan version must be correct in having ὁ υἱὸς τοῦ
ἀνθρώπου representing an original בר אנש, as this makes a
straightforward parallel to Luke 12.8 and enables us to explain
all the variants.[9] Matt. 10.33 renders with ἐγώ exactly as at
Matt. 10.32, the translator having taken pains to ensure that
the reference to Jesus was carefully brought out, while the
Lucan tradition took Luke 12.9 as a general statement and
replaced a possible Son of man statement with a passive to avoid
the apparent contradiction with Luke 12.10. The original
saying had nothing other than the term בר אנש to link it with
Dan. 7.13, and this cannot be regarded as sufficient to demonstrate a connection. The question then is whether Dan. 7.13 has
been used in the secondary development of this saying 'when
he comes in the glory of his father with the holy angels'. We
shall see that Mark 13.26 and 14.62 provide evidence of the
Western Christian interpretation of Dan. 7.13 of the parousia of
Jesus. This is the interpretation which is required here. Thus
general considerations favour the possibility of an allusion, and
this is supported by the detailed description. ἔλθῃ could represent אתה; δόξῃ recalls ויקר; and angels must be presupposed
as the subject of הקרבוהי (as explicitly in Midr. Ps. 21, 5).
The decisive factor is the collocation of 'Son of man' and
'coming'. Jesus was expected to come according to New Testament writers whose work shows no trace of the use of Dan. 7:
see 1 Cor. 4.5; 11.26; 2 Thess. 1.10; Heb. 10.37 (Hab. 2.3);
likewise the day of the Lord (1 Thess. 5.2), God (Jude 14), even
Antichrist (1 John 2.18; 4.3). Similarly the Acts of the Apostles,
where we shall find no clear or conscious trace of Dan. 7, refers
to the coming of Jesus (Acts 1.11), and the coming of 'times of
refreshment' when he will be sent (Acts 3.20). Hence the
Marcan expansion of a reference to Jesus at the End with a
reference to his coming is not surprising.

But the Gospel examples have a peculiarity. In the synoptic

Gospels, where influence of Dan. 7.13 is certainly to be found at Mark 13.26||Matt. 24.30||Luke 21.27 and Mark 14.62||Matt. 26.64, it is invariably 'the Son of man' who will come, and there are no less than five further examples: Matt. 24.44||Luke 12.40; Matt. 10.23; 16.28; 25.31; Luke 18.8. There is one exception, whose origin is easily traced. At Mark 13.35, 'for you do not know when the lord of the house is coming', we are clearly dealing with the application of parabolic material, and it is from the parable that the expression 'the lord of the house' comes. This is also the source of Matt. 24.42, so that the Matthean 'your Lord comes' has its origin in parabolic material. This is the only exception to the general rule that in the synoptic Gospels all statements which say with reference to the parousia that Jesus will come take the form of saying that the Son of man will come.

The fourth Gospel is different. In this Gospel there is no certain trace of Dan. 7 at all, and nowhere is it said that the Son of man will come. Mostly, it is true, it is the Paraclete who will come, but there are a few passages where Jesus says 'I come' of his return (John 14.3, 18, 28; 21.22, 23). The consistency of these sayings is very striking. It must be deduced that the collocation of ὁ υἱὸς τοῦ ἀνθρώπου and ἔρχομαι has a specific origin. This collocation cannot be explained by any particular feature of the Aramaic language. It is not a grammatical item at all. Two of the eight synoptic examples certainly are dependent on Dan. 7.13, where they have turned כבר אנש into ὁ υἱὸς τοῦ ἀνθρώπου and taken up אתה with ἔρχομαι. It follows that Dan. 7.13 is the source of all these statements that the Son of man will come. Mark 13.26; 14.62 provide indubitable evidence of midrashic use of this text. It is possible that all the other examples depend on this midrashic use, and it is possible that Mark was not aware of the influence of Dan. 7.13 at Mark 8.38, that is to say, it may be that the influence of Dan. 7.13 was indirect.[10] Whether this influence of Dan. 7.13 was consciously felt is difficult to decide. But it is clear that Dan. 7.13 really did exercise this influence, and this is an important finding. Furthermore, we have noted that Mark 8.38c is an expansion of a Son of man saying of which a more original version is to be found at Luke 12.9/Matt. 10.33. But the term 'Son of man' was in the original saying, whereas ἔρχομαι was not. Therefore the expan-

163

sion of this saying with influence from midrashic use of Dan.
7.13 was the work of the early Church, not of the historical
Jesus, and this midrashic use of Dan. 7.13 in this particular
saying is demonstrable only at a stage of the saying's development other than that at which the expression 'the Son of man'
originated in it.

Matthew omitted the first part of Mark 8.38, no doubt
because he already had Matt. 10.33 from Q. But he retained the
secondary addition with a fresh beginning to include the Son of
man: 'for the Son of man will come in the glory of his Father
with the holy angels' (Matt. 16.27). Then in true midrashic
fashion he added a quotation from Ps. 62.13. One cannot be
certain whether he recognized any allusion to Dan. 7.13. Luke
9.26 is an abbreviated version of Mark 8.38 with minor modifi-
cations. Here, too, it is impossible to say whether the author
saw any allusion to Dan. 7.13 in his Marcan source.

Mark 9.12‖Matt. 17.12

Mark 9.12 explicitly refers to the Old Testament for the suffering of the Son of man, and Moule, taking up an earlier reference
to Dan. 7.21, argues that Dan. 7 is the scriptural passage referred
to; the suggestion has been fully worked out with reference to
all the suffering Son of man sayings by M. D. Hooker.[11] It is not
acceptable because, as we have seen, there is no suffering Son
of man in Dan. 7; the imagery of this chapter is inconsistent
with the idea that the man-like figure suffers.[12] Moreover, I
have found no ancient exegete who thought there was a
suffering Son of man in this chapter. This removes the basis for
Moule's conjecture.[13]

Mark 10.45‖Matt. 20.28

Gaston has suggested that Mark 10.45 is a correction of Dan.
7.14.[14] Correction of the book of Daniel is not, on the face of it,
a probable line for Jesus to have taken, so that if Gaston's
hypothesis is to be accepted, clear evidence is required that
Dan. 7.14 is in fact being referred to, but this is just what Gaston
has failed to supply. The sense of 'be served' suggested by the
context in Mark is hardly that of Dan. 7.14, and the tense of
$ἦλθεν$ shows that, if it were understood in the normal sense of

ἔρχομαι and referred to Jesus' coming to earth for his earthly life, it could not refer to the אתה of Dan. 7.13 as it was understood when we know it was used at that time. It is therefore to be concluded that Dan. 7.14 was not in mind.

Mark 13.26||Matt. 24.30||Luke 21.27

The dependence of Mark 13.26 on Dan. 13 is universally recognized. The occurrence of the Christian term ὁ υἱὸς τοῦ ἀνθρώπου is not consistent with the view that this verse was part of a Jewish apocalypse taken over by Mark. This view, motivated by theological rather than historical considerations, is based on arguments which are unsound of method.[15] In particular, the demonstration that an item of belief was Jewish does not show that it was not Christian; the contrary assumption has the function of making early Christianity as unJewish as possible, and the effect of rendering its origins inexplicable. As well as the Christian term, 'the Son of man', Mark 13.26 has 'coming' and 'in clouds'. Its dependence on Dan. 7.13 is therefore clear. In view of this, it is natural to suppose that 'power' and 'glory' are derived from Dan. 7.14. Too much should not be made of the change from 'with' to 'in' (the clouds) when formal considerations are brought into view. Mark 13.26 is not a translation of Dan. 7.13, but part of a new apocalyptic work in which creative use has been made of Dan. 7.13 to form a new piece of Christian material. Greater precision should therefore not be expected, especially if the new work was written in the first place in Greek. Subsequent Christian interpreters were quite happy to interpret Dan. 7.13 as the parousia of Jesus when they read ἐπί, μετά, or a variety of other prepositions. The position of ἐν νεφέλαις after ἐρχόμενον helps to make it clear that the clouds are the vehicle for the Son of man's journey.

One aspect of the interpretation of Dan. 7.13 implied by Mark 13.26 is easy to recover: the man-like figure has been interpreted as Jesus. This much is a straightforward example of the Western Christian tradition. Other aspects of the interpretation of this verse are bound up with the question of its authenticity. If Jesus said it, he said it in Aramaic. A reconstruction should therefore be attempted: ואדין יחזון בר אנשא אתה בענני עם שלטן שגיא ועם יקר. The main problems here are the use of בר אנשא and the likelihood of

165

there being any Aramaic background to ὄψονται. The difficulty with בר אנשא is that it is an ordinary Aramaic term for 'man', so that the first question that would arise on this sentence being heard would be 'which son of man?' A feasible answer might be 'the one in Dan. 7.13'.

In the first place, let us suppose that Jesus held the original corporate interpretation of the man-like figure in Dan. 7.13, a possibility made more reasonable by the demonstration that this interpretation of the man-like figure was known among the Jews at the time of Jesus.[16] This interpretation of Mark 13.26 is, however, improbable. Dan. 7.13 is not suitable for midrashic use like this because of the obscurity of the resulting statement; no one would have understood what Jesus meant. It is significant that there are no comparable Jewish examples,[17] despite the fact that this interpretation of the man-like figure was preserved right through the rabbinical period. Of the two examples of the use of Dan. 7.13 interpreted like this in Jewish midrashim, one, Midr. *Ps.* 21, 5, is due to the apparent contradiction with Jer. 30.21: this kind of problem was indulged in by the static bibliolatry of the well-developed rabbinical tradition, and is alien to the early Christian tradition. The other example, Tanch. *Tol.* 20, uses Dan. 7.13 because it is the only OT passage that can offer support for the identification of 'Anani in 1 Chron. 3.24 as the Messiah. Secondly, if Jesus held and used the corporate interpretation of the man-like figure, and did so in sayings which were remembered and written down in the Gospels, its absence in the Western Christian tradition would be very remarkable. Thirdly, the context is against this view. The subject of ἀποστελεῖ at the beginning of Mark 13.27 must be a person. An Aramaic version might have continued . . . ואדין ישלח מלאכיא ויכנש בחירוהי. The subject of ישלח (ἀποστελεῖ) would have to be God. It is possible that the assumption that it must be God who would gather the elect was so strong that this could be done, but the suddenness of the change of subject perhaps adds cumulative weight against the hypothesis under consideration. Moreover, it is difficult to see how Dan. 7.13 could be fulfilled in this sense when the elect had not yet been gathered. Finally, the uniform misinterpretation of the term בר אנשא in the traditions which culminated in the Gospels would be difficult to explain. These same reasons forbid the conjecture that this is an early Christian midrash using the corporate interpretation of the man-like figure.

Let us next suppose that this saying goes back to Jesus and that he interpreted the man-like figure as himself. It must first be noted that this is linguistically sound only if בר אנשא in this saying really is a reference to Dan. 7.13–14. It cannot be a simple circumlocution for 'I' because Mark 13.26 cannot be understood as a general statement, and all Aramaic examples of the use of בר אנש with reference to the speaker are general statements.[18] Therefore it can refer to the speaker only if it is primarily a reference to a separate figure in the scriptural text, with whom the speaker has also identified himself. It is not difficult to suppose that there is a reference to Dan. 7.13 here, because of the number of contacts between these two passages, but if Jesus is the subject of vs. 27, he should have reverted there to the first person singular, and it is just this which he so strikingly never does. However, it is still possible that vs. 26 is a genuine saying, and that Jesus was so confident of the assumption that it was God who would collect the faithful that he could proceed to vs. 27 without explicitly stating the subject of ישלח (ἀποστελεῖ). A second objection to the authenticity of this saying is that Jesus never expresses his belief in his return except by speaking of the coming of the Son of man. This raises the larger problem of this whole group of sayings, and we shall return to it.[19] For the time being, it is to be noted that, so far, detailed arguments against the authenticity of this saying understood in this sense have not been decisive. A further possibility is that this is a genuine saying in which Jesus referred to the coming of a messianic figure other than himself. This possibility is excluded by the fact that he did not believe in the advent of such a figure. The contrary impression is derived only from Son of man sayings, and it can be otherwise explained.[20]

The next possibility to consider is that the proposed Aramaic reconstruction is sound but that it originally formed part of an early Christian midrash done in Aramaic, interpreting the man-like figure as Jesus. From the point of view of the Aramaic, the saying is now sound provided that it is seen as a midrash deliberately using the terms of Dan. 7.13. It has so much in common with Dan. 7.13–14 that it is not difficult to see it like this. The change from כבר אנש to בר אנשא is not difficult to account for once it is remembered that this verse is a new creative work. Daniel might have seen Jesus looking 'like a son of man', but as a result it could be said that people would see 'the son of man' (sc. the one whom Daniel saw); there is no need to repeat the characteristically visionary 'like' because the people of the last days would not have a vision of Jesus at his parousia, they would actually see him coming. Verse 27 could proceed in the third person because everyone knew that Jesus was the Danielic son of man just referred to, or alternatively on the assumption that the subject must be God. The articles in τὸν υἱὸν τοῦ ἀνθρώπου are then to be explained as a function of the translation of the material into Greek. Even if the difference between the absolute and emphatic states of the Aramaic noun was breaking down, it is probable enough that the emphatic state would be used in this sentence, and the natural tendency of a translator to use the Greek articles for rendering it would be reinforced by the fact that he knew he was referring to a definite person.[21] General support for this view of Mark 13.26 comes from the fact that a *Sitz im Leben* in the early Church can be found for this whole group of sayings.[22]

Moreover, there are some reasons for believing that this midrash was first constructed in Greek. If this could be demonstrated, it would be a decisive reason for attributing this saying to the early Church rather than to Jesus. The first is ὄψονται. Though this is a satisfactory translation of יחזון, its appearance here might be considered somewhat coincidental, because it also occurred in a non-Septuagintal version of Zech. 12.10 in midrashic use in the early Church, or at least in an early church midrash which had ὄψονται in it as a translation from Zech. 12.10. This occurs in its simple form in the Gospel which shows no certain trace of Dan. 7.13, at John 19.37, ὄψονται εἰς ὃν ἐξεκέντησαν. It recurs in modified version as ὄψεται, with the Semitic impersonal giving way to the specification of a general subject, at Rev. 1.7 πᾶς ὀφθαλμὸς καὶ οἵτινες αὐτὸν ἐξεκέντησαν (though the variant ὄψονται should be taken seriously). It is striking that here it is joined midrashically to Dan. 7.13 Ἰδοὺ ἔρχεται μετὰ τῶν νεφελῶν. Also ὄψεται (or ὄψονται) gives word-play with κόψονται quoted with Dan. 7.13 from Zech. 10.10–12 at Rev. 1.7.[23] ὄψονται also occurs with the certain allusion to Dan. 7.13 at Mark 13.26, and Mark 14.62 has ὄψεσθε introducing what is certainly a midrashic combination, as it clearly depends on Ps. 110.1 as well as Dan. 7.13. Matt. 24.30 expands Mark 13.26, and this expansion includes a certain quotation from Zech. 12.10–12, κόψονται πᾶσαι αἱ φυλαὶ τῆς γῆς. Thus all demonstrably conscious allusions to Dan. 7.13 in the New Testament occur in midrashic combination with other OT allusions, and all have either a citation from Zech. 12.10ff or are introduced with ὄψονται or ὄψεσθε. It is therefore rather probable that Zech. 12.10ff. is the source of this word. This explains very simply why Mark has changed from the second person address of the discourse of Mark 13 to the (Semitic) impersonal plural of 13.26—it was like that in the midrashic source. The consistency of the use of ὄψομαι suggests that this midrash was done in Greek, and shows that the version of Zech. 12.10f. employed was not the LXX, which represents הביטו with ἐπιβλέψονται.

However, it is difficult to feel that this argument has been raised to the level of proof. ὄψομαι is not a rare word, and the number of occurrences here is perhaps not too great for the Marcan examples to be independent. Belief in the return of Jesus was widespread in the early Church, and the conclusion that people would see him at the End is not a surprising one. If the sayings are genuine, a similar view may still be taken of Mark 13.26, and in addition תחזון at 14.62 would have made a very dramatic threat. It is not improbable that חזה should be rendered with ὄψομαι in both these sayings. It should perhaps be concluded that the introduction of both Mark's certain allusions to Dan. 7.13 with ὄψομαι strongly suggests the influence of an early Christian midrash done in Greek, but does not demonstrate it.

Glasson is outstanding among scholars who have tried to show that Mark 13.24–7 as a whole is dependent specifically on the LXX version of the Old Testament and therefore originated in Greek. His attempts to show that it is the LXX rather than the MT which is in mind are not always convincing even according to his own standards of judgement, and a major difficulty is that of demonstrating that the OT passages suggested really were in mind in any version to the extent that particular words must be derived from them. Thus Glasson argues that Mark 13.25 οἱ ἀστέρες ἔσονται . . . πίπτοντες, . . . αἱ δυνάμεις αἱ ἐν τοῖς οὐρανοῖς is dependent on Isa. 34.4 LXX. But it is not verbally identical with the LXX, and the sentiment is really found in the Hebrew: כל צבאם יבול gives the only item for which Isa. 34.4 is a unique OT source.[24] At 13.27 Glasson and others see dependence on Zech. 2.10 LXX. Seitz put the argument clearly: 'In its present form this appears to be the creation of a Hellenistic community, rather than a deposit from Palestinian tradition, since the Hebrew of Zech. 2.10 says nothing of gathering but only of scattering'. 'For Hebrew פרשתי אתכם LXX reads συνάξω ὑμᾶς, an alteration of the original which permitted its midrashic combination with Deut. 30.3f.'[25] But the LXX is not always a translation of our MT, and the possibility that its authors and the early Christians were dependent on a version that read מארבע רוחות השמים אספתי cannot be excluded.[26] Moreover, the LXX testifies to a reasonable interpretation of the whole passage of Zechariah which Jesus and early Aramaic-speaking Christians may have shared. Another difficulty is that of showing that Zech. 2.10 was in mind at all. The gathering of the elect has been a standard Jewish belief from the OT period onwards. ἐπισυνάγω is a reasonable enough term for expressing it. The four winds are so common an item that it can hardly be asserted that ἐκ τῶν τεσσάρων ἀνέμων must come from here. If OT origin for ἐπισυνάξει is sought, other plausible (though uncertain) sources can be found. If the four winds are not derived from Zech. 2.6 (2.10 LXX), the gathering can easily be taken from Deut. 30.4 (יקבצך, LXX συνάξει). Zech. 12.10 probably lies behind ὄψονται; midrashic use of Zech. 14.5 has been plausibly suggested as an OT source of the angels in Mark 13.27. Ancient exegetical method, Jewish and Christian alike, would not be above finding the gathering at Zech. 14.2 ואספתי את כל הגוים (LXX accurately καὶ ἐπισυνάξω πάντα τὰ ἔθνη); Mark's τοὺς ἐκλεκτοὺς αὐτοῦ is then but interpretation. Thus in the absence of clearly decisive evidence of verbal identity (this caveat is important, because the reasons why the argument of Glasson and others has not achieved proof are practical as well as theoretical), this view founders on two factors: the possibility of use of a Hebrew OT text like that underlying the LXX, and the possibility that the OT passages suggested were not directly in mind.

France has tried to show that on the contrary the MT has

been used rather than the LXX, but his argument is unconvincing for much the same reasons. For example, he asserts that
Mark translates the MT אוֹרִין (Isa. 13.10) by τὸ φέγγος αὐτῆς
(Mark 13.24) as against LXX τὸ φῶς αὐτῆς, but his reference to
Joel 2.10 neatly undermines his assumption that it must be Isa.
13.10 that φέγγος is derived from.[27] It is moreover possible that
early Christian exegetes who read the Old Testament in
Hebrew put together this midrash in Greek. In general, Mark
has reused the biblical tradition to form a genuinely new
creation, so that the majority of words which can be derived
from one particular biblical text could also be derived from
another. The argument that 13.24–7 is dependent on the LXX,
though plausible, is not decisive.

Another aspect of the interpretation of Dan. 7.13 in Mark
13.26 which has been much discussed is the direction of movement. The answer to this problem is that the movement is
downwards to the earth, and the event is the parousia of Jesus.
The whole of Mark 13 up to this point takes place on earth;
even the heavenly phenomena of 13.24–5 may be seen from an
earthly point of view; the subject of 'they shall see' are people
in general, who must be assumed to be still on earth. If the Son
of man then comes, he must come towards them. This interpretation can be consistently maintained for all sayings about
the coming of the Son of man, and it corresponds to early
Christian belief about the return of Jesus. Mark 13.27 should
not be brought against this.[28] Firstly, the subject of ἀποστελεῖ
(יִשְׁלַח) may be God; secondly, since Jesus does not habitually
send out angels to gather the elect in the Gospels, we have no
adequate reason for supposing he must be in heaven rather than
on earth when he does so in Mark 13.27. However, the main
thrust of the argument against seeing the parousia at Mark
13.26 is based on misinterpretation of Dan. 7.13 and failure to
accept the nature of Jewish and early Christian exegesis.[29] It
would not matter if in Dan. 7.13 the movement had been
upwards, since early Christian exegetes who believed in the
parousia of Jesus could so easily have interpreted it differently.
In fact the movement is downwards in the original Danielic
text, and this interpretation was preserved by both Jews and
Christians, of whom the latter saw here the parousia of Jesus;
the view that his exaltation is portrayed at Dan. 7.13 is an

offshoot of the normal Western Christian tradition first attested by Cyprian. Thus the Gospel interpretation of Dan. 7.13 as portraying the parousia of Jesus merely represents the beginning of the Western Christian tradition, and it constitutes a simple development of the original tradition in which the movement was already downwards to the earth, a development paralleled in the messianic interpretation of this text by the Jews.

Since patristic times, some exegetes have argued that the reference in Mark 13.26 is to the fall of Jerusalem, not to the parousia at all. This suggestion, involving as it does the assumption that a straightforward statement of one event 'really' means quite a different one, is worthy of an ancient exegete rather than a modern scholar, but its periodic recurrence in modern scholarship means that we must examine it. A recent presentation of this view has been provided by France.[30]

France begins by limiting ταῦτα . . . πάντα in the introductory question of vs. 4 to the destruction of the Temple predicted in vs. 2. This is unjustifiable, and when he refers to the more obvious suggestion that ταῦτα . . . πάντα also refers to the 'eschatological consummation', his argument that 'In the *Marcan context* this seems improbable' assumes his result. He then suggests two reasons why the events of vss. 5–13 should be taken to be 'preliminaries to the fall of Jerusalem, not to the Parousia'. The first is that 'the whole section is couched in terms of what his actual hearers are to witness and experience'. But this is perfectly compatible with the view that at least some of his hearers would see the parousia. France's second reason is the close link with the following section, but while the following section is intelligible as events leading to the fall of Jerusalem, it contains nothing which is not equally intelligible as the time of distress before the End. France's view that putting forward reasons for seeing these verses as preliminaries to the fall of Jerusalem actually demonstrates that they are not preliminaries to the parousia depends on one of the conclusions he is trying to reach, namely that the parousia does not occur at the same time as the fall of Jerusalem.

France goes on to argue that vss. 14–23 'then describe the events connected with the siege of Jerusalem but without describing the actual fall of the city. This leads one to expect a further section which will complete the prophecy by stating that

172

the city will actually be destroyed, and mentioning the significance and effects of this destruction.' But the foundation of
France's expectation is a dogmatic belief in the authenticity and
accuracy of Jesus' predictions so strong that he expects the
Marcan prophecy to read like some pedant's account of the
event written after it. Mark 13 is a prophecy written before
Jerusalem was destroyed.[31] This is sufficient to remove the
grounds of France's expectations. Mark 13.5ff. is an apocalyptic
piece whose contents cannot be governed by the separate
question of vs. 2. France has done nothing to show that the
tribulations of vss. 14–23, a widespread feature of the apocalyptic schema of the period before the End, must lead up to the
destruction of Jerusalem rather than the parousia. Verses 19–20
are especially characteristic of contemporary prophecies of the
End. France's further assertion that 'all these things' in vs. 30
must refer to the fall of Jerusalem because this expression did so
in vs. 4, is too rigid a description of the general expression which
must be governed by the preceding verses and cannot be
allowed to govern them,[32] and it fails because he did not in fact
succeed in demonstrating that this was the reference in vs. 4.
His view that 'that day' in vs. 32 cannot be one of 'those days'
(vss. 17, 19, 24) is quite arbitrary; vs. 32 does mention the single
day of the parousia rather than all the days leading up to and
including it, but to fasten on the expression by means of which
this distinction is conveyed and call it 'new' when it is the
singular of the expression already used is merely to carry this
arbitrary feature into the linguistic description. As throughout
his book, the real ground of France's expectation is the conclusions which he seeks to reach. He has simply failed to set up
the view that the fall of Jerusalem must be described in vss.
24–7. Mark had already mentioned it in vs. 2, and it is not
obvious that he would feel a need to repeat himself at a mundane level. Whether the fall of Jerusalem is described in vss.
24–7 must be discovered by examining the text of these verses.

In dealing with vss. 24–7 France employs the same method
as he used in dealing with the whole of Mark 13, taking first
vss. 24–5 and using them to set up an expectation that vs. 26
would refer to the fall of Jerusalem. He notes the OT phrases of
which these verses appear to be made up, and says that in OT
prophecy these phrases 'are used to describe especially political

disasters, and the destruction of cities and nations'. This is misleading because of its assumptions that predictions which involve the day of Yahweh as well as political disaster were fulfilled in the sense intended by straightforward political disasters, and that Jesus, Mark, and their contemporaries must have been aware of this. In fact France has simply read the conclusions which he wishes to reach for Mark 13.24–5 straight into his interpretation of the OT passages,[33] so that his argument is a form of concealed circle. He then asserts that Jesus' use of such language is intended in the same sense as a prediction of national disaster(s). This does not follow at all. There is nothing 'consistent' about restricting the application of Jesus' words to their OT sphere of reference, because the OT sphere of reference has been misleadingly stated and because in the intertestamental period it was common to describe new events in OT language. Any attempt to use OT language to describe the parousia of Jesus was bound to result in some shift of use of OT phrases because there is not really any OT description of the parousia of Jesus, but this does not constitute a good reason for supposing that the parousia of Jesus could not be described in OT terms, which is the necessary effect of arguing that the OT phrases must be used according to France's idea of consistency. France further ignores the use of this imagery in contemporary apocalyptic writings, an omission of relevant evidence that would be remarkable if it were not still distressingly common. What would he make of 1 Enoch 80; IV Ezra 5.4ff?

In fact the celestial portents of Mark 13.24–5 might intelligibly have been used by a writer of this period to lead up to a description of either the fall of Jerusalem or the parousia of Jesus or both, and the only way to find out what they lead up to is to turn to vs. 26. Here we find a prediction that the Son of man will be seen coming in clouds with great power and glory. A blunter brief description of the parousia would be difficult to provide, but it is not enough for France, who refers to his discussion of Dan. 7.13 as showing 'that its keynote is one of vindication and exaltation to an everlasting dominion, and that the "coming" of vs. 13 was a coming to God to receive power, not a "descent" to earth'.[34] But the second of these points is incorrect, and the first does not mean that any act of vindication

174

and exaltation can be fathered on Daniel or on Mark. France then asserts that nowhere in Jesus' use of Dan. 7.13 was this verse interpreted of his coming to earth at the parousia (the authenticity of all the relevant sayings is assumed). His discussion of Mark 14.62 argues, following Glasson and others, that Jesus was referring to his immediate exaltation; this is unconvincing,[35] and France seeks to support it by arguing that 'it is reasonable to assume that Jesus used Daniel 7.13 in its intended sense unless there is evidence to the contrary'; but the mere fact that the man-like figure is interpreted as Jesus instead of as a symbol of the Saints of the Most High, and ὡς υἱὸς ἀνθρώπου altered to ὁ υἱὸς τοῦ ἀνθρώπου, is very straightforward evidence to the contrary. France continues 'also by the word ὄψεσθε ("you will see"), which implies that those sitting in judgement over Jesus will in fact witness the "coming", i.e. that it will occur within their lifetime.' As an argument against a parousia reference, this appears plausible to France only because he assumes that the prediction of Mark 14.62 is correct, a view which he everywhere assumes and nowhere demonstrates. It is the same argument that he used at Mark 13, and it is especially unconvincing in dealing with a verse in which the interpretation of Dan. 7.13 attributed to Jesus is not correct. Moreover, France's admission that some allusions to Dan. 7.13 are eschatological makes it necessary for him to distinguish different uses of Dan. 7 in texts which are very similar, so that the coming of the Son of man can refer both to Jesus' exaltation immediately after the Resurrection, and to the culmination of the same authority in the final judgement (Matt. 19.28; 25.31). It is much simpler to suppose that the predictions of the coming of the Son of man refer uniformly to the parousia. In his discussion of other allusions to Dan. 7.13, France constantly makes reference to his discussion of Mark 13.26 to show that they too refer to the fall of Jerusalem.[36] Thus his assertion in his discussion of Mark 13.26 that there are no references to the parousia in Jesus' other references to Dan. 7.13 completes a circular argument. Moreover, his view that the fall of Jerusalem is referred to involves attributing to Jesus and to Mark an exegesis of Dan. 7.13 unexampled in the material under review.

France concludes the main part of his argument by declaring,

'Where Jesus used the symbolic language of the Old Testament, it is perverse to look for a literal application of his words.' Where Jesus (or the early Church) took the symbol of the man-like figure and clearly interpreted it as a description of Jesus, ὁ υἱὸς τοῦ ἀνθρώπου, some such shift is simply demonstrated, and it is not in the least perverse to observe this and apply it to the rest of the verse, a view amply confirmed by the continual usage of the Christian West, and by a large section of Jewish exegesis too, which saw in Dan. 7.13 the coming of the Messiah. France's whole argument consists in the detailed and complex application of the blunt assumptions with which he began, much assisted by misinterpretation of Dan. 7.13 itself. At Mark 13.26 this has led him to deny the plain meaning of the scriptural text which he believes that he venerates. The whole New Testament, Gospels, Acts, Epistles, and Revelation alike, testifies to belief in the return of Jesus, an event often referred to as his coming. In the synoptic Gospels, the influence of Dan. 7.13 has caused this to be described as the coming of the Son of man. It is perverse to assert that this must mean a quite different event, which the evangelists could easily have described as the fall of Jerusalem. Thus France's arguments are quite unconvincing, and the more straightforward interpretation of Mark 13.26 as a reference to the parousia of Jesus should be preferred.

Finally, Mark 13.26 is best understood as a literal rather than as a figurative description of the parousia. This plain meaning of the text has often been controverted by exegetes who wish to follow Jesus and yet are so far removed from his *Weltanschauung* that they must pour scorn upon a picture of the last times which was certainly held by some of his contemporaries and may have been shared by him. But there are no difficulties in a literal interpretation, as long as difficulties are not imported from an alien culture. Jesus was believed to be in heaven above, and he was expected to come. Mark 13.26 simply states that he will come, that his coming will be powerful and glorious (to early Christians it could hardly be otherwise), that his mode of transport would be a standard one for this purpose,[37] and that people would see this great event. This is indeed striking, but scholars who cannot believe it should place Jesus and Mark firmly on the side of their comrades who can. The symbolic nature of the Danielic text should not be urged against this. The man-like figure of Dan. 7.13 is placed clearly within a symbolic vision which is followed by an angelic interpretation; in the Marcan text he has been replaced by the title 'the Son of man', which Mark understood as a designation of a very concrete person, Jesus of Nazareth. This is straightforward evidence that at least the central item of Daniel's symbolic vision has been interpreted literally, and the natural assumption that the rest of the description has been interpreted in the same way is the only consistent one.

It is therefore to be concluded that Mark 13.26 is one of the earliest examples of the Western Christian tradition of interpretation of Dan. 7.13. Some of the evidence surveyed suggests that it is not an authentic saying but the result of early Christian exegesis, first composed in Greek. This evidence has not, however, been found decisive, so that before any final decision about its authenticity can be reached, the rest of the use of Dan. 7.13 in the Gospels must be surveyed.

Matt. 24.30 is a much expanded version of Mark 13.26. 'Of heaven' is added as in Dan. 7.13, and for 'in clouds', Matthew has 'on the clouds', as in the LXX of Dan. 7.13. It should be deduced that Matthew was aware that this was a reminiscence of Dan. 7.13 and that, like Mark, he belonged to the Western Christian tradition of interpretation of this verse. The man-like figure is Jesus, and the scene is his parousia. This is immediately preceded by a quotation from Zech. 12.12. This is the same text used with Dan. 7.13 at Rev. 1.7, and this constitutes prima facie evidence of an early Christian testimonium.[38] ὄψονται, as well as Dan. 7.13 in the Marcan text, will have reminded Matthew of it and caused him to add the text from Zechariah. In Matt. 24.30a Matthew has another Son of man saying. It fills out his picture of the parousia, but there is no further specific reference to Dan. 7.13.[39]

Luke 21.27 is a fairly accurate reproduction of Mark 13.26. There is one stylistic alteration, πολλῆς being moved to a new position after δόξης. A second alteration is more interesting: νεφέλαις has become νεφέλη. This is clearly intended to look forward to Acts 1.9–11, and it suggests that Luke did not regard the cloud as symbolic. It represents a move away from the Danielic text. It may be seriously questioned whether Luke perceived any connection with Dan. 7.13; Luke 21.27 suggests

that he was thinking only of a prediction of the parousia of
Jesus, not of Dan. 7.13 at all.

Mark 14.62∥Matt. 26.64∥Luke 22.69

Mark 14.62 is the second passage in the Gospels which clearly
uses Dan. 7.13. Here again we have 'the Son of man' and
'coming': this time we have also 'with the clouds of heaven', a
literal and accurate rendering of the Aramaic identical to that
of Theodotion. Thus the allusion to Dan. 7.13 is somewhat
more precise than at Mark 13.26. Of itself, this does not show
that either allusion is secondary to the other. Developments
both towards and away from the Danielic text are detectable in
the parallels in Matthew and Luke, and either could have taken
place in the pre-Marcan tradition; Jesus, anonymous early
Christians, and Mark alike could have created two similar
pictures of the End which vary in their detailed use of this text.
The interpretation of Dan. 7.13 which is presupposed is the
same as that which lies behind Mark 13.26: Jesus is the man-like
figure, and the scene is his parousia. ὄψεσθε is interesting as a
possible reflection of the same midrashic use of Zech. 12.10–12
as is found at Matt. 24.30; Rev. 1.7.[40] Here we certainly have
midrashic combination of Dan. 7.13 with Ps. 110.1, a well-used
OT text in early Christianity.[41] An Aramaic reconstruction can
be provided; it shows no features that make an Aramaic original
unbelievable:

אנה הוא ותחזון בר אנשא מן ימינא
יתב די גבורתא ואתה עם ענני שמיא׃

If the position of גבורתא is found odd, it is not difficult to
explain. מן ימינא יתב goes together because it is based directly
on Ps. 110.1; now that it is no longer in the first person some
gloss such as די גבורתא is required, and has been placed
simply at the end. ἐκ δεξιῶν καθήμενον is reminiscent of the LXX
κάθου ἐκ δεξιῶν μου because both are based on the same Hebrew
text; this cannot constitute a satisfactory argument that this was
first done in Greek. ὄψεσθε is the only word that this could be
built on; it is perhaps not sufficient on its own, though it is
striking. It is therefore to be concluded that this text itself does
not allow us to make a final decision as to whether its midrashic
combination of OT texts was first done in Aramaic or Greek.

Several scholars have argued that in the Marcan text as it stands the reference is not to the parousia of Jesus but to his Ascension. The fundamental attempt to demonstrate this is that of T. F. Glasson, and he has received strong support from J. A. T. Robinson.[42] Glasson begins by asserting that in Dan. 7.13 the man-like figure does not descend, but he simply assumes that the Ancient of Days must be in heaven, and we have seen that this is incorrect.[43] He proceeds on the assumption that Jesus must have followed the original exegesis of Dan. 7.13. There is no reason to suppose that he did or did not do so in any instance until the evidence of the particular case has been examined, and in this instance the hypothesis that he did so would have to suppose that he interpreted the man-like figure as a symbol of Israel. Glasson admits that the early Church 'later, in defiance of the original context' interpreted Dan. 7.13 of the parousia. The Church used the same general exegetical principles as Jesus; what they did, he might have done; the evidence must be examined to see whether he did so or not. Glasson then asserts, 'The meaning of Jesus' reply would therefore seem to be that although He was about to be put to a shameful death He was really entering upon his reign.' This assertion, together with the texts he quotes in support, is simply remote from the text of Mark 14.62. It is partly a result of Glasson's presuppositions concerning what eschatological beliefs may be deemed appropriate for the Son of God, but it is also a consequence of his view that the coming is a coming to God. If this is the case, a straightforward interpretation of the verse becomes impossible, since Jesus patently cannot come to God either at the same time as, or shortly after, he is already sitting at his side. This is particularly clear in the discussion of Robinson, who goes on to state that 'Such spatial terms are, in any case, only an accommodation of language, and it is finally of no significance whether man is conceived as coming to God or God coming to man.'[44] It may not be important to Robinson *qua* theologian, but it is very important in getting the meaning of Mark right, and it was very important in enabling Robinson to interpret Mark figuratively.

Glasson next argues that Mark 14.62 originally contained an expression 'from now'. The only manuscript evidence for this that Glasson could cite was the single Ms of the sinaitic Syriac;

he and his supporters subsequently added one Ms of the sahidic version, and they might have noted a sahidic lectionary. This evidence is extremely weak, and its weakness is amplified by Origen's assertion in his commentary on Matt. 26.64 that Mark has no such expression. The 'agreement' between Matthew and Luke which it is held to explain is illusory, because ἀπαρτί should be read at Matt. 26.64.[45] The sinaitic Syriac in fact reads *mekīl*, which cannot be dismissed forthwith as assimilation to Matt. 26.64 and Luke 22.69, because the Syriac of both these verses has a different expression. The possibility that it is a translation made from a Greek Ms that had been assimilated should perhaps not be altogether ruled out, but where a single Syriac Ms is in error it is simplest to look for mechanical error in Syriac, and the occurrence of *mekīl* at Mark 14.63 should probably be regarded as the source of this mistake. As for the sahidic, 'from now on' is read by 108 and m[1]. The expression which they use is identical to that employed by this version at both Matt. 26.64 and Luke 22.69, and is absent from other witnesses at Mark 14.62. 108 is to be dated in the second millennium, m[1] to the fourteenth century.[46] It should be clear that this is a genuine case of late Mss assimilating to Matthew or Luke, a not uncommon phenomenon in late Mss. Finally Glasson gives no satisfactory account of the omission of these words from all other manuscripts, including those known to Origen, and it is difficult to see how any such explanation could account for the lack of similar textual interference with Matt. 26.64.

Thus the text of Mark 14.62 should be left intact, and it makes excellent sense. At the time of the parousia people on earth, including those condemning Jesus, will see him sitting at the right hand of God and coming to earth with the clouds of heaven. His Ascension is assumed, but not mentioned. That he will have been sitting at the right hand of God for a period of time is also presupposed, but what is actually stated is that at a particular moment in the not too distant future they will see him sitting there (it may reasonably be assumed that the heavens will open for this purpose), and then coming with the clouds. It is not suggested that they will see him sitting there as soon as he arrives there, so that even if the parousia is delayed, a lengthy interval between them seeing him sitting and seeing him coming is not presupposed. On the contrary, though he will be seen sitting, the text implies that they will not have recovered from the shock of seeing him sitting at the right hand of God before he comes with the clouds of heaven.

Perrin has tried to show that there was an ascension tradition of interpretation of Dan. 7.13 developing from an interpretation of the Resurrection in terms of Ps. 110.1: he finds evidence of this at Mark 14.62, though he does not think that this was Mark's interpretation of it. He says

> we must seek a factor in the Christian tradition which could be the occasion for the development of the conception of Jesus 'coming with the clouds' as Son of man, and we claim that the only factor sufficient for this purpose would be an interpretation of the resurrection as Jesus having ascended to heaven as Son of man. In other words, there must be a moment in the Christian tradition where the resurrection of Jesus is interpreted in terms of Dan. 7.13.[47]

This is not convincing. We may need an interpretation of the Resurrection of Jesus involving or culminating in his Ascension to heaven, in order to get him coming back on the clouds, but we do not need him going up as Son of man or in terms of Dan. 7.13. We simply need him going up; after this he can be brought back in terms of Dan. 7.13. It is only because Perrin has fed this interpretation in at the beginning of his discussion that it comes out at the end; by his own confession there are no examples of it, and his hypothesis that it existed at an early stage encourages him to use very low standards of proof. He comments on Mark 14.62a

> Let it be noted that there is here no parousia reference; were it not for the 'you will see' which comes before, and the explicit parousia reference which comes after, also alluding to Dan. 7.13, there would be no hint of a parousia, only of an ascension, in the '. . . Son of man sitting at the right hand of power' of Mark 14.62a.

The trouble with this is that we have no reason to think that Mark 14.62a ever existed separately; 'you will see' and 14.62b do actually occur in the text as we have it. There is no evidence here that the term 'Son of man' originally occurred in exegesis of Ps. 110.1. In Greek there is no particular reason why it should, and Perrin's truncated version of Mark 14.62 would not make satisfactory Aramaic. It is the combination of Ps. 110.1 with Dan. 7.13 and the introductory 'you will see', with the natural result that the object of 'you will see' has been put before 'sitting on the right hand of Power', which has produced the Son of man sitting on the right hand of Power. Here, as everywhere else, 'the Son of man . . . coming' is evidence of the Western Christian tradition of interpretation of Dan. 7.13 of the parousia of Jesus. When this text is interpreted of the parousia, the exaltation of Jesus is implied, because he must be exalted before he can come with the clouds. It is then useful to have another OT text which portrays his exaltation, and Ps. 110.1 performs this function excellently. So far from providing evidence that Dan. 7.13 was interpreted of Jesus' exaltation, Ps. 110.1 functions very well as a complement to Dan. 7.13 interpreted of his parousia.

There is therefore no need to suppose that there was another OT passage which was used to connect Ps. 110.1 and Dan. 7.13 and was subsequently dropped; Pss. 8 and 80 are the commonest suggestions,[48] but perhaps the best is the succeeding verses of Ps. 110.[49] It is not in any way improbable that any exegete considering the interpretation of Ps. 110.1 would move on to the subsequent verses, and several coincidences can be noted, with $\mu\epsilon\tau\grave{a}$ $\sigma o\hat{v}$ $\dot{\eta}$ $\dot{a}\rho\chi\dot{\eta}$ recalling the gift of $\dot{a}\rho\chi\dot{\eta}$ to the man-like figure in Dan. 7.14, and $\tau\hat{\omega}\nu$ $\dot{a}\gamma\iota\omega\nu$ corresponding to the multitude of Daniel's angels; moreover, unconscious reminiscence of $\delta\upsilon\nu\acute{a}\mu\epsilon\omega\varsigma$ by an exegete who had just read it twice in Ps. 110.2–3 could be the immediate cause of the choice of it as a circumlocution of God. In any of these forms the suggestion of a linking passage is not in any way unJewish nor, on the face of it, generally unlikely; it is simply vacuous. The joining together of Ps. 110.1 and Dan. 7.13 can be explained on grounds of their content and the requirements of early Christian exegesis, and the explanation is complete without these further suggestions, none of which can be satisfactorily verified.

The question of the authenticity of this saying is difficult. The Aramaic original which I have proposed makes satisfactory Aramaic. The use of בר אנשא in it is not quite normal, in that

it is a self-reference in a statement which is not a general statement,[50] but this divergence from the norm is acceptable as long
as this is a deliberate use of an OT text; בר אנשא became
a self-reference only when Jesus applied an OT text to himself, and there could not be grammatical reasons for him not
to do this. Therefore this divergence from the norm in the use
of בר אנשא is the kind of new use of words which occurs when
native speakers of languages create new sentences all the time,
and cannot be held against the authenticity of the saying. Thus
Aramaic usage excludes the possibility that Mark 14.62a alone
is authentic, because the end of the verse is necessary in order
to make clear a reference to Dan. 7.13, but it does not exclude
the authenticity of the whole verse. ὄψεσθε can be brought
against the authenticity of this saying; as we have seen in discussing Mark 13.26, it strongly suggests, but scarcely proves,
that this is the deposit of midrashic activity which was carried
out in Greek. However, it is significant that Jesus' return is
spoken of in the synoptic Gospels only in terms of the Son of
man coming, and when the remaining evidence of the use of
Dan. 7.13 in the Gospels has been surveyed, general considerations will be brought to bear against the authenticity of this
saying.

   Matt. 26.64 has two interesting alterations: μετά is changed to
ἐπί, the same Septuagintal alteration that Matthew made at
24.30. Here, as there, Matthew knew that he was dealing with
Dan. 7.13. Of the alterations at the beginning of this verse, the
one that might affect the interpretation of Dan. 7.13 is the
addition of ἀπαρτί, meaning 'certainly'. This standard Greek
word gives excellent sense in the context. Matthew took over
Mark's expectation of the parousia of Jesus within a generation,
and here he adds emphasis to Jesus' prediction of it. The usual
reading of Matt. 26.64 with ἀπ' ἄρτι, 'from now on', does not
make good sense at all, because a prediction beginning 'From
now on you will see' must be followed by a continuous state, not
a single event, as the object of the vision. The first clause can be
made to conform to this (though not without some difficulty),
especially if its meaning is assimilated to that of Luke 22.69, but
it will not fit the coming on the clouds of heaven, which is a
single event, not a continuous state. Hence many exegetes,
reading ἀπ' ἄρτι, can indulge in 'figurative' meanings remote

from the text of Matthew, and go on to argue that if this can be shown to be the meaning of Matt. 26.64 it can hardly be denied for Mark 14.62.[51] It is better to keep to the straightforward meaning of the text, which enables us to link it up in the simplest possible way both with Matthew's intensification of the primitive eschatology and with the interpretation of Dan. 7.13 elsewhere. Matthew interpreted Dan. 7.13 of the parousia of Jesus, just as Mark before him. We should not attempt to assimilate Matthew to Luke, who made more radical alterations and did in fact mean something different. It follows that this is different from Mark 14.25 and parallels, where Matthew and Luke both agreed with Mark but independently wrote better Greek of the same meaning, ἀπ' ἄρτι from Matthew and ἀπὸ τοῦ νῦν from Luke (the latter possibly from another source).

Luke 22.69 omits 'and, coming with the clouds of heaven' altogether; in place of 'and you shall see' it has 'from now on will be'. Thus the present exaltation of the risen Christ is described instead of his future coming. Luke could retain the term 'the Son of man' because to him it was a title of Jesus, but his omission removed all definite trace of Dan. 7.13. Therefore this cannot be an authentic saying of Jesus independently transmitted because, devoid of pointers to Dan. 7.13, it will not make reasonable sense in Aramaic at all. Here the presence of the term 'the Son of man' is ultimately due to Dan. 7.13, but all trace of this dependence has been removed by Luke's editorial activity; this process may have gone on elsewhere. Once Luke decided that the present exaltation of the risen Christ was to be referred to, Dan. 7.13 had to go; this would not have been the case if Luke thought Dan. 7.13 referred to the Ascension. Its removal is however not a sign that Luke did not believe in the parousia; he expected Jesus to return at length in a cloud (Luke 12.40; 18.8; 21.27; Acts 1.9). But after Mark's mistake, as Luke will have seen it, and the lapse of time, he concluded that mention of the parousia was not appropriate at this point. With his alterations to Mark 13.26 and 14.62 Luke achieved the omission of direct reference to Dan. 7.13 in his Gospel. It is tempting to conjecture that this is because he did not interpret Dan. 7.13 of the parousia of Jesus; in view of the other motivation for these alterations, however, it must be admitted that this conjecture goes beyond the evidence.

Matt. 10.23

Matt. 10.23 is another passage dealing with the coming of the Son of man. General reasons have been given for regarding all such texts as indirect references to Dan. 7.13.[52] There are no further contacts between the two passages. A hypothetical Aramaic original of the most relevant part of the verse may be reconstructed as follows:

לא תהשלמון קריה די ישראל
עד די יאתא בר אנשא·

Here the use of בר אנשא is all right if, and only if, a deliberate reference to Dan. 7.13 is intended. This seems satisfactory for the saying as I have reconstructed it, and it is a plausible, though speculative, conjecture that it could have ended with a quotation, עד די בר אנש אתה, and that a Greek translator, knowing that the reference was to Jesus, could still have produced the end of our present Matt. 10.23 from this. The only reasonable interpretation of it, whether authentic or not, is that, like the other references to the Son of man coming, it refers to the parousia of Jesus. Other suggestions are vulnerable to the same decisive objections as those urged above in the case of Mark 13.26; 14.62. This is how Matthew interpreted the verse, and it is how he interpreted Dan. 7.13, but it is uncertain whether Matthew recognized a reference to Dan. 7.13 here. He wrote in Greek, and accepted 'the Son of man' as a title of Jesus; he may therefore have accepted the coming of the Son of man as an item of belief without seeing any clear reference to this text. However, we have seen that he did find it there at Matt. 24.30; 26.64, so it is possible that he picked up the reference here, too.

The authenticity of this saying is a difficult problem. Since it refers to the completion of the mission to Israel, it is not inconsistent with the passage of several years between the time when it was spoken and its expected fulfilment.[53] The common argument that it must go back to Jesus because it is an unfulfilled prediction is unsatisfactory, because it could have originated as a word of the Lord to a Christian prophet who had in mind the Church's mission to Israel.[54] He will have been influenced by the use of Dan. 7.13 found in Mark 13.26; 14.62, and will not have expected his prophecy to remain unfulfilled.

When the remaining evidence of the use of Dan. 7.13 has been discussed, general reasons will be brought forward for thinking that it did originate in the early Church rather than with Jesus.

Matt. 13.41

Matt. 13.41 belongs to the Matthean interpretation of the parable of the tares. The interpretation is secondary, as Jeremias has shown.[55] The verse contains angels and a kingdom as well as the Son of man, and hence it has been classified as an 'indirect reference' to Dan. 7.13.[56] There is certainly not sufficient evidence here for it to be classified as a direct reference. The source of Matthew's belief in the Son of man sending his angels, an event which does not occur in Dan. 7.13–14, is to be found in the tradition represented by Mark 13.26–7. Since the occurrence of the term 'Son of man' in Mark 13.26 is in fact due to the influence of Dan. 7.13, this is another reason for admitting Matt. 13.41 as an indirect reference to Dan. 7.13, even though the development has gone a long way beyond the Marcan use of this text. The use of βασιλεία in Matt. 13.41 is developed beyond Dan. 7.13–14, and Zeph. 1.3 appears to have been utilized. It is notable that in Dan. 7.14 the man-like figure is given βασιλεία, and in Matt. 13.41 this is what he has got. Matthew nowhere makes it clear that he associates this with Dan. 7.14, and his other example of the association between Son of man and kingdom (Matt. 16.28) is not very helpful here because it too is associated with indirect use of Dan. 7.13, and explicable without conscious use of this text. It is therefore to be concluded that the influence of Dan. 7.13–14 can be detected at Matt. 13.41; that this influence is indirect; and that Matthew has not said anything which indicates that this influence was consciously felt.

These results are interesting not only in themselves, but also for their bearing on Vielhauer's dilemma, which becomes especially acute if Son of man sayings are derived in any quantity from Dan. 7.13.[57] The kingdom is given to the man-like figure in Dan. 7.14, but Son of man and the kingdom are closely associated only in this demonstrably Matthean text and at Matt. 16.28, which is demonstrably secondary to its Marcan source and does not show clear signs of new influence of Dan. 7.13–14. In view of Jesus' high position in the Gospels, occasional attribution of the kingdom to him in secondary material is not surprising, and it is interesting that it does not occur more with the use of the term 'Son of man' than without it (Matt. 20.21; Luke 22.30; 23.42. Cf. Luke 1.33). Perhaps, however, it is significant that indirect influence of Dan. 7.13–14 is detectable with the term Son of man in Matthew (13.41; 16.28), whose interests in the parousia have led to increased indirect use of Dan. 7.13, and that the attribution of the kingdom to Jesus occurs only without the use of the term Son of man in the Gospel writer who deliberately removed all clear trace of this text (cf. 1 Cor. 15.24; Eph. 5.5; Col. 1.13; 2 Tim. 4.1, 18; Heb. 1.8; 2 Pet. 1.11; Rev. 11.15). If only a small group of Son of man sayings are dependent on Dan. 7.13, Vielhauer's dilemma is satisfied by Matt. 13.41; 16.28.

Matt. 16.28

Matt. 16.28 is directly based on Mark 9.1. Here Matthew has introduced the term 'Son of man', replacing Mark's 'the kingdom of God come in power' with his own formulation 'the Son of man coming in his kingdom'. This verse and Matt. 13.41 have been noted as the only two examples of the combination of kingdom of God and Son of man in the Gospels. This revision of Mark shows the great importance of the coming of the Son of man to Matthew, who has carried out this revision in order to make it quite clear that the reference of the saying recorded in Mark 9.1 ought to be to the parousia. We have seen that the combination of 'Son of man' and 'coming' goes back ultimately to Dan. 7.13, but there is no sign of the deliberate use of this text here. It seems probable that we are dealing with indirect influence.[58] Matthew did believe that Dan. 7.13 portrayed the coming of the Son of man at his parousia, as is shown by Matt. 24.30; 26.64, but it seems probable that this was to him an important item of belief which he did not associate exclusively with this single biblical text.

Matt. 19.28‖Luke 22.30

At Matt. 19.28, Matthew has inserted a Q saying into the Marcan context; its parallel occurs in a different context at Luke 22.30. Only the Matthean version contains the term 'Son of man', in a clause belonging to that part of the verse which has no parallel in Luke. Luke had no reason to omit it, and it fits Matthew's conceptions very well. It is difficult to avoid the conclusion that Matthew has provided what seems to him a most appropriate setting for the final part of the verse.[59] But is either or both parts of this verse dependent on Dan. 7.9–13? It is difficult to be certain. The part which both Gospels have in common may be dealt with first. The use of the thrones here certainly makes good sense when understood of the thrones in Dan. 7.9–10. Presumably the disciples are the heavenly court; Matthew has introduced a limitation to twelve thrones to correspond to twelve apostles and twelve tribes. The judicial function of the apostles has been traced back to Dan. 7.22,[60] but this is unconvincing because there is no clear reference to this verse, the exegesis of it which is presupposed is unexampled in the material under review, and the general tendency in this period for intermediary figures to take over functions previously divine had already manifested itself in the ascription of a judicial function to the righteous (Wisd. 3.8; 1QpHab V, 4; cf. 1 Cor. 6.2); thus Dan. 7.22 does not provide a suitable link between the conception of the righteous judging the nations in these latter passages and the apostles judging Israel here. Even a reference to vss. 9 and 10 is possible rather than certain. Hay concludes his survey of some of the relevant evidence:

> In ancient paganism and Judaism generally the right side symbolized potency and honour. Long before the Christian era pagans spoke of kings and gods exalted to thrones at the right of other gods, and they sometimes described bliss after death in terms of a right-hand location. The Hebrew scriptures and later Jewish writings spoke of men and supernatural beings gaining right-hand or heavenly thrones, often without implying that any particular function was linked with such elevation. The notions of Jesus sitting at the right hand of God and of his followers gaining similar honour seem to have widely fired the imagination of early Christians. This development may be attributed in part to the use of Ps. 110.1, but it must have been encouraged by the fact that wholly apart from the psalm such notions would be richly meaningful to contemporary pagans and Jews.[61]

It may be that we should seek here the background to the

concept of Jesus' followers sitting on thrones (cf. especially Rev. 3.21; I Enoch 108.12–3), and that for the judicial function we should consider the tendency just noted in the religious thought of this period for intermediary figures to take over the active functions once carried out by God alone.

On the other hand there is nothing improbable about the supposed use of Dan. 7.9–10. It fits into the eschatological structure of the Western tradition used in demonstrable NT references to this chapter. While the rabbinical problem of the occupants of the thrones should not be antedated, the variety of solutions illustrates the potential of this text; the members of the court and occupants of the thrones are not specified, and it would have been as easy for Jesus or the early Church to read the apostles in here as it was for the rabbis to read in their various suggestions.[62] Hence Western Christian exegetes found no difficulty at all in reconciling these texts and putting the apostles on the Danielic thrones, and this view is found as a solution to the Jewish problem of the plurality of thrones in the Syrian Christian, Isho'dad of Merw. It should be noted that the version which mentions the Son of man (Matt. 19.28) distinguishes him clearly from the apostles; in Matthew's view he was so obviously Jesus that this did not require comment, so that support for a corporate interpretation of the Son of man should not be drawn from this verse. Matthew's addition does not make it clear that he saw a reference to Dan. 7.13. It is therefore to be concluded that use of Dan. 7 behind this passage is uncertain.[63]

Matt. 24.27∥Luke 17.24

This saying does not appear to be dependent on Dan. 7.13. Vermes classifies it as indirect reference, but this opinion is difficult to justify, for the saying does not show any of the elements which Vermes appears to regard as indications of indirect influence, 'the coming, or the glory, or the kingship of the *son of man*, or to the clouds transporting him'.[64] The eschatological placement of the Son of man cannot be regarded as sufficient evidence of the use of this text in early Christian writers who believed in the great importance of the eschatological function of Jesus and used the term 'Son of man' as a title of him.

189

Matt. 24.44‖Luke 12.40

Matt. 24.44‖Luke 12.40 is a Q saying containing the collocation of 'Son of man' and 'coming' which is a sign of the influence of Dan. 7.13. The event referred to is clearly the parousia of Jesus. An Aramaic original can be reconstructed:

ואנתון הוו עתידין די בה שעתא די לא מסברין
בר אנש אתה.

This sentence does not contain any features that make it un-acceptable. The last three words constitute a brief quotation from Dan. 7.13, and for this reason the reference to this text seems clear enough to be satisfactory and the use of בר אנש is sound Aramaic. It is not difficult to find a *Sitz im Leben* for this saying in the early Church,[65] but it is more difficult to show that it is not a genuine saying of Jesus which the early Church found relevant to its own situation. His coming would be just as dis-astrous for some of his contemporaries as for later unbelievers, and the author of the Gospel of Thomas was not likely to have retained this saying if he found it. General considerations which can be brought against the authenticity of this whole group of sayings will be discussed below.[66]

Matt. 25.31

Matt. 25.31 is the introduction to the purely Matthean parable of the sheep and the goats. It has many Matthean features, including the use of 'the Son of man' as the title for Jesus at the eschatological consummation, whereas 'the king' is used in the parable itself. Jeremias suggests that this change 'may be due to the stylization of the introduction by Matthew, since it is closely connected with Matt. 16.27, and the session of the Son of man on the royal throne only occurs in Matt. 25.31; 19.28'.[67] The indirect influence of Dan. 7.13–14 is clear because of the collocation of 'Son of man' and 'coming'. Further parallels can be drawn between the two texts—glory, the accompanying angels, the sitting on a throne, and, from Matt. 25.32, πάντα τὰ ἔθνη. However, the man-like figure is not enthroned in Dan. 7.13–14, and it is not clear that Matthew thought he was. Moreover, these other features all belong to the standard Judaeo-Christian picture of the End, the distinctively Christian feature being the role of Jesus, a factor according with the tendency in the Judaism of this period for divine activities to be taken over by intermediary figures. They may owe their origin to these beliefs rather than to this specific biblical text. Moreover, if Matthew intended to make a clear reference to this text, even without a quotation (cf. Matt. 24.30; 26.64), it is perhaps surprising that he does not have the Son of man coming on the clouds of heaven. It is therefore probable that the influence of Dan. 7.13–14 here is indirect, even though it can certainly be established, and it is doubtful whether these other features are in fact derived from this text.

The setting is clearly the final judgement, as is normal in Western traditions of interpretation of Dan. 7. The coming of the Son of man has been understood as the parousia of Jesus, which again fits very straightforwardly into the Western Christian tradition. T. W. Manson used this passage as an argument in favour of his corporate concept of the Son of man; here the Son of man is 'the Danielic Kingdom of the Saints, of which Jesus is the head: and the parousia is the elevation of this body to supreme power over all the nations of the world'.[68] This is unconvincing. The king's brethren are distinct from the sheep and goats because this is a parable in which the salvation of the Jews as a group is in accordance with normal Jewish belief taken for granted; the Gentiles (πάντα τὰ ἔθνη) are split into sheep and goats.[69] Matthew will not have found it difficult to assume that the brethren are Christians; he will have come from an environment in which most Gentiles were not. The king is not said to be a spokesman for anyone, though in the present form of the parable he could legitimately be treated as a spokesman for the Father (25.34 only); he is king of his brethren, rather than their spokesman. His solidarity with them is not to be connected with the use of the term 'Son of man' because this term is not used in the body of the parable, as it could so easily have been, just as it is not used at Mark 9.37||Matt. 18.5||Luke 9.48; Matt. 10.40|| Luke 10.16; Mark 9.41||Matt. 10.42. Some statements about the coming of the Son of man must be interpreted of an individual, as Manson admits in the case of Mark 14.62, and all make excellent sense so interpreted, including this one. Moreover, 'then he shall sit on the throne of his glory' (Matt. 25.31) is clearly a statement about an individual, and does not lend itself to assimilation to the twelve thrones of Matt. 19.28. In short the Son of man is an individual, namely Jesus, and no convincing reason has been given for considering him to be anything else.

Matt. 28.3

Gundry has suggested that Matt. 28.3 contains an allusive quotation of Dan. 7.9.[70] Unconscious influence is not out of the question, but deliberate use is improbable and cannot be demonstrated. Matthew's account is so different from his Marcan source that it is misleading to represent him as simply conforming the description of the heavenly figure to the phrases of Dan. 10.6; 7.9. Heavenly figures were often clothed in white, and the comparison of something white to snow is too obvious to constitute satisfactory evidence of literary dependence. The contrast between εἰδέα (not in the OT texts to which Gundry refers) and ἔνδυμα, together with the fact that ἔνδυμα is not a rare word, means that this too cannot satisfactorily be regarded as evidence of the use of Dan. 7.9. Matthew had a tradition of description of the heavenly world to rely on, and it is difficult to see why he should appropriate Daniel's description of God in order to produce so straightforward a description of an anonymous angel. It is difficult not to conclude that the multitudinous examples of this kind produced by Gundry testify to his diligence in searching the Bible, but show no appreciation of the ability of authors to write from within a tradition without perpetually utilizing individual texts.

Matt. 28.18

Several scholars have suggested that Matt. 28.18–20 is dependent on Dan. 7.13–14, but the thorough discussion of Vögtle has shown that this is not correct.[71] Gundry, seeing a reference to Dan. 4.14 LXX as well, argues that 'The double allusion produces a very fine contrast between Nebuchadnezzar, divested of his authority, and the Son of man, to whom all authority in heaven and upon earth is given.'[72] It should be clear that this contrast is quite absent from the text of Matthew, who mentions neither figure and is not likely to have had Nebuchadnezzar in mind at all. The absence of terms which point exclusively to Dan. 7.13–14 is noteworthy. If the fulfilment of this text was consciously in Matthew's mind, the absence of the term 'Son of man' is especially remarkable. Of the common terms on which the hypothesis of an allusion is based, 'all the nations' is inappropriate, because Dan. 7.14 is not suggestive of the Gentile mission, a major aspect of early Christianity which did not require this text for its justification. The decisive argument is the fact that the fulfilment of Dan. 7.13–14 would have to be seen as having taken place immediately after the Resurrection. This is contrary to its interpretation wherever it can certainly be shown to be used. In view of this, the coincidence of ἐδόθη and ἐξουσία, already found together at Mark 11.28, may not be regarded as sufficient evidence of such use. This is rather to be regarded as a Matthean expression of the early Christian belief in the exalted status of their risen Lord.

Luke 1.32–3

Luke 1.32–3 is a suggestion which we owe to C. H. Dodd, who comments: 'Luke 1.32–3 echoes Isa. 9.7 (with a glance also at 2 Sam. 7.13–16, and Dan. 7.14)'.[73] What are the criteria for a glance? This is a Christian expression of standard Jewish messianic hope. The eternity of the Messiah's kingdom is a normal feature of this, and cannot be regarded as sufficient evidence of the use of an Old Testament text, so that there is no reason to believe that Dan. 7.14 was in mind here. This example illustrates the fact that, though Dodd's work on the use of the OT was an important advance over his predecessors, his criteria in determining the influence of OT texts are often too loose to be helpful. In particular, the assembling of a large number of references of this kind cannot demonstrate anything of real significance.

Luke 12.8

Luke 12.8 is a Q saying. The Lucan version is the more original,[74] and it includes the two items, the Son of man and the angels, which might be thought to link it with Dan. 7.13. The term 'the Son of man' is not enough on its own, and the angels do not perform the same function as in Dan. 7.13. It might be urged that they perform the function of being the tribunal which sat on the thrones in Dan. 7.9–10, but this in itself makes clear that the picture of the judgement has been developed beyond and differently from that of Dan. 7.9–14, and it is therefore not

sufficient to validate the hypothesis that there is a reference to
Dan. 7. The point is perhaps most easily made in Aramaic. A
possible Aramaic original behind Luke 12.8||Matt. 10.32 might
be reconstructed thus:

כל די יודי בי קדם אנשא
בר אנש יודי בה קדם מלאכיא די אלהא·

In this saying the context does not provide enough markers for
the unconscious question 'which son of man?' to receive the
answer 'the one in Dan. 7.13'. Therefore it cannot be seen as a
deliberate reference to this text. But if it is not a deliberate
reference to this text some other use of the Aramaic term
בר אנש must be found if the saying is to be acceptable Aramaic
at all, and once this is done, any theory of unconscious or
indirect reference must collapse as well. It is reasonable to
suggest that this reconstruction is in fact an example of an
Aramaic idiom whereby a speaker used a general statement to
say something about himself.[75]

Luke 12.32

The connection between Luke 12.32 and Dan. 7 has been
pressed by a few scholars, largely on the ground that 'the kingdom of God is connected with the verb "to give" only in Dan. 7
in the pre-Christian literature'.[76] It is however doubtful whether
this argument can be maintained. The concept of the kingdom
of God is a fundamental Jewish concept which Jesus made much
use of. The idea that it is God's kingdom, and that entry into it,
or possession of it, is a matter that lies within the divine control,
is basic to the conception of the kingdom. That his faithful
servants will enter or inherit it is also part of this widespread
concept. To express these basic ideas several different terms
were used, and it is not surprising that the author of Dan. 7
himself used more than one. 'Give' occurs in the symbolic 7.14,
and in the full interpretation of 7.27; the briefer summaries
have 'receive' (vs. 18), and 'possess' (vss. 18, 22). Of the rather
meagre intertestamental evidence the most relevant expression
of this thought occurs in Wisdom's praise of the righteous
(Wisd. 5.16): 'they shall receive royal splendor'. Other sayings
attributed to Jesus speak plainly of the kingdom as the gift of
God; especially notable are Luke 22.29 and Matt. 21.43, where

God can take the kingdom away from the Jews and give it to the righteous. Even so in Midr. *Esth.* I, 13 when Israel sinned, God took the kingdom away from them and gave it to the Gentiles; when they repent, he will restore it to them. It is not usually suggested that these passages are dependent on Dan. 7, and indeed this should not be supposed. If God gives the kingdom, others can receive it (Mark 10.15‖Luke 18.17, where the parallelism shows clearly that receiving the kingdom is the same as entering it), or inherit it (Matt. 25.34). To Peter, Jesus can give its keys (Matt. 16.19). Elsewhere in the New Testament, Jesus can be said to restore the kingdom to Israel (Acts 1.6). The wicked do not inherit it (1 Cor. 6.9–10 *bis*; Gal. 5.21; Eph. 5.5); nor do flesh and blood or corruption (1 Cor. 15.50); the faithful will inherit it for he promised it to those who love him (Jas. 2.5). The concept of the kingdom as a gift of God is basic to the idea of the kingdom. I have selected those New Testament texts whose manner of expression comes closest to Luke 12.32, but it is important that there is real variety of expression about this basic theme. Given that the theme is basic, and the expression varied, it is to be expected that δίδωμι might be among the words used to express it. It is a common Greek word meaning 'to give', and hence much used in the New Testament to refer to divine gifts to men. When a biblical text contains more than one common item, these items are bound to recur independently in works that offer no more than the most general contact of thought. There is no need of a specific OT text to explain the expression of Luke 12.32, which contains no rare expression found in the Danielic text, where the kingdom is given to the man-like figure (7.14) and the people of the Saints of the Most High (7.27); the former is not found in Luke 12.32, and the latter, more characteristically Danielic expression, neither here nor anywhere else in the New Testament.

It is therefore to be concluded that Luke 12.32 cannot be regarded as an allusion to Dan. 7.

Luke 17.22

Luke 17.22 has been classified as an 'indirect reference' to Dan. 7.13[77] but the saying does not appear to have sufficient in common with Dan. 7.13 to justify this view. The occurrence of ὄψεσθε is interesting, but this is a very well developed Son of man

195

saying which does not lend itself to a convincing reconstruction in Aramaic, and it may be ultimately dependent on the traditions first found in Mark 13.26; 14.62, and known to Luke, who reproduces ὄψονται at Luke 21.27. If this is the ultimate source of some of the terminology of this verse, it could be classified as testimony to the indirect influence of Dan. 7.13, but even if this hypothesis were right, the reference is so indirect that such a classification is of very doubtful value, and it is perhaps better to say that influence of Dan. 7.13 as such cannot definitely be detected here.

Luke 18.8

Luke 18.8 is the final example of the collocation of 'Son of man' and 'coming' which indicates the influence of Dan. 7.13. There is no direct reference to this text, so that here, too, this influence appears to be indirectly mediated. This final clause is usually, and rightly, regarded as an addition to the parable of the unjust judge.[78] While the parable deals with the imminence of the End, this final clause of Luke 18.8b links it more precisely with the subject of the previous paragraph, the final revelation of the Son of man, that is, Jesus (Luke 17.22–37). Verse 1 is indicative of the community situation to which Luke considered the parable to be relevant. Thus the saying has a satisfactory *Sitz im Leben* both in the primitive community and in the structure of Luke. A reconstruction must be attempted:

להן בר אנש אתה הישכח המנותא בארעה

It is very difficult to feel any confidence that this saying existed in Aramaic before I made it up. The use of τὴν πίστιν appears to be Christian, and it is difficult to regard the article as an Aramaism when it can be read as perfectly satisfactory Greek. Even if some sense can be found for the Aramaic word המנותא, it is very doubtful whether a *Sitz im Leben* can be found in the teaching of Jesus for the sense of the saying as a whole. It appears to belong to a period when the parousia has been delayed and some people are losing heart. To assert that Luke never uses the expression 'Son of man' independently begs the question: if he uses it twenty-five times in his Gospel, the possibility that he uses it independently once or twice should be admitted and cannot be excluded by examining the other examples.[79] Here he had good cause, in the provision of a link with the previous paragraph; at Acts 7.56 he probably had another reason to do the same, and it is difficult to exclude the possibility that he did so at Luke 21.36; 24.7. In all these cases he had precedent for using the term in known traditions before him. The actual indirect reference to Dan. 7.13 does not run as smoothly as at Matt. 10.23; Matt. 24.44‖Luke 12.40, perhaps because it is even more secondary. It should therefore be concluded that the saying probably originated in the Greek-speaking Church, and may well be a Lucan construction.

John 1.51

John 1.51 is difficult to interpret. It appears to depend primarily on Gen. 28.12, which was interpreted by some rabbis to mean that the angels went up and down on Jacob (cf. *Gen. R.* 61, 18). This suggests the possibility of an exegetical amalgam in which the term 'the Son of man' is derived from Dan. 7.13. In general, Son of man sayings in the Fourth Gospel say what is said of Jesus elsewhere in this Gospel without the use of this term,[80] but it is noteworthy that in most cases this is true in a very straight-forward sense, whereas in this case it is only true if this verse is interpreted symbolically of the contact between Jesus and the words of his Father in Heaven, and reference made to passages such as 14.10–11. While such an interpretation is not wrong, the fact that there is not a straightforwardly similar saying without the use of the term 'Son of man' does further suggest that this Son of man saying may have a specific origin. It is then tempting to derive ὄψεσθε from Zech. 12.10 as at John 19.37; Rev. 1.7; and perhaps Mark 13.26; 14.62,[81] and add Num. 19.8–9 to the mixture (John 3.14). The use of the term 'the Son of man' is then the last remaining sign of the influence of Dan. 7.13, as at Luke 22.69 and perhaps Luke 17.22. It can be added that John 1.51 reads like a detached saying, having the plural ὄψεσθε despite the singular of its own special introduction (αὐτῷ), and it is easy to conjecture that it was added on the catchword principle, ὄψεσθε suggesting the verse as an illustration of μείζω τούτων ὄψῃ. The *Sitz im Leben* of the saying is the same midrashic use of Dan. 7.13 by the early Church as is to be supposed behind Mark 13.26; 14.62. On the other hand, it is interesting to conjecture that the corporate interpretation of the man-like

figure was preserved, that the Saints of the Most High have
been correctly seen as the faithful of Israel, and that this
explains the midrashic interpretation of בו (Gen. 28.12) as
Jacob = Israel = Saints of the Most High = man-like figure
= the Son of man.[82]

However, this hypothesis is extremely conjectural, and it is
difficult to feel any confidence in it. It is to be noted that, even
if something on these lines were to prove correct, the use of Dan.
7.13 would lie so far behind the Gospel that its influence would
be present only in a rather remote sense and, what is important,
would not be consciously felt by the author. The selection of the
term 'the Son of man' does not require the influence of Dan.
7.13 to explain it; once it is shown that the term 'Son of man'
functions as an alternative title of Jesus by pointing out that in
most instances what is said of the Son of man is also said of Jesus
without the use of this title, the perfect neatness of every single
Son of man statement being paralleled in this literal way should
not be required. Rather this evidence shows that the author
could use the term 'Son of man' as one of several alternative
designations of Jesus, and that does in fact explain why he or his
source has used it here, to designate Jesus as the person referred
to at Gen. 28.12. Moreover, the way the term 'Son of man' is
used here is not in itself suggestive of Dan. 7.13 at all. It is
therefore to be concluded that the influence of Dan. 7.13 is
probably not to be found here, and that if a complex conjecture
tracing it ultimately to that source be allowed, it is still the case
that the author of the Gospel shows no awareness of it.

John 5.27

John 5.27 is the only Johannine reference to be seriously
suggested as a straightforward direct reference to Dan. 7.13, and
it too is unconvincing. This occurrence is anarthrous, and as
Leivestad[83] has noted, 'Jesus has been given authority to pass
judgement not because he is *the* Son of man, but because he is a
son of man.' The most striking parallel is Test. Abr. XIII,
where God, in delegating the function of judgement to Abel,
comments: 'I will not judge you, but every man shall be judged
by a man.' This interpretation fits very well into the Johannine
context. The judicial office of the Son of man in Jewish apocalyptic should not now be urged against this, because it has been

shown that there was no such concept in Judaism.[84] The fact that the expression is anarthrous cannot point to a specific biblical text because this is too general a feature of language to point anywhere and because the anarthrous expression yields a sound sense without such a reference. Colwell's law may explain the absence of one article, but it is doubtful whether it explains the absence of both, and even the attribution of judgement to Jesus because he is 'the Son of man' would establish only that the judicial function was inherent in his being 'the Son of man', not that there was a reference to Dan. 7.13. The man-like figure in Dan. 7.13 is not the judge, and the synoptic evidence which suggests he was seen as such is notably foreign to the fourth Gospel. Like his contemporaries, John believed that judgement was the prerogative of God; like Test. Abr. XIII, he saw advantage in its being carried out by a man. Only a Christian could take the latter view and still believe that God himself did the judging. John assumed that God judges; John 5.27 explains why Jesus, rather than God the Father, carries out this function. Reference to Dan. 7.13 is unhelpful as well as unnecessary. John took the expression 'Son of man' from Christian tradition, and it is at least feasible to suppose that, like many later Western Christians, he believed it to express the human nature of Christ.[85]

Acts 1.11

Acts 1.11 does not show any definite trace of Dan. 7.13. The possible connection lies only in Jesus' return in a cloud, and the fact that Luke took the trouble to alter the more Danielic ἐν νεφέλαις to ἐν νεφέλῃ at Luke 21.27 shows that he did not intend such a reference. The origin of this belief is rather to be found in the widespread early Christian expectation of the return of the Lord, an expectation which Luke imagined would be accomplished in the manner heavenly journeys were often conceived of in the Hellenistic world.[86]

Acts 7.56

Acts 7.56 contains the only New Testament occurrence of 'the Son of man' outside the Gospels. Here it occurs in a brief utterance of the dying Stephen. Elsewhere in the New Testament, it occurs on the lips of Jesus everywhere except John

12.34. The occurrence of this term is the only feature of Acts 7.56 that recalls Dan. 7.13. Luke had already written a Gospel, and the immediate origin of the term appears to be the Gospel traditions that he had used. It is especially reminiscent of Luke 22.69,[87] a radical alteration of Mark 14.62 which does depend on Dan. 7.13. In this sense, the occurrence of the term 'the Son of man' can be ascribed ultimately to the influence of Dan. 7.13. But Luke eliminated direct reference to this text at Luke 21.27; 22.69, and it is reasonable to deduce that if he had associated this term exclusively with Dan. 7.13 he might well have dropped it altogether, so that its continued use by him is really dependent on its occurrence many times in the traditions which he knew, and most of these occurrences are not dependent on Dan. 7.13 at all. Thus the ultimate influence of Dan. 7.13 can be detected at Acts 7.56 only in a remote sense, and reference to it was not intended by the author. Therefore it does not constitute evidence of the application of Dan. 7.13 to Jesus immediately after his Resurrection.

The term ἑστῶτα has caused much difficulty, and it has been suggested that it may be derived from the LXX of Dan. 7.13.[88] But the presence of οἱ παρεστηκότες does not explain why Jesus should be standing, and there is nothing about the LXX of Dan. 7.13 that would cause an early Christian exegete to keep him standing. Like the suggestion that ἑστῶτα simply means 'positioned', this view suffers from a lack of definiteness. Dan. 7.13 is not explicit enough to be the cause of the Son of man standing, though this could certainly be read into Dan. 7.13 by current exegetical method after it had been thought of.

Perrin has argued that Acts 7.56 is a pre-Lucan formulation which is independent of Mark 14.62 and has the same combination of Ps. 110.1 and Dan. 7.13.[89] This view is unsatisfactory because of the lack of use of Dan. 7.13 in this text, but Perrin's reasons for thinking that Luke has a different *Vorlage* require discussion. He first argues that Luke uses the term 'Son of man' only in dependence on a *Vorlage*. This is however difficult to prove.[90] At Luke 6.22 it appears secondary to the parallel Matt. 5.11; Luke 17.22, 30 are only Lucan; Luke 18.8 is intelligible as a Lucan construction; Luke 21.36 makes especially good sense as a Lucan ending to the eschatological discourse; and Luke 24.7 may have been formulated by Luke himself on the basis of the traditions which he used earlier in his Gospel. Some at least of these examples may be at least indirectly dependent on a *Vorlage* containing the term 'Son of man' and it is fair to comment that they scarcely constitute proof of independent Lucan use of the term, but if Luke used the term 'Son of man' no less than twenty-five times he felt no need to run away from it. Moreover, in the sense that these occurrences may be held to require a *Vorlage*, Mark 14.62 provides a perfectly satisfactory *Vorlage* for the use of this term at Acts 7.56. Perrin's second argument is the 'clumsy' combination of the singular οὐρανόν in Acts 7.55 and the plural οὐρανούς in vs. 56. Luke normally uses the singular and has the plural only five times, suggesting that Acts 7.55 is Lucan but 7.56 dependent on a *Vorlage*. The singular is Greek, the plural semitizing. Luke was better than most New Testament authors at writing Greek, so his proportion of singular to plural is higher than average, but he was not above semitisms. He really did use the plural of οὐρανός no less than six times on any hypothesis. It should be deduced that he has a pronounced tendency to use the singular, not that he is incapable of using the plural. Authors generally have tendencies where grammarians have rules, and their exceptions may be caused by unconscious recollections. Ezek. 1.1 might have been at the back of Luke's mind; Perrin's evidence is accounted for if it was right at the back.

It is to be concluded that there is no clear sign of Dan. 7 in Acts. Its absence from all the speeches in the early chapters is especially significant, and confirms the evidence of the Epistles that it was not a passage of fundamental importance throughout the early Church.

The results of this survey are striking indeed. There are no formula quotations from Dan. 7 anywhere in the New Testament. Dan. 7.13 was certainly used in Mark 13.26; 14.62; and Matthew appears to have been aware of this when he took over these sayings into Matt. 24.30; 26.64. Luke, on the other hand, seems not to have accepted any reference into Luke 21.27; 22.69. Indirect evidence of the influence of Dan. 7.13 is to be found at Mark 8.38‖Matt. 16.27‖Luke 9.26; Matt. 10.23; 16.28; 24.44‖Luke 12.40; Matt. 25.31; Luke 18.8. This is secondary at Mark 8.38; Matt. 16.28; and it appears to be secondary at Matt. 25.31 and Luke 18.8 as well. That this indirect use of

Dan. 7.13 goes back to Jesus is not thereby excluded, but it does not look very probable. Moreover, this indirect use of Dan. 7.13 may have been unconscious in all these references. There are a few further sayings where Dan. 7.13 was or may have been influential at one remove, as it was in Luke 21.27; 22.69 (Matt. 13.41; Luke 17.22; John 1.51; Acts 7.56). This evidence shows Dan. 7.13 being added in to some sayings by the early Church, and being removed from others so as to leave the expression 'Son of man' behind. Since both processes are attested, a simple tendency in one direction has not been demonstrated. Sayings in the latter group may leave the influence of Dan. 7.13 so difficult to detect that the group may be suspected of having been larger. This does not legitimate the lowering of criteria to a point at which dependence on this text is accepted where it cannot be demonstrated, but it does necessitate further arguments to show that this group was not very significantly larger.[91]

There is possible use of Dan. 7.9–13 at Matt. 19.28||Luke 22.30, but even if this is right, it is striking that this classic text of the heavenly world is not more used. Of the four kingdoms there is no trace. The teaching of Jesus includes the expectation of the kingdom of God, but shows no concern for the destruction of the Roman empire. In itself this is a good reason why he should not have made use of the whole of Dan. 7. The same consideration applies for the most part to the early Church. Verse 13 is interpreted of the parousia of Jesus only, and there is no sign of a double level of interpretation of any OT text in this material. Logic and later empirical evidence alike imply that the fourth kingdom be taken as the Roman. To this same exegetical tradition belongs the 'abomination of desolation' of Mark 13.14, but of the little horn there is no sign. The Saints of the Most High, the fundamental group of Dan. 7 who receive the kingdom, do not occur at all.

Two conclusions follow. Dan. 7 was not an exceptionally important chapter for the early Church, and it was not an important formative influence on the thought of Jesus.

This is a very significant result. Most Son of man sayings show no direct influence of Dan. 7.13. If Dan. 7 was not a formative influence on the thought of Jesus, and was not an exceptionally important chapter for the early Church, the Gospel term 'the Son of man' cannot in general be derived from it. This does not exclude the possibility of its being derived from it in a saying or two, such as, clearly, Mark 14.62. It does mean that another source or sources must be found for the majority of the occurrences of this term.

These conclusions are contrary to the views of so many established scholars that we must examine the main attempts to demonstrate that Dan. 7 was much more important than this. C. H. Dodd classified Dan. 7 as a 'primary source of testimonies', having concluded his detailed discussion of it by commenting, 'There is amply enough here to show how deeply this chapter of Daniel is embedded in the foundations of New Testament thought.' This enabled him to see Dan. 7 as a source of the New Testament use of the title 'Son of man'.[92] There are two main faults in the argument of Dodd's book. The first is his failure to appreciate the absence of important parts of OT passages in the work of New Testament writers. This fault is evident in his failure to observe the absence of so much of Dan. 7 from most of the NT. The second main fault in Dodd's whole discussion is that his criteria for accepting that a New Testament passage does in fact contain a reference to or reminiscence of an Old Testament passage are not precisely defined by him and are evidently too loose. For this reason I have repeatedly rejected his suggestions.[93]

These faults completely undermine Dodd's argument, which is not improved by the bare assumption, characteristic of attempts to find the origin of 'the Son of man' in Dan. 7.13, that this term must have a scriptural origin. His stress on the suffering of Israel anticipates Moule's view of a suffering Son of man in Daniel, and this is unsatisfactory, too.[94] It leads him to link up the Son of man with the Suffering Servant of second Isaiah, but the influence of the latter figure in the New Testament has been very much exaggerated.[95] It is therefore to be concluded that Dodd's view is quite unsatisfactory.

Gaston's view is more original and more subtle, but it too is exposed to fatal objections. He believes 'that when the evangelists use the phrase Son of Man they use it nearly consistently as a designation of Jesus, but when Jesus used the phrase he used it just as consistently as a designation of the community he came to found.' The source of this designation is to be found in Dan. 7.[96] Gaston has realized that it is necessary to establish criteria for use in deciding when an OT passage is being referred to, but his attempts to do so are not satisfactory, and show little appreciation of the theoretical problems involved, especially when dealing with a period of history for which our sources are meagre. Thus he asserts that a connection with Dan. 7 can be assumed wherever exaltation is combined with riding on clouds and in support of his view he cites Oepke's statement that 'The cloud was not originally a vehicle of rapture.'[97] This is however misleading. In the first place, the limitation to 'rapture' places an unwanted restriction on our appreciation of the use of clouds in contemporary literature. Secondly, Oepke also pointed out that 'Gods . . . conceal themselves in clouds. . . . The gods also conceal their assistants and favourites in clouds. . . . Finally the cloud is the chariot of the gods which leads the hero to them. . . . In later writers the cloud has a stylized part in divine appearances or journeys.'[98] When the Jews came to believe in heavenly journeys for the faithful, they too put them on clouds.[99] Moreover, Dan. 7 is not an exaltation text, and was not seen as one in the early Church. Gaston's loose criteria necessarily enable him to suggest examples of its use as an exaltation text, but this is not satisfactory when only a different exegesis is demonstrable by means of more precise criteria. Again, in pressing the corporate interpretation of 'Son of man', Gaston argues, 'if we find some of the exaltation aspects applied to Jesus' followers this is more unusual, and a connection with Daniel can perhaps be assumed'.[100] It is not surprising that the application of such a vague criterion should result in a large quantity of references: Matt. 28.18; John 6.27; Mark 2.10; Matt. 16.19; 18.18; John 20.23; Mark 3.15; 6.7; Luke 10.19; 9.1; Matt. 10.1; Rev. 2.26f.; John 1.12; 17.22; Rom. 8.18; 1 Pet. 1.11. But it is an illusory list, produced by a vague criterion rather than by NT use of Dan. 7. That this development is connected with the corporate interpretation of Dan. 7.13 requires demonstration in an altogether more precise manner. Consistent use of similar criteria leads Gaston to accept every one of the possible NT allusions to Dan. 7 that I have discussed and rejected.[101]

When more precise criteria are applied, the important fact emerges that Son of man sayings with so-called 'corporate' characteristics show no clear sign of Dan. 7, whereas sayings which do show clear signs of Dan. 7 consistently use the term

'Son of man' with reference to Jesus at his parousia. All Gospel writers clearly assume that the Son of man is Jesus, and it is because the phrase refers both consistently and obviously to Jesus that they can leave it unexplained. But if Gaston's argument that they were aware of a corporate interpretation of Son of man (even though they used the term nearly consistently to refer to Jesus) be disallowed, it becomes difficult to explain how they consistently misinterpreted all genuine Son of man sayings and thought their misinterpretation obvious. Gaston's view may therefore be rejected on these grounds alone, apart from its less original faults.

The recent theory, first clearly adumbrated by Moule and most fully worked out by Hooker, that Dan. 7 is the scriptural source of the suffering Son of man, was a major cause of the investigation reported in this book.[102] The first, and decisive, fault in this theory is that there is no trace of a suffering Son of man in Dan. 7: on the contrary, the man-like figure was deliberately chosen as a symbol of Israel in triumph, and any suggestion that he suffers is inconsistent with the author's symbolism.[103] Secondly, this investigation produced no ancient exegete who thought that there was a suffering Son of man in Dan. 7. Thirdly, only the broad assumption of the suitability of this text, backed by the difficulty of explaining the origin of the Gospel term 'Son of man' without recourse to the few scriptural texts in which it occurs, can provide a connection between the suffering Son of man sayings and Dan. 7; they do not show detailed features indicative of literary dependence, so that once the broad assumption is removed, all reason for connecting them is removed. Moule's second essay does not help by suggesting that Jesus could have referred to the man-like figure as ברה דגברא, a piece of Christian translationese which could not function as a reference to Daniel without adequate contextual markers, just as בר אנש could not, but the more so because it is a different phrase; furthermore, it should have been rendered into Greek either freely as ὁ ἄνθρωπος or ὁ ἀνήρ, or literally as ὁ υἱὸς τοῦ ἀνδρός. Moule further suggests that 'the figure in Dan. 7 could have been alluded to by various specific Aramaic phrases';[104] but his grounds for this are only the translation variants of the Ethiopic Enoch[105] and the translation variant of the Old Syriac of the Gospels which occasionally uses *breh dgabra* instead of the normal Syriac translationese *breh d'nasha*. These attempts to translate ὁ υἱὸς τοῦ ἀνθρώπου after it had become established do nothing to help explain its origin; in particular, Moule offers no explanation of how various specific Aramaic phrases all came to be rendered into Greek in, it would seem, different sources, by the identical term ὁ υἱὸς τοῦ ἀνθρώπου.

To a large extent this theory has the same basic faults as the traditional view that the sufferings of the Son of man are to be found in the suffering Servant of Isa. 53. The first is the selection of a single passage of Scripture as the source of the suffering Son of man, when the flexibility of ancient exegesis demands that the early Christians should have assembled many such passages. The second factor is that contemporary Jewish exegesis is laid on one side; Isa. 53 was not interpreted by Jesus' contemporaries of the suffering and death of the Messiah, and Daniel's man-like figure was not thought to suffer at all. The third fault lies in the criteria of assessment of the use of OT passages, which have to be set loose in order to allow sufficient references to the chosen passage. The fourth is the philological background, which has to be maltreated by devotees of Isa. 53 in order to produce references behind such texts as Mark 10.45 which do not contain them in their present form, and which Hooker sets on one side: 'Previous discussion of these subjects has shown, however, that our evidence is insufficient to give us any firm conclusions on these points.'[106] The meaning and use of the Aramaic term בר אנש will not retreat in the face of scholarly failure to reach and apply firm conclusions.

These discussions are the best substantial attempts to demonstrate that Dan. 7 was an especially important chapter for Jesus and/or the early Church, and all suffer from fatal faults. They proceed from inadequate criteria for demonstrating that an OT passage is really being used, and they ignore evidence that some parts of the chapter were clearly not in use. A major motivating factor in the case of Dan. 7 has always been the difficulty of solving the Son of man problem. The philology really is difficult; since Tertullian there has been a tradition that the answer is to be found in Dan. 7: and bible-centred Christians have a built-in tendency to look to the Bible for the answer, a tendency which can easily be justified by observing quite correctly that Jesus himself treated the Old Testament unhesitatingly as the

Word of God. But the evidence is decisively against this theory. Dan. 7 was not a chapter of major importance to Jesus or to the earliest Christians, and such traces of its use as are found in the synoptic Gospels are not consistent with any theory that Jesus' profound meditations on it were the main source of his use of the term 'Son of man'.

So far we have considered this theory in its most straightforward form; it is proposed that the occurrence of this title is due to abundant use of Dan. 7, so the use of Dan. 7 has been tested and found to be much too little for the purpose. We must now consider a more refined form of the theory: let us suppose that Dan. 7 was the starting-point, and that it gave rise to the title בר אנש, which Jesus then used as a self-reference without continually referring to the text with which he began. In view of the evidence already surveyed in this chapter, this might be considered to be merely pushing the theory in the direction of unverifiability, but in this case it is useful because the theory when thus handled does not become unverifiable at all—it becomes exposed to decisive objections of a different kind. These same objections also show that the term 'Son of man' is not derived from undetectable use of Dan. 7 in a significantly larger number of sayings than this investigation has suggested.[107]

In the first place some general points may be made. It has been shown above that the term 'Son of man' was not already a title in Judaism.[108] Therefore Jesus cannot have utilized a Son of man concept in his interpretation and use of Dan. 7; it will have to be supposed that he used Dan. 7 alone. Secondly, the process whereby the term became a title has never been satisfactorily explained; suppose Jesus did interpret Dan. 7.13 of himself—why should this make him extract the term בר אנש from it and use it as a title? Here it is relevant to mention the now universally recognized fact that בר אנש was a normal term for 'man'. It is perhaps too much to claim that this makes it completely impossible as an Aramaic title; it was not a Jewish title at a time when Judaism hardly produced any titles for its intermediary figures, and its pejorative sense is perhaps too occasional to be relevant here. Nevertheless this does not enhance its usefulness; it is a strange item to extract from Dan. 7.13, and its use as a title should have caused difficulties for Jesus' hearers, difficulties of which there is in fact no trace in the synoptic tradition. In addition, if it be held that Jesus used no other title,[109] the use of titles to categorize this dynamic religious figure has its *Sitz im Leben* in the early Church, and this suggests that, in so far as it is a title (as בר אנש *per se* is not), ὁ υἱὸς τοῦ ἀνθρώπου may have its *Sitz im Leben* in the early Church as well.

More detailed arguments can be added. We may begin with Vielhauer's dilemma. Sharman noted, and Vielhauer made notorious scholarly use of the fact, that while the kingdom of God and the Son of man both appear central concerns in the teaching of Jesus, they do not appear together in sayings that may reasonably be considered authentic.[110] Finding that the kingdom of God was indeed a central concept of the teaching of the historical Jesus, Vielhauer argued that all Son of man sayings originated in the early Church. If Dan. 7 is regarded as the origin of the term 'Son of man', Vielhauer's dilemma becomes the more acute, for at vs. 14 the man-like figure is given a kingdom which will not be destroyed.

The attempts to meet this dilemma have not been convincing. It is not sufficient to argue that Vielhauer's main conclusion, that all Son of man sayings have their origin in the early Church, is on other grounds incorrect. This is true, but it does not meet Vielhauer's dilemma. Secondly, it is clear that 'kingdom of God' and 'Son of man' are not interchangeable terms—it would be quite incongruous to suggest that the kingdom of God might forgive sins or the Son of man be given to the little flock (cf. Mark 2.10; Luke 12.32). But if they are not interchangeable terms, arguments designed to show that they are intimately connected at a different or profound level, or that both appear in the different sources or layers of the tradition, do not explain why they are not mentioned together in authentic sayings; on the contrary, if there is genuine connection between them they should be mentioned together. Thirdly, it is not sufficient to draw attention to passages such as Mark 8.38–9.1; Luke 21.27–31.[111] Both these passages appear to consist of originally detached sayings, so that if the material does go back to Jesus it does not show him speaking about the kingdom of God and the Son of man on the same occasion. Mark 8.38 has undergone secondary development, and the earlier version of Luke 12.8||Matt. 10.32 appears in a quite different context.[112] Luke 21.31 is a particularly unfortunate example, since it is verbally identical with Mark 13.29, excepting only that it has 'the kingdom of God' where Mark has 'at the doors', so that the mention of the kingdom is evidently secondary. Moreover, this objection does not meet Vielhauer's dilemma at a more fundamental level. If these two concepts, 'kingdom of God' and 'Son of man' are both fundamental and somehow related to each other, they ought to occur together, as they do in secondary sayings (Matt. 13.41; 16.28). It is this kind of association which is conspicuous by its absence in primary tradition.

Moreover, if the Son of man has been transmogrified from Dan. 7.13 in the manner sometimes suggested, he should have obtained kingship when he obtained authority (Dan. 7.14), and the two concepts, 'kingdom of God' and 'Son of man', should be associated in sayings referring to Jesus' earthly life; again, sayings of this kind do not occur at all. If however Dan. 7.13 is the cause only of the small group of sayings that I have proposed, Vielhauer's dilemma can be met for this group of sayings. If any are authentic, they are so few in number that Vielhauer's dilemma cannot apply, and for the Church's additions it is met by Matt. 13.41; 16.28. If none are authentic, the proportion of them in which the kingdom of God and the Son of man are associated should be regarded as sufficiently large. It is significant that the association occurs only in eschatological sayings, for it is only in sayings of this type that the influence of Dan. 7.13–14 is in fact demonstrable. Furthermore, the absence of the kingdom of God in the basic core of this group of sayings can be accounted for analytically in considering the purpose for which Dan. 7.13 was used. The Church had the preaching of the kingdom and searched the Scriptures to find the coming of their Lord.[113] To begin with, it was the only item which they needed to extract from Dan. 7.13, and they took it in the form of the coming of the Son of man under the direct influence of the formulation found in this text. Association with the kingdom of God then follows in the latest sayings of this group.

The next difficulty for the theory that the Son of man is derived from Dan. 7 is that in the New Testament the term occurs only on the lips of Jesus. The only exceptions are John 12.34 and Acts 7.56, and it is notable that neither exception belongs to the synoptic Gospels. So simply put, this objection should be weakened by the observation that Jesus in fact does most of the talking, though even then it is not negligible. If, however, it is added that the term 'Son of man' was in any way ambiguous, veiled, or mysterious,[114] this objection becomes decisive, since we can no longer explain why there is no discussion of the term either with the crowds or with the disciples. On the contrary, the Gospel writers assume that the meaning of the term was straightforward for themselves and everyone else. This objection is met for the small group of sayings which I have derived from Dan. 7 by supposing that any authentic sayings, together with the inner core of this group, whether authentic or not, contained a clear reference to Dan. 7.13 and that secondary additions followed the pattern of this basic group. The point of the formation of these sayings necessitates that they be authoritative pronouncements of the Lord, and they do not require discussion because they are not ambiguous, veiled, or mysterious.

Many Son of man sayings have alternative forms which say the same things about Jesus but which do not contain the term 'Son of man'. This does not however apply to any of the sayings which speak of the Son of man coming, that is, the group which shows clearly demonstrable influence of Dan. 7. If Dan. 7 is the origin of Son of man sayings in general, this is difficult to explain. This group of sayings can hardly be the oldest stratum, because some of them are clearly secondary (cf. Mark 8.38c; Matt. 16.28; 25.31), and it is very difficult to believe that the tendency of the tradition was uniformly in favour of the insertion of the term, especially in the case of Luke 12.8–10 and parallels. If, however, Son of man sayings are not largely derived from Dan. 7, this phenomenon is easy to explain. Sayings in this group have no alternative form because they, and they alone, have their origin in a direct reference to this text.

If Son of man sayings in general are derived from Dan. 7, the content of some of them produces difficulty. To some extent this applies to all Son of man sayings which refer to his earthly life, but it is especially acute in the case of sayings which predict his sufferings. If Jesus wanted to say that he had to suffer, why use a term from Dan. 7.13 to say it? To meet this kind of difficulty, scholars have suggested that the Son of man has been combined with the Suffering Servant, or that a suffering Son of man is to be found in Dan. 7; both theories have been found wanting.[115]

This difficulty does not apply if only the group of Son of man sayings which concern his coming is derived from Dan. 7.

Some Son of man sayings have features which suggest that they may be true not only of Jesus himself but also of a larger group of people. Some scholars have tried to associate this with the fact that in Dan. 7 the man-like figure is a symbol of the Saints of the Most High, and when interpreted as an individual he is naturally seen as their representative and leader.[116] This interpretation cannot be said to have received any support from ancient exegesis of Dan. 7; only the brief comments of Rashi's uncertain text show any sign of anything that might be termed 'oscillation'. Messianic interpreters may regard the Messiah as the leader of the Saints, but they do not regard the man-like figure as a symbol of the Saints as well as the Messiah; many of them try to find the Messiah somewhere in the interpretation, and Polychronius, who did not, bluntly declared that he was not mentioned there. When Ibn Ezra correctly took up the corporate interpretation, he dropped the messianic view to which he had previously adhered. The corporate interpreters of the Syrian tradition, subjected to theological pressures for finding Jesus in Dan. 7.13, did not oscillate, but used a complex exegetical method with two levels. Israelite notions of 'corporate personality' have been misapplied to Son of man sayings.[117] But the remarkable fact about 'corporate' Son of man sayings is that they do not show detectable signs of the influence of Dan. 7.13, whereas the group of sayings that show clear signs of this influence do not show corporate characteristics. These sayings fit the Western Christian tradition which consistently interpreted the man-like figure as Jesus alone. It should be deduced that 'corporate' features have their origin elsewhere.

If Son of man sayings are in general derived from Dan. 7, the absence of both 'the Son of man' and Dan. 7 from so much of the New Testament is difficult to explain. In particular, Dan. 7.13 does not reappear with Ps. 110.1, with which it is combined at Mark 14.62, a text often thought to have been influential as well as authentic. The first of these two points has been glossed over by drawing parallels between what is said of Jesus as Son of man in the Gospels and what is said of him, especially with the use of the term ἄνθρωπος, in the Pauline epistles,[118] but the absence of the term remains. It was obviously not too Semitic for the author of Revelation, and it is difficult to claim that it was both too barbaric for Paul (despite Eph. 3.5) and not too barbaric for Luke. Moreover, if Jesus, having begun from Dan. 7, used it as the characteristic expression for referring to his own vocation, its absence from all confessions of faith is especially remarkable.[119] If, however, Dan. 7 was responsible only for one group of parousia sayings it was not important enough to be taken up outside Revelation, and if these sayings are all the product of the early Church, the fact that one or more groups of Christians searching the Scriptures found the second coming of Jesus in Dan. 7.13, whereas others show no signs of having done so, is not in any way remarkable.

Finally, this theory would make several sayings in any proposed Aramaic so ambiguous that their intelligibility must be cast in serious doubt. It is remarkable how many scholars have published research on the Son of man problem without reconstructing any Aramaic originals of sayings known to be difficult because they contain the outstanding Aramaism of the New Testament. Nevertheless, this factor has been observed. Taylor, commenting on Mark 2.10, goes so far as to suggest that it 'is a genuine utterance, which Jesus spoke without the expectation of being immediately understood'.[120] Remarks like this remove the need to make sense of Jesus' sayings at all; if they need not be comprehensible, traditional belief, or any other belief, can continue unhindered by them. Nor should this factor be associated with the Messianic secret, for the Gospel which is most concerned with this theory assumes that the term 'Son of man' is so clear that it does not require explanation. The Pharisees may not have liked Mark 2.10, and Peter did not like Mark 8.31, but both were spoken openly, and no one shows any sign of finding the use of the term 'Son of man' in any way ambiguous or difficult. If Jesus had used בר אנש as a title, his sayings would have been ambiguous because בר אנש is an ordinary term for 'man', and if he had used it as a simple self-reference, he would have produced a linguistic innovation; Dan. 7.13 can mitigate these factors only when the context provides clear reference to Dan. 7.13, and the synoptic tradition fails to show any signs of the difficulties which such ambiguity or linguistic innovation would necessarily have produced. The actual evidence of the synoptic tradition thus sets the seal on the general improbability that any Aramaic speaker would have formed the title 'Son of man' on the basis of Dan. 7.13.

All these points combine to form a cumulative argument of overwhelming weight: Dan. 7 is not the source of a large number of Son of man sayings, and it is not the origin of Jesus' use of this term.

But what of the small group of Son of man sayings in which the influence of Dan. 7 really is detectable? Mark 8.38c; Matt. 16.28; 25.31; and Luke 18.8 appear to be secondary, thus establishing that this influence of Dan. 7.13 has a satisfactory *Sitz im Leben* in the early Church. But this still leaves Mark 13.26; 14.62; Matt. 24.44||Luke 12.40; and Matt. 10.23. Are these authentic? Mark 14.62 and Matt.10.23 in particular have often been defended, and not only by conservatives or by scholars who found their authenticity congenial. Nevertheless, I propose to argue that the whole group derives from the exegetical activity of the early Church.

In the first place I shall argue simply that all this group of sayings has a satisfactory *Sitz im Leben* in the early Church. We may begin with those sayings which must be seen as conscious allusions to Dan. 7.13, namely Mark 13.26||Matt. 24.30; Mark 14.62||Matt. 26.64; and we may add Rev. 1.7. These are the only New Testament passages to contain demonstrably conscious allusions to Dan. 7.13, and all of them have it in midrashic combination with other OT texts. This is a known activity of the early Church. 'The New Testament writers believed that the life, death, and resurrection of Jesus Christ, under whose authority they lived, had been predicted in the Old Testament. The events to which they themselves bore witness were thus the proof that they were living in the age of fulfilment.'[121] To find these events in the Old Testament they searched the Scriptures. Moreover, they did not expect the age of fulfilment to continue in its present form for ever. Some of them at least expected a radical change to take place very soon. Jesus had predicted that the kingdom of God would shortly be established, but what part had he given himself in the final events? Acts, the Epistles, and the Book of Revelation testify to the fact that the early Church, reasonably enough in the light of contemporary Jewish belief that a redeemer figure would appear as God's agent to deliver them, expected his return and

searched the Scriptures to find it. In the Epistles, they appear
to have found it in a few passages which originally referred to
the coming of Yahweh on the day of the Lord.[122] This is not
surprising, for the coming of Yahweh is the only dramatic
supernatural coming in the Old Testament. It is to be noted
that the resulting picture often combines 'echoes' of several
different OT passages, a procedure which Jewish evidence
should lead us to anticipate.

One group of early Christians, however, found the coming of
their Lord in Dan. 7.13. This is very intelligible. The early
Church inherited a flexible and actualizing method of exegesis.
It is probable enough that they also inherited the Western
tradition of interpretation of the Book of Daniel. They were in
a very similar position to the Enoch circle, who also found their
man in this verse.[123] Both believed in a supreme human figure
who was now in heaven and was of such majesty that he must
play an important role in the last times that were already upon
them. Both followed the actualizing Western tradition according to which Dan. 7.9–14 dealt with eschatological events. With
these factors in the background, it is not surprising that both
identified the man-like figure as their own. When his interpretation as the Saints of the Most High is lost to view (neither
the Similitudes nor the Gospels show clear signs of the four
kingdoms or of the interpretative section of Dan. 7), this figure
is indeed mysterious; the questions of 1 Enoch 46.2 are very
appropriate, and the two answers, Enoch and Jesus, correspond
to the general beliefs of these two communities. On the other
hand, none of this is necessary, least of all in exegetes who were
not especially concerned with the Book of Daniel: the Epistles
show both assertions of the early Church's faith without scriptural backing and exegetes who could find the second coming
elsewhere in the OT. The confidence of their faith and the
flexibility of ancient exegetical method provide sufficient explanation of the absence of this interpretation of Dan. 7.13 from
a considerable part of the NT, and it is not necessary to turn to
the suggestion, plausible but unverifiable, that some of these
early Christians may have interpreted the man-like figure as a
pure symbol of the Saints of the Most High.

Thus we can explain the use of Dan. 7.13 to describe the
second coming of Jesus, and the fact that it is used together with

midrashic echoes of other texts at Mark 13.26; 14.62; Rev. 1.7. Matthew received it from Mark, and the author of Revelation may well have been dependent on the same grouping of OT texts as these two Gospel writers, though he certainly did cast his eye over the whole of the chapter. It is to be observed that the degree of originality and creativity required does not surpass that which is normally to be found in documents of this period, so that it is not incredible that the exegetical work on Dan. 7.13 behind the Similitudes and the Gospels alike should have been carried out by exegetes whose names are unknown to us. Moreover, the Book of Revelation apart, the exegesis of the early Christians and the Enoch circle alike does fit into, but does not utilize, a consistent exegetical tradition of the whole chapter.

> If anything is clear about ancient Jewish hermeneutics, it is that 'context' is not understood in modern literary and historical categories. The context of any Scripture text is rather the whole of Scripture and contemporary needs. Doeve put the matter quite correctly when he pointed out that Jewish hermeneutics can depend on the immediate context or completely ignore it according to its needs. . . . 'Atomistic' and 'harmonistic' are two sides of the same coin in ancient Jewish hermeneutics.[124]

The earliest Christians were Jews, and they inherited and used these same hermeneutics. Thus both groups made use of the short passage of Daniel which gave them the scriptural information they required. Their interpretation does fit a consistent exegetical tradition, but both could happily ignore the four kingdoms and the interpretative section of Dan. 7. Their interpretations are both incorrect, but follow the normal pattern of the actualizing traditions of the West.

That the Church should have attributed its exegesis to Jesus himself accords with its normal practice. The form of the eschatological farewell discourse was well enough known to the Jews; Mark utilized it in Mark 13 and put Jesus' prediction of his coming at its climax. However, while few will object to such an explanation of Mark 13.26, Mark 14.62 is more often defended. To begin with, I observe simply that it has a satisfactory and similar *Sitz im Leben* in the early Church. If the Church did not know what Jesus said at his trial, Mark might

215

well follow the normal practice of ancient historians of putting into his mouth a speech of the kind he was expected to have made. The result is very good: brevity, the conclusion of the Messianic secret, all three of the titles of Jesus that were important to Mark, the community's hope and the confounding of the Jews in pure Old Testament terms.[125]

This same group of Christians whose exegesis lies behind the synoptics then produced another group of sayings in which the influence of Dan. 7.13 is indirect but detectable. All speak of the Son of man coming. Mark 8.38c; Matt. 16.28; 25.31 and Luke 18.8 have already been noted as secondary, their *Sitz im Leben* therefore in the early Church. We now suppose that the rest of this group originated there too. In discussing the details, a possible *Sitz im Leben* in the early Church has been suggested for both Matt. 10.23 and Matt. 24.44||Luke 12.40. It remains to argue that this group of sayings does not have a satisfactory *Sitz im Leben* in the life of Jesus.

The two main sayings, Mark 13.26 and 14.62, the only two in the oldest Gospel that can plausibly be regarded as authentic, both lie in combinations of OT allusions. This consideration has often been brought against the authenticity of 13.26;[126] it should be brought against both, because it is uncharacteristic of the teaching of Jesus as well as characteristic of the early Church. The other sayings, however, appear secondary to this main group of two. It would be very difficult to argue that Jesus used Dan. 7.13 allusively as at Matt. 10.23; Matt. 24.44||Luke 12.40 without allowing the authenticity of Mark 13.26; 14.62. Secondly, apart from the parabolic Mark 13.35||Matt. 24.42, Jesus in the synoptic Gospels never refers to his second coming except by using Dan. 7.13 and making reference to the Son of man coming.[127] This is difficult to explain, and may not be connected with any motif of secrecy because the Gospel writers evidently do not treat these sayings as ambiguous.[128] It is not characteristic of Jesus to deal with a topic only in such rigidly scriptural terms, but we have seen that this is explicable if the sayings have their origin in the early Church. It is paradoxical, but it is the case, that only this will explain the impression that the Son of man might be someone other than Jesus. If Jesus used Dan. 7.13 in this way, he was bound to explain that he was speaking of his own coming. The early Church, however, as the uniform attitude of the Evangelists demonstrates, could expound the coming of Jesus in scriptural terms without ever supposing that the faithful might imagine the coming of anyone else.

Thirdly, it has often been noted that, in spite of the fact that he speaks of the death and Resurrection of the Son of man and of the coming of the Son of man, Jesus never combines the two. This is very odd if these sayings in fact go back to him, and it is not sufficient to assert that they are alternative ways of speaking of vindication, since this does not explain why they should be alternatives which cannot be combined. However, this aspect of the evidence is readily explained if all the parousia sayings are due to early Christian exegetes who already had materials about the death and Resurrection, and who then formed new sayings in OT terms precisely in order to provide information about Jesus' coming.

The cumulative weight of these arguments must be regarded as a sufficient demonstration. This group of sayings which utilize Dan. 7.13 to speak of the Son of man coming have their *Sitz im Leben* in the early Church. The distinctively Christian version of the Western tradition of interpretation of Dan. 7, that which sees the parousia of Jesus in vs. 13, originated there and at length became universal in the Christian West.

It follows that Jesus himself did not speak of his second coming.[129] He preached the establishment of the reign of God, together with his Resurrection and the final judgement, but not until there was a Church waiting for his return was there any need to insert his coming. This need not be regarded as a fundamental shift. From the perspective of the teaching of Jesus, any coming that he might need to do would have been a very minor detail. When the different perspective of the early Church made his coming an important event, they did not thereby alter the basic expectation of the establishment of God's kingdom; they merely assimilated the picture to the standard Jewish idea that the last times would include the coming of a redeemer figure, and naturally identified that redeemer figure as their Lord. However, the new detail had to be searched for in the Scriptures, and exegetes found it in Dan. 7.13 and went on to produce this group of Son of man sayings.

It is therefore to be concluded that the Western Christian

217

tradition of interpretation of Dan. 7 began in the work of early
Christian exegetes some time after the death and Resurrection
of Jesus. This exegetical work resulted in the production of a
small group of Son of man sayings, which were incorrectly
attributed to Jesus and are now to be found in the synoptic
Gospels. The term 'Son of man' occurs in them because it occurs
in Dan. 7.13, and it has the articles because it refers to a definite
person. Where the reference to the scriptural text is very clear,
as at Mark 13.26 and 14.62, the option was open to Mark or his
predecessors not to include the articles, but it is not surprising
that this single Gospel writer, on whom Matthew was dependent
for the only other Gospel sayings that make equally clear
reference to Dan. 7.13 (Matt. 24.30; 26.64), chose to use the
articles and thereby reproduce exactly the title of Jesus which
he knew from other sayings in the tradition. All other sayings
in this group make only indirect reference to Dan. 7.13, so that
even if some of them did have an Aramaic substratum, the
translators would be strongly motivated to use the articles in
order to make their meaning clear. This is readily seen if we
consider, for example, Matt. 10.23b: οὐ μὴ τελέσητε τὰς πόλεις
τοῦ Ἰσραὴλ ἕως ἔλθῃ υἱὸς ἀνθρώπου.

Here the very fact that υἱὸς ἀνθρώπου is indefinite makes the
saying unsatisfactory, so that if it were being translated from
Aramaic, the articles would be a help. They could easily be put
in because the translators were referring to a particular person,
Jesus, and may have been conscious of referring to a particular
scriptural vision of him. Moreover, it is difficult to believe that
any of them did not know the title 'the Son of man' from an
earlier layer of genuine tradition. This is probably the decisive
factor which would cause even independent translators to use
the term with both its articles. It follows that the occurrence of
the articles is not sufficient to show either that there must have
been some connection between the translators of such sayings as
could have come from the Aramaic-speaking Church, or that
this group of sayings must have originated in Greek among
exegetes who already knew the Greek title ὁ υἱὸς τοῦ ἀνθρώπου
with both articles. It may be added that if any of the few sayings
was translated into Greek without the articles, the Gospel
writers themselves would almost certainly insert them to conform the sayings to other Son of man sayings. Finally, this group

of sayings is so small that the level of probability that translators and Gospel writers would consistently work like this must be regarded as sufficient.

Thus the theory expounded in this chapter gives a completely explanatory account of one small group of Son of man sayings, and it marks the limit of certainly verifiable use of Dan. 7 in the Gospels. It is, however, clear that a complete solution to the Son of man problem is not to be found along these lines. The *prima facie* case for supposing that a title so common in the Gospels, yet absent from the Epistles and all early confessional material, must in some sense go back to Jesus, has not been overthrown, and it has been demonstrated that the influence of Dan. 7 can account for the presence of the term 'the Son of man' in only a small group of Son of man sayings. The final chapter of this book is therefore devoted to a brief exposition of a more complete theory of the origin of the Gospel term 'Son of man' and its use by the historical Jesus.

NOTES

1 T. W. Manson, *BJRL* 32 (1950), 191 = *Studies in the Gospels and Epistles*, 143.

2 G. Vermes, App. E in M. Black, *An Aramaic Approach to the Gospels and Acts* (³1967), 310–28.

3 C. H. Dodd, *According to the Scriptures* (1952), 69.

4 C. H. Dodd, *The Parables of the Kingdom* (²1961). Cf. e.g. W. G. Kummell, *Promise and Fulfilment* (ET ²1961), especially 19–25; H. Ridderbos, *The Coming of the Kingdom* (ET 1962), 36–47; R. Schnackenburg, *God's Rule and Kingdom* (ET 1963), 77–86.

5 A. M. Farrer, *A Study in St Mark* (1951), 267–75; Tertullian, *Adv. Marc.* IV, 10, discussing Luke 5.24 (cf. supra, 97); so also A. Feuillet, *RScR* 42 (1954), 171f, and cf. H. van der Loos, *The Miracles of Jesus* (1965), 446 n. 2, relying on the methodologically uncontrolled J. W. Doeve, *Jewish Hermeneutics in the Synoptic Gospels and Acts* (1953).

6 Cf. G. Vermes, *Jesus the Jew* (1973), 68–9, 180; infra, 228–9.

7 Infra, 228–9.

8 J. Jeremias, *New Testament Theology* I (1971), 7 n. 2.

9 Infra, 193–4, 232.

10 So G. Vermes, op. cit., 178–9, 184–5.

11 C. F. D. Moule, *BSNTS* III (1952), 40–53, reprinted in C. F. D. Moule, *The Phenomenon of the New Testament* (1967); M. D. Hooker, *The Son of Man in Mark* (1967).

12 Supra, 24–7, 38–9.

13 On this theory see further infra, 205–6.

14 L. Gaston, *No Stone on Another* (1970), 395, 401–2.

15 On the background to modern dissection of Mark 13, G. R. Beasley-Murray, *Jesus and the Future* (1954).

16 Supra, 24–7, 58, 62–6, 69, 81–5, 88, 135; P. M. Casey, *NT* XVIII (1976), 167–80.

17 Supra, 89.

18 Infra, 224–8.

19 Infra, 213–19.

20 Infra, 216–17, 233.

21 Cf. infra, 218–19, 230–1.

22 Infra, 213–17.

23 Cf. supra, 143–4; N. Perrin, *Rediscovering the Teaching of Jesus* (1967), 175–85.

24 T. F. Glasson, *ExpT* LXIX (1957–8), 213–15; cf. L. Hartman, *Prophecy Interpreted* (1966), 156–7; R. T. France, *Jesus and the Old Testament* (1971), 255–6.

25 O. J. F. Seitz, *StudEv* VI (1973), *TU* 112, 489.

26 G. R. Beasley-Murray, op. cit., 247.

27 R. T. France, op. cit., 242 and n. 10; similarly R. H. Gundry, *The Use of the Old Testament in St Matthew's Gospel* (1967), 51–2.

28 As it is by Jeremias, op. cit., 273–4.

29 Cf. H. K. McArthur, *NTS* 4 (1957–8), 156–8.

30 France, op. cit., 227–39.

31 E.g. Beasley-Murray, op. cit., 244–6.

32 Cf. Beasley-Murray, op. cit., 260–1.

33 Cf. Beasley-Murray, op. cit., 170, 201–2.

34 France, op. cit., 235, referring to pp. 169–71; for a more accurate view of Dan. 7.13, supra 24–9.

35 Infra, 178–82; cf. France, 140–2.

36 France, op. cit., passim, e.g. p. 140, discussing Mark 8.38 and Matt. 10.23.

37 Cf. infra, 199, 204.

38 Supra, 143–4, 168–9.

39 On its interpretation, T. F. Glasson, *JThS* XV (1964), 299–300.

40 Supra, 143–4, 168–9, 177.

41 D. M. Hay, *Glory at the Right Hand. Psalm 110 in Early Christianity* (1973); W. R. G. Loader, *NTS* 24 (1977–8), 199–228.

42 T. F. Glasson, *The Second Advent* (³1963); id., *NTS* 7 (1960–1), 88–93; J. A. T. Robinson, *Jesus and his Coming* (1957), 43ff.

43 Supra, 22, 24–9.

44 J. A. T. Robinson, *ExpT* LXVII (1955–6), 339; op. cit., 50–1.

45 Infra, 183–4.

46 *The Coptic Version of the New Testament in the Southern Dialect* (7 vols, 1911–24); the dates of the Mss are given in vol. III, *St John* (1911), 378, 382, 383.

47 N. Perrin, op. cit., 175–6.

48 E.g. A. Gelston, *SJTh* 22 (1969), 189–96; W. O. Walker, *JBL* 91 (1972), 487–9.

49 J. W. Doeve, *Jewish Hermeneutics in the Synoptic Gospels and Acts* (1954), 152–3.

50 Infra, 224–8.

51 E.g. Glasson, op. cit.; Robinson, op. cit.

52 Supra, 162–3.

53 D. Hill, *The Gospel of Matthew* (1972), ad loc.

54 Cf. especially P. Vielhauer, in *Festschrift für Günther Dehn* (1957), 59–61.

55 J. Jeremias, *The Parables of Jesus* (ET ²1963), 81–5.

56 G. Vermes, *Jesus the Jew* (1973), 178–9.

57 P. Vielhauer, in *Festschrift für Günther Dehn* (1957), 51–79; infra, 208–9.

58 Cf. Vermes, loc. cit.

59 J. Dupont, *Bib* 45 (1964), 355–92, esp. 365.

60 P. Grelot, *Bulletin du Comité des études (Compagnie de S. Sulpice)* 45 (1964), 27.

61 Hay, op. cit., 58.

62 Supra, 87–8.

63 So Dupont, op. cit.

64 Vermes, loc. cit.

65 Jeremias, op. cit., 48–51.

66 Infra, 213–19.

67 Jeremias, op. cit., 206; likewise H. E. Tödt, *The Son of Man in the Synoptic Tradition* (ET 1965), 73.

68 T. W. Manson, *The Teaching of Jesus* (1931), 265; cf. P. M. Casey, *JSJ* VII (1976), 11–14.

69 On the Jewish background, cf. especially C. G. Montefiore, *Rabbinic Literature and Gospel Teachings* (1930), 332–40.

70 R. H. Gundry, op. cit., 146; similarly E. Lohmeyer, *Das Evangelium des Matthäus* (²1958), 405 n. 4.

71 A. Vögtle, *StudEv* II, TU 87 (1964), 266–94, esp. 266–77.

72 Gundry, op. cit., 147.

73 C. H. Dodd, *According to the Scriptures* (1952), 81.

74 E.g. W. G. Kümmel, *Promise and Fulfilment* (ET ²1961), 44–5.

75 Infra, 224ff.

76 Gaston, op. cit., 406; among others Glasson, op. cit., 53.

77 Vermes, loc. cit.; cf. supra, 189.

78 E.g. Tödt, op. cit., 99; for a recent defence of the unity and authenticity of Luke 18.2–5, 7–8, D. R. Catchpole, *NT* XIX (1977), 81–104.

79 Cf. infra, 200–1; G. Schneider in *Jesus und der Menschensohn*. Für Anton Vögtle (1976), 267–82.

80 Cf. especially E. D. Freed, *JBL* 86 (1967), 402–9.

81 Supra, 143–4, 168–71, 178.

82 Cf. C. H. Dodd, *The Interpretation of the Fourth Gospel* (1953), 244ff.

83 R. Leivestad, *NTS* 18 (1971–2), 252–3.

84 Supra, 11–17 24–40.

85 Leivestad, loc. cit.

86 Cf. infra, 204.

87 G. H. Dalman, *The Words of Jesus* (ET 1902), 250–1; C. K. Barrett, *BZNW* 30 (1964), 32–8.

88 Tödt, op. cit., 303–4; for other suggestions, cf. Barrett, op. cit.

89 Perrin, op. cit., 178ff.

90 Cf. supra, 196–7.

91 Infra, 207–13.

92 C. H. Dodd, *According to the Scriptures* (1952), 67–70, 107, 116–23. Cf. M. P. Miller, *JSJ* II (1971), 65–7.

93 Supra, 144–5 (Rev. 1.13); 151 (1 Cor. 6.2); 153–4 (1 Thess. 4.7); 158–9 (Mark 1.15); 193 (Luke 1.32–3); 199 (Acts 1.11).

94 Supra, 24–7, 38–9, 164; infra, 205–6.

95 C. K. Barrett in *New Testament Essays. Studies in Memory of T. W. Manson* (1959), 1–18; M. D. Hooker, *Jesus and the Servant* (1959).

96 Gaston, op. cit.: the quotation is from pp. 394–5.

97 Gaston, op. cit., 387 and n. 2: A. Oepke, *TWNT* IV, 911 = *TDNT* IV, 909.

98 Oepke, *TDNT* IV, 904.

99 Vermes, op. cit., 186–8; cf. Oepke, op. cit., 907.

100 Gaston, op. cit., 405.

101 Supra, *passim*, especially 164–5.

102 C. F. D. Moule, op. cit.; M. D. Hooker, *The Son of Man in Mark* (1967); C. K. Barrett, *Jesus and the Gospel Tradition* (1967), 41ff.; C. F. D. Moule in *Neues Testament und Kirche*, Für Rudolf Schnackenburg (1974), 413–28; id., *The Origin of Christology* (1977), 11–22.

103 Supra, 24–7, 38–9.

104 Ibid., in *Neues Testament und Kirche*, 471–2.

105 Supra, 101–2; P. M. Casey, *JSJ* VII (1976), 17–18.

106 Hooker, op. cit., 78.

107 Cf. supra, 201–2.

108 Supra, 24–40, 99–139, *passim*.

109 So e.g. J. Jeremias, *New Testament Theology* I (1971), 258–9; of the abundant literature, cf. especially Vermes, op. cit.

110 H. B. Sharman, *Son of Man and Kingdom of God* (1943), 89; P. Vielhauer, in *Festschrift für Günther Dehn* (1957), 51–79; id., *ZThK* 60 (1963), 133–77; id., *EvTh* 25 (1965), 24–72. In support of Vielhauer, cf. especially H. Conzelmann, *ZThK* 54 (1957), 277–96. Against him, H. E. Tödt, op. cit., 329–47; E. Schweizer, *ZNW* 50 (1959), 185–209; *JBL* 79 (1960), 119–29; M. Black, *BJRL* 45 (1962–3), 306ff.; F. Hahn, *The Titles of Jesus in Christology* (ET 1969). Cf. supra, 186–7.

111 M. Black, *BJRL* 45 (1962–3), 310.

112 Cf. supra, 162–4, 193–4.

113 Infra, 213–15.

114 So among many scholars, e.g. C. E. B. Cranfield, *The Gospel According to St Mark* (1959), 275–6; M. Black, *An Aramaic Approach to the Gospels and Acts* (³1967), 328–30.

115 On the Suffering Servant, C. K. Barrett in *New Testament Essays. Studies in Memory of T. W. Manson* (1959), 1–18; M. D. Hooker, *Jesus and the Servant* (1959). On the suffering Son of man in Dan. 7, supra 24–7, 38–9, 205–6.

116 E.g. T. W. Manson, op. cit.; C. F. D. Moule, op. cit.

117 Cf. J. W. Rogerson, *JThS* XXI (1970), 1–16.

118 Cf. supra, 151–5.

119 Leivestad, *NTS* 18 (1971–2), 253.

120 V. Taylor, *The Names of Jesus* (1954), 27.

121 C. K. Barrett, *The Cambridge History of the Bible* I (1970), 399.

122 Cf. especially T. F. Glasson, op. cit.

123 Supra, 99–107.

124 M. P. Miller, *JSJ* II (1970), 66, referring to Doeve, op. cit.

125 Among many scholars who now regard Mark 14.62 as a Marcan construction, P. Vielhauer, *Festschrift für Günther Dehn* (1957), 65; P. Winter, *On the Trial of Jesus* (1961), 20–30; A. Suhl, *Die Funktion der alttestamentlichen Zitate und Anspielungen im Markusevangelium* (1965), 64–6; R. H. Fuller, *The Foundations of New Testament Christology* (1965), 109–11, 145–7; Vermes, op. cit., 183–4.

126 E.g. Robinson, op. cit., 57, 119f; Glasson, op. cit.; cf. supra, 165–71.

127 Cf. supra, 162–4.

128 Supra, 210, 212.

129 Cf. Glasson, op. cit.; Robinson, op. cit.

9

The Son of Man Problem

If the Gospel term 'the Son of man' did not come from Dan. 7, what is its origin? Does the term go back to Jesus, and if so, what did he mean by it? To answer these questions we must turn to the use of the Aramaic term בר אנש.[1] It is now generally accepted that this was a normal Aramaic term for 'man', and our knowledge of its use has been greatly increased by the important collection of evidence made by Vermes.[2] One of his contentions has, however, become controversial. He argued that the Aramaic בר נש was used as a surrogate for 'I', but most scholars have dismissed his examples with remarks to the effect that they are general statements.[3] We must therefore consider one of his examples in detail, and for this purpose I have selected *Gen. R.* 79, 6.

In this passage the capture and escape of several birds is summed up by R. Simeon in a general statement, 'A bird is not caught without the will of Heaven.' It is natural to interpret the succeeding statement which is so closely bound to it as a general statement also: חד כמן וכמן נפש דבר נש, 'How much less the soul of a son of man.' This interpretation of it is in perfect accordance with the normal meaning and usage of the term בר אנש, as agreed by all investigators on the basis of ample evidence. However R. Simeon said it, not in order to make general statements about man, but for the sake of the implicit application of the general statement to himself. This is clear from the way that he acted on this general statement by emerging from the cave himself. Thus there are two observations to be made about the statement, 'How much less the soul of a son of man', both of which are important for our understanding of the origin of Son of man statements in the Gospels. The first is that the statement really is a general statement. The second is that the function of this statement really is that the speaker is saying something about himself.

The story in which this saying is found is extant in three other
224

versions, at pT *Sheb.* IX, 1; *Eccl. R.* 10, 8; and *Esth. R.* 3.7. For
the story as a whole, the four recensions form close parallels. As
at *Gen. R.* 79, 6, the versions at pT *Sheb.* IX, 1 and *Eccl. R.* 10, 8
have R. Simeon using a general statement with the term בַּר
נָשׁ, though with minor variations in the rest of the sentence.
Vermes denies that this statement is a general statement.[4] The
first of his four arguments refers to the version in pT *Sheb.* IX, 1.

> In the crucial last phrase, although a differentiation is no
> doubt intended between צִיפּוֹר (bird) and בַּר נָשָׁא, it is
> noteworthy that whereas the former is indefinite, *bar nasha* is
> not. Hence, it is justifiable to assume that the speaker has in
> mind not some random member of the human race, but one
> particular person, and that person cannot but be himself.

But Vermes has himself said that, in regard to the use of
בַּר נָשׁ(אָ) in general, 'the employment of the definite or
indefinite forms does not substantially affect the meaning', and
he comments in the middle of his discussion of this particular
idiom, 'In all the examples so far examined, reference to the
speaker is effected by means of the indefinite form בַּר נָשׁ. It
will be shown now that בַּר נָשָׁא, also, can be used in the same
way.'[5] His inconsistency on this point underlines his failure to
explain the presence of the articles in the Gospel phrase ὁ υἱὸς
τοῦ ἀνθρώπου. It is noteworthy also that בַּר נָשׁ is indefinite in
the parallel statements in *Gen. R.* 79, 6 and *Eccl. R.* 10, 8. In fact
the general variation in the state of בַּר נָשׁ(אָ) in Vermes'
evidence as a whole simply reflects its date, but in this particular
idiom it is to be supposed that this variation was already to be
found at the time of Jesus.[6] It is arbitrary, as well as inconsistent,
to isolate the examples of the use of the definite state and draw
such conclusions from them alone.

Vermes' second argument refers to the version of this story in
Gen. R. 79, 6. 'In this version, the *bar nāshā* saying is immediately
followed by Simeon's departure from his hiding place, so we
may once more conclude that *bar nāshā* whose soul will not
perish must be the speaker himself.' This argument is too simple.
Simeon's departure indicates the function of the general statement which he made, but it is difficult to see how it could show
that it is not a general statement. Vermes' third argument is
based on a textual variant. One manuscript reads נַפְשִׁי, 'my

soul', instead of נפש דבר נשא and Vermes regards this as decisive evidence; '*bar nāshā* is definitely a circumlocution for "I" in this instance at least.' This deduction is methodologically unsound. In their edition of the text, Theodor and Albeck read the general statement חד כמן וכמן נפש דבר נש. In the variant cited by Vermes, this has been replaced by a direct reference to the speaker, חד כמן וכמן נפשי. Transcriptional probability is decisively in favour of the reading adopted by Theodor and Albeck (other variants do not affect the point at issue). This text has been altered by a scribe to a more straight-forward reading, in which the speaker refers directly to himself. But this cannot constitute evidence that the original text חד כמן וכמן נפש דבר נש is not a general statement. This is a logical error, and together with a very similar fault of method in the use of parallel narratives, it runs right through Vermes' whole discussion.

His fourth argument is a rather tentatively expressed example of this fault in the treatment of parallel material. He refers to the parallel statement in *Esth. R.* 3, 7, commenting 'Another, though less direct, confirmation is provided by *Esth. R.* 3. Here, נפשנא (our soul) or נפשתנא (our souls) is substituted for נפש דבר נשא, implying that Simeon was thinking of both himself and his son.' But the text of *Esth. R.* 3, 7 is in fact different from that of the parallel narratives, and the difference is precisely that it is not a general statement, whereas all three parallel versions do have a general statement with בר נש(א) at this point. This cannot undermine the general nature of the parallel statement in *Gen. R.* 79, 6‖pT *Sheb.* IX, 1‖*Eccl. R.* 10, 8. As to the origin of the different readings, we are bound to draw the same kind of conclusion as in the case of the textual variant to *Gen. R.* 79, 6. The earliest form of this narrative will have contained a general statement at this point which has been altered in the version of *Esth. R.* 3, 7 to the more direct נפשתנא.

Similar criticisms could be made of Vermes' discussion of other examples of this idiom. All his examples may be inter-preted as I have interpreted *Gen. R.* 79, 6, so that the idiom may be described as follows: in Aramaic a speaker could use a general statement, in which the expression for 'man' was בר אנש, in order to say something about himself. Vermes has accurately described the circumstances in which this idiom was used. 'In most instances the sentence contains an allusion to humiliation, danger, or death, but there are also examples where reference to the self in the third person is dictated by humility or modesty.'[7] This is a more accurate and helpful description than that offered recently by Bowker, who argues that בר נש carries the generic nuance 'man born to die'.[8] While it is true that בר נש was a suitable term for an Aramaic speaker to use in discussing human beings as subject to death, and it is also the case that its association with human frailty explains its use in this idiom in all the circumstances referred to by Vermes, Bowker's selective employment of mostly late evidence does not show that the precise nuance 'man born to die' would be picked up in any significant sense from the term alone; rather it is a function of the use of the term in an appropriate context and this suits, for example, Mark 14.21a rather than Mark 2.28. Vermes' description is to be preferred; it is above all a more complete description of the circumstances in which this particular idiom was used.

Fitzmyer[9] has questioned the date at which this idiom began to be used, but there is sufficient evidence that the generic use of בר אנש was in operation before the time of Jesus, so there should be no doubt that general statements using this term were part of normal usage in Middle Aramaic. Vermes' view of this idiom gave it the appearance of being new, but my description of it shows it to be no more than a particular application of this well-known Aramaic locution. Since general statements using בר אנש were in normal use, the application of one to himself by an Aramaic speaker is the sort of development of existing usage that could occur on the lips of native speakers of the language at any time. The evidence which Vermes collected shows clearly that this development did in fact occur. New Testament evidence that it had occurred already in Middle Aramaic should on these grounds be regarded as sufficient, and the absence of examples in Middle Aramaic sources should be ascribed to the paucity of surviving Middle Aramaic. Vermes' examples lack the initial א of אנש because of the late date at which they were written down.

An outstanding problem is the state of (א)אנש in this idiom. This is difficult, because surviving examples come from a period when the difference between the absolute and emphatic states of the Aramaic noun had in general broken down. However, there is good reason to conjecture that in the time of Jesus the absolute and emphatic states of (א)בר אנש(א) were already in use in this idiom without any difference in meaning. General statements in Aramaic originally used the absolute state, and there is no reason to expect this to be altered when a speaker used such a general statement to say something about himself. The breakdown of the difference between the absolute and emphatic states of the Aramaic noun was already under way long before the time of Jesus, being evident already in 11QTgJob and more advanced in 1QApGen.[10] The predominant manner in which this breakdown first becomes evident is the use of the emphatic state where the absolute would previously have been expected. It is therefore to be supposed that examples of this idiom will have occurred with the emphatic instead of the absolute state. The nature of the idiom is such that this variation could not affect the meaning. On purely Aramaic grounds, therefore, such variation is to be conjectured by the time of Jesus, and this will enable us to explain the Gospel evidence in which the articles are invariably found in the expression.

This idiom may now be applied to the Son of man sayings in the Gospels. Each example has two levels of meaning. The first level is that of the general statement, which will be unfamiliar in many cases. The second level is that at which the speaker says something about himself. In each case this is related to the sense in which the sayings have been traditionally understood, but the fact that a general statement is being used results in these sayings being understood of Jesus in a sense that they were believed by him to be true of other people as well as of himself.

Nine Gospel sayings may be suggested as relatively straightforward examples of this idiom. Mark 2.10 has often been thought of as a general statement in the original Aramaic, which was then misunderstood. I suggest that it was a general statement, but Jesus deliberately used it to say something about himself in accordance with normal Aramaic idiom. It was not misunderstood, but some shift of meaning took place when it was translated into Greek. The general statement used was 'a man has power to forgive sins on earth'. Belief in the connection between sinfulness and illness was widespread in the Judaism of

228

this period, and it had long been accepted that men could announce God's forgiveness of sins. Evidence that in popular Jewish religion this belief could be formulated in the same way as it was here by Jesus comes from 4QOrNab, which shows that at a popular level the widespread belief in the need for sins to be forgiven so that a person could be healed found expression in saying that healers forgave people's sins. This does not mean that, in the popular view, they usurped divine prerogative; it means that some people expressed their beliefs in a comparatively blunt and straightforward manner. The small quantity of the evidence is due to the fact that we have so little evidence of popular religion in this period. The implications of 4QOrNab should nevertheless be clear, and Matthew was so far from embarrassed by the concept that men might forgive sin that he reintroduced it, no doubt quite independently, at Matt. 9.8.[11]

The function of the general statement which Jesus used is its implicit application to the speaker, who thereby declared that he had the power to forgive sins on earth. This point was retained when the saying was translated into Greek, but the original Aramaic idiom was lost. This explanation reinforces the view taken above that reference to Dan. 7 is unnecessary and unhelpful in understanding this saying.[12]

General statements have likewise been perceived behind Mark 2.28; Matt. 8.20‖Luke 9.58; Matt. 11.19‖Luke 7.34; and Matt. 12.32‖Luke 12.10,[13] all of which can now be seen as examples of this idiom. Luke 22.48 can easily be added. At the level of a general statement it draws attention to the fact that this is a particularly cynical way of betraying someone. Jesus here used his native idiom to ask Judas if he would really do such a terrible thing to him. Mark 10.45 may be seen as a general statement concerning the significance of life. Jesus used it to say that the purpose of his life was service, especially martyrdom.[14]

Behind Mark 14.21a lies a general statement, 'a man goes to his death as it is written of him'. It is simplest to suppose that this involves scriptural justification for the mere fact of death. There are many OT passages that could be in mind—among the more obvious are Gen. 2.17; 3.19; Isa. 40.6–8; Eccl. 12.5–7. The point of this general statement is its application to the speaker—Jesus announces that he is about to die, as all men do, by divine decree according to the Scriptures. This provides an excellent context for Mark 14.21b. At the level of a general statement this is a condemnation of traitors, a sentiment which is almost universal. Jesus used it to declare that Judas would come to a bad end.

With these examples in mind, we can consider the process of translation of these Aramaic sayings into Greek. Apart from the articles, the use of the literalistic υἱὸς ἀνθρώπου rather than the more idiomatic Greek ἄνθρωπος is probably due simply to the difficulties inherent in translating an exclusively Aramaic idiom. I know of no genuinely equivalent idiom in Greek, and translators of all periods tend to be literalistic when they cannot see how to translate an idiom idiomatically. The articles have caused more trouble. Here the random variation between בר אנש and בן אנשא in this idiom set a problem for the translator, because it meant that the state of אנש(א) did not tell him whether he should use the Greek articles or not. Therefore he had to use other criteria, and the obvious criterion to a Greek speaker would be normal Greek usage. In Greek the definite article is used to indicate a particular, previously known entity.[15] To any early Christian, Jesus was a particular, previously known entity. Thus a translator of a saying which employs this idiom, selecting the most important level of meaning of such a saying, that at which Jesus is saying something about himself, would use the articles on the ground that the entity represented by בר אנש(א) was a particular, previously known entity. Knowing that the saying was on another level a general statement, he would find his decision to use the articles perfectly in order because of the so-called 'generic' use of the definite article in Greek.

One practical example may be given. Matt. 12.32a‖Luke 12.10a may be reconstructed thus:

וכל די יאמר מלה לבר אנש ישתביק לה

The translators agreed on ן = καί, מלה = λόγον, and ישתביק לה = ἀφεθήσεται αὐτῳ. For כל די יאמר the Lucan version is as literal as possible, πᾶς ὃς ἐρεῖ, while Matthew prefers ὃς ἐὰν εἴπῃ. ל = εἰς in Luke, κατά in Matthew. The point of the saying is the pronouncement of forgiveness for anyone who speaks against Jesus, a particular and previously known person. Hence (εἰς) τὸν υἱὸν τοῦ ἀνθρώπου and (κατὰ) τοῦ υἱοῦ τοῦ ἀνθρώπου. The articles make generic sense as well, approximating to the sense of the general statement used by the speaker in the original Aramaic. So far, no one has misunderstood anything. Once the statement was in Greek, however, ὁ υἱὸς τοῦ ἀνθρώπου could easily be taken as a title of Jesus. Moreover, to anyone who in ignorance of the original Aramaic comes along and reads the saying in Greek, it appears to be a saying by and about Jesus only, no longer a general statement. This shift of meaning has taken place with the transmission of the saying from Aramaic into Greek. The Aramaic idiom has been lost. The point of the saying, however, has not been lost at all. It still pronounces forgiveness for anyone who speaks against Jesus.

A second false impression could be gained by someone who took the saying in isolation, not knowing what it meant or, what is more relevant, trying to work out what it originally might have meant. ὁ υἱὸς τοῦ ἀνθρώπου could easily be another figure altogether; the saying does not explicitly identify him with the speaker. This impression is simply a function of the fact that Son of man sayings are translationese.

The shift of meaning which took place when the saying was translated from Aramaic into Greek, and the false impression which can be gained if the saying is removed from its context in a Christian Gospel, could hardly be avoided, and the translator should be considered to have done as well as possible. Few alternatives were open to him. He could boldly render with ἐγώ, but this is a considerable change which abandons the general level of meaning altogether, so there are no more than two verifiable examples (Matt. 10.32, 33). He could render with ἄνθρωπος, but this would not help with the problem of translating this idiom at all, so it is not surprising that the Gospel translators uniformly preferred to be more literal. He could omit the articles, but that would produce a general statement which would not clearly refer to Jesus. The Aramaic idiom set the translator a real conundrum, and an ancient translator was bound to produce the results we have got. Modern scholars who think that Son of man statements cannot be translationese should reconstruct them in Aramaic, translate them into better Greek and demonstrate that ancient Christian translators could reasonably be expected to have done the same.

231

We can now consider three more complex examples of this idiom. Behind Luke 12.8b lies a general statement, 'a man will confess him before the angels of God'. This utilized current belief in the role of the exalted righteous as witness at the last judgement; Jesus used it to say that he would confess such a man before the angels of God. Matt. 10.32b is primarily an alternative translation, in which בר אנש is rendered with ἐγώ. Once a saying exists in Greek in an individual form it may undergo further development, as here with τοῦ πατρός μου. This kind of development also helps to conceal the original Aramaic idiom.

Mark 8.38 is another development, parallel to Luke 12.9‖ Matt. 10.33, with ὁ υἱὸς τοῦ ἀνθρώπου representing the original בר אנש. However this saying has undergone even further development in an individualizing direction, and it is at this stage that the influence of Dan. 7.13 was shown to be detectable.[16] This process of the selection and development of the individual level of meaning is in this instance carried to its final conclusion by the parallel Matt. 16.27, in which all thought of a general statement has become quite obscured. Thus these sayings provide a clear example of the process of selection and development of the individual level of meaning being carried a very long way, so that the original idiom is quite obscured. Moreover, they show this process going on behind the Gospel of Mark.

It is reasonable to conjecture that this process went on elsewhere behind Mark. It has often been noted that the Marcan predictions of the passion are in effect different versions of the same prediction, and it has been justly conjectured that details have been added in from the traditional accounts of the actual events. If Jesus used the indirect idiom as I have suggested, it is likely that he would do so above all in predicting his death and subsequent vindication. To obtain an original Aramaic example of this idiom we must remove individualizing features from the tradition common to Mark 8.31; 9.31; 10.33–4. One might suggest something on the following lines:

ימות בר אנש ולתלתתה יומין יקום

Here we have a general statement, 'a man will die, but he will rise again at three days'. At this general level ימות בר אנש is an obvious commonplace, but it provides an interesting connection with Mark 14.21. That Jesus believed in the general resurrection of the dead is well enough known, and there is some evidence which suggests that he could have expressed this belief by saying that a man will rise 'at three days'.[17] Perhaps this is how Jesus predicted his death and subsequent vindication. Translated into Greek, a statement of this kind could be taken to be simply a statement by him about himself, and it could then be expanded with details which apply only to him.

All these Gospel sayings may reasonably be held to be derived from this Aramaic idiom. None of them should be considered ambiguous, and in view of the indirect mode of expression, it is reasonable to trace them back to Jesus himself. I therefore suggest that these sayings go back to twelve authentic sayings of Jesus, and that, with the exception of Mark 9.12, where בר אנש was probably used in a simple general statement, all other Son of man sayings in the Gospels are to be attributed to the activities of the early Church. It may be that further research will alter the number of authentic sayings somewhat, but for the moment it is more important to suggest a basic distinction between authentic sayings which derive from Aramaic idiom and inauthentic sayings which do not, with this rough estimate of the approximate quantity of each. It has already been shown that the theory that most Son of man sayings are derived from Dan. 7 is open to insuperable objections which include most of the classic problems of Son of man research, whereas my view that one small group of sayings results from the influence of Dan. 7.13 is not vulnerable to these objections.[18] It must now be shown that the hypothesis that a basic group of twelve authentic Son of man sayings used this Aramaic idiom enables us to provide a more complete solution of the traditional problems of Son of man research.

In some sayings 'the Son of man' appears to be someone separate from Jesus, though he is manifestly identical with him in all the Gospels.[19] This is a false impression resulting from the translation of this Aramaic idiom into Greek.

In the Gospels the term 'Son of man' appears to have connotations of authority, exaltation, and humiliation. This is due to the circumstances in which this idiom was used. This explains how the Son of man can suffer. When Jesus came to speak of his impending martyrdom he naturally used this indirect mode of speech, and its translation into Greek gave it the expression ὁ υἱὸς τοῦ ἀνθρώπου. The reason why the Son of man must die is to be sought firstly in the fact that since the fall of Adam all men must die, and secondly in the current theology of martyrdom. The flexibility of contemporary Jewish exegesis will have enabled Jesus to find support for these beliefs in many passages of Scripture.

Vielhauer's dilemma[20] has a twofold explanation. In the first place, the Son of man is not a being or title which holds any place in contemporary Judaism or a central place in the teaching of Jesus. It is a reflection of an Aramaic idiom. In the second place, the relationship between Jesus and the kingdom is not the same as that between other men and the kingdom. Therefore he could not use a general statement to say anything about himself and the kingdom of God.

It has always seemed remarkable that the term 'Son of man' appears in the Gospels always on the lips of Jesus himself (except at John 12.34, rightly suspected as secondary). The reason for this is that he is the only person in the Gospels who talks about himself to any extent.

Much of the evidence cited in favour of the view that the term 'Son of man' in the Gospels is a corporate expression[21] finds its real explanation in the fact that the statements used in this Aramaic idiom are general statements, and that what is thus said of Jesus is therefore necessarily presupposed as true of other men also.

If the occurrence of ὁ υἱὸς τοῦ ἀνθρώπου in the Gospels is translationese, a simple explanation of its absence in the rest of the New Testament (apart from Acts 7.56) is obtained. This also accounts for its rarity in early Church literature of the second century.

This hypothesis accounts for the origin of the Gospel term ὁ υἱὸς τοῦ ἀνθρώπου. Once this term had got into Gospel traditions which circulated in Greek, it is only to be expected that it should be used in the development of those traditions where there was no occurrence of it in any underlying Aramaic. It is here that the group of Son of man sayings which have been the primary concern of this book should probably be fitted in. It was probably exegetes who already knew the term 'Son of man' as a term used by Jesus to refer to himself who found his second coming in the text of Dan. 7.13. This could have been done in Aramaic, for ancient exegetes could have seen special significance in the occurrence of בר אנש where speakers of the language would normally regard it as an ordinary term for 'man'. If the term בר אנש was already known from sayings of Jesus, it would for this reason reinforce the suggestion, which could be made on the grounds of the content of Dan. 7.13, that כבר אנש was in fact Jesus, and such was ancient exegetical method that the mere occurrence of the term in the text of Dan. 7.13 could be the origin of the suggestion that the man-like figure was Jesus even among Aramaic-speaking Christians. On the other hand, reasons have been noted for thinking that some of these Son of man sayings originated in Greek.[22] This again suggests that the production of this whole group of Son of man sayings may have been done in Greek by exegetes who already knew the term ὁ υἱὸς τοῦ ἀνθρώπου as a title of Jesus. This would put them in the position of their multitudinous successors who have been struck by their apparent discovery of this title of Jesus in Dan. 7.13. However, it has not been possible to raise this suggestion to the level of proof. This use of Dan. 7.13 could have originated in the Aramaic-speaking Church together with the earliest sayings in this group. That the Greek-speaking Church continued to form sayings on this basis is however demonstrable (Matt. 16.28; 25.31 and probably Luke 18.8, at least).

These two groups of sayings, those derived from Jesus' use of an Aramaic idiom and those resulting from the influence of Dan. 7.13, account for all Son of man sayings in Mark and about half of the other Son of man sayings in Matthew and Luke. At the same time they do not account for any sayings in the fourth Gospel (with the possible exception of John 1.51), and they provide for no authentic sayings from material special to Matthew. Moreover, this hypothesis entails the conclusion that none of the Son of man sayings which first occur in post-canonical sources is to be considered genuine. Thus this hypothesis fits very neatly into the general results of Gospel criticism. I have therefore provided a fresh classification of Son of man sayings in Table 5. It has been carried out on a new basis, though it will be clear that it corresponds to a considerable extent to the results of the work of some scholars who have used

TABLE 5

	1 Aramaic idiom	2 Prediction	3 Daniel 7	4 Others
MARK	2.10 2.28 8.38 9.12 10.45 14.21 (*bis*)	8.31 9.9 9.31 10.33 14.41	8.38c 13.26 14.62	
Q	Matt. 8.20 || Luke 9.58 Matt. 11.19 || Luke 7.34 Matt. 12.32 || Luke 12.10 Luke 12.8		Matt. 24.44 || Luke 12.40	Matt. 12.40 || Luke 11.30 Matt. 24.27 || Luke 17.24 Matt. 24.37, 39 || Luke 17.26 Luke 6.22
MATTHEW		26.2	10.23 16.28 25.31	13.37 13.41 16.13 19.28 24.30a
LUKE	22.48	17.25 24.7	18.8	17.22 17.30 19.10 21.36
JOHN				All

the now conventional threefold classification. It is not intended
as a permanent classification, especially in that col. 4, 'others',
consists of sayings that may yield to a more useful analysis after
further work, but it seems to me to be more useful than existing
classifications. Purely secondary parallels have been omitted.
Col. 1 consists of sayings that may reasonably be considered to
be authentic examples of sayings spoken in accordance with
correct Aramaic idiom. It is to be noted that the general shape
and validity of the theories advanced in this book would not be
seriously affected if this group were somewhat reduced in size
by the removal of its more conjectural examples. In col. 2 I have
isolated the suggested prediction of Jesus' death, because it has
received so much secondary development by all three synoptic
evangelists that a simple classification of these sayings as
authentic or inauthentic, and as conforming or not conforming
to Aramaic idiom, would be too simple to be useful. Col. 3 lists
those sayings which were produced by the early Church under
the influence of Dan. 7.13. Here I have drawn a line between
those sayings which show straightforward indirect evidence of
the influence of Dan. 7.13 by talking of the Son of man coming,
and Matt. 13.41 and any other sayings in which the possible
influence of this text is less fundamental and lies further back in
the tradition. This is not the only possible place to draw the line,
but it is convenient and will not be misleading if it is borne in
mind. Col. 4 is a disparate group. It is possible that further
work may not only result in some reclassifying of this group, but
may produce one or more further examples of authentic
Aramaic idiom. Be that as it may, the present contents of col. 4
do not give rise to serious concern. The appearance of ὁ υἱὸς τοῦ
ἀνθρώπου in Gospel traditions from the original group, and its
use in Dan. 7 sayings, was bound to be followed by further Son
of man sayings as long as inauthentic Gospel sayings were in
general developed. This group is not too big, nor does it show
features in any way so odd, as to call into question the general
hypotheses proposed in this book.

A few observations may be made on the development of Son
of man sayings as this appears from Table 5. Most authentic
sayings deal with Jesus' life on earth, including his death. His
Resurrection and the last judgement also appear, but as part of
a picture of the last times generally accepted in the Judaism of

this period; his own role is hardly the subject of any great emphasis. The absence of a suffering Son of man in Q now appears in a useful perspective. Mark had a single prediction of this kind, but he used it a great deal; it is not surprising that Matthew and Luke did not find occasion to use yet another form of the same prediction. The majority of inauthentic synoptic sayings deal with the time of the End, and give Jesus a fundamental role in these last events. It is within this broader framework that the Dan. 7 group of sayings belong. As the early Christians sought Jesus' role at the End, some of them found his coming in Dan. 7.13, and used it in this group of sayings. It is nevertheless to be noted that this verse is not the sole cause and content even of this group of sayings. Further analysis of inauthentic sayings which do not appear to make use of Dan. 7 lies altogether beyond the scope of this book.

If this general hypothesis is correct, the solution of the Son of man problem removes an important obstacle to the writing of a developmental Christology running from the historical Jesus up to the fourth Gospel.[23] Here the results of the new analysis of the Similitudes of Enoch carried out in ch. 5 again become important. This analysis releases Enoch to join Melchizedek and Moses as an incomparable human redeemer figure in the sectarian Judaism of this period. These three men were believed by some Jews to have lived human lives on earth, to have ascended to heaven, and to be on the point of playing a vital role in the deliverance of their people. If 11Q Melchizedek is outstanding for its demonstrably early date, the Similitudes are especially useful for their comparatively full account of the Enoch circle's beliefs about Enoch at a sufficiently early date for an analysis of the material to yield information which can profitably be applied to our understanding of the categories in which the early Church put Jesus. Moreover, the elevation of these figures to such a high status was clearly not due to anything which they actually did in the years immediately preceding their elevation. In the face of several Gospels, I do not suggest that Jesus did nothing, but the common assumption that the early Church's view of him could only have arisen from the impact which he made on those who knew him while he was alive on earth is in some important respects, relating to both his status and his function, falsified by this Jewish evidence.

238

Son of man sayings can now serve as signposts on the way through the Gospel traditions. The term בר אנש has its *Sitz im Leben* in the life of Jesus, but ὁ υἱὸς τοῦ ἀνθρώπου as a title has its *Sitz im Leben* in the work of the early Church. The increasing status of the risen Lord provided a setting within which ὁ υἱὸς τοῦ ἀνθρώπου could be accepted as a title, once the translation process had produced it. It is hardly as barbaric as scholars have often suggested. All evangelists believed that Jesus was a unique man, the son of God; the child of Fortune was now very old (παῖδα τῆς Τύχης Soph., *Oed. T.* 1080), though not as old as υἷες Ἀχαιῶν, and a distinguished man could be υἱὸς πόλεως or even υἱὸς τῆς πατρίδος; for communities who had read the LXX, the Son of man, described in a type of phrase with which they were familiar, would form an acceptable description of the exceptional man. Thus the release of Enoch and of the Jesus of history from the Son of man should enable us now to write a full account of the development of New Testament Christology, linking together the Jesus of history in the Aramaic-speaking Jewish world with the Christ of faith as he was eventually perceived among the Greeks.

NOTES

1 I am grateful to Dr Lohse for publishing an earlier draft of this discussion in *ZNW* 67 (1976), 147–54.

2 G. Vermes in M. Black, *An Aramaic Approach to the Gospels and Acts* (³1967), 310–28.

3 E.g. C. Colpe, *TDNT*, VIII, 403–4; F. H. Borsch, *The Christian and Gnostic Son of Man* (1970), 5 n. 19; J. Jeremias, *New Testament Theology* I (1971), 261 n. 1. Cf. I. H. Marshall, *The origins of New Testament Christology* (1976), 64–5.

4 Vermes in M. Black, op. cit., 325–6; G. Vermes, *Jesus the Jew* (1973), 162–3.

5 Vermes in M. Black, op. cit., 315, 323; cf. Colpe, op. cit., 404.

6 Infra, 227–8.

7 Vermes in M. Black, op. cit., 327.

8 J. Bowker, *JThS* XXVIII (1977), 19–48.

9 J. A. Fitzmyer in *Jesus aux origines de la christologie* (Journées Bibliques de Louvain 24ᵉ, 1975), 73–102.

10 Cf. e.g. T. Muroaka, *JJS* XXV (1974), 425–33.

11 Cf. Vermes, op. cit., 67–9, 180.

12 Supra, 159–61.

13 Cf. Colpe, op. cit., 405, 431–3, 442–3; Jeremias, op. cit., 261–2; Vermes, op. cit., 180–1.

14 On the Aramaic background to this saying, J. Jeremias, *ZNW* 58 (1967), 166; on the interpretation of the context, C. K. Barrett in *New Testament Essays. Studies in Memory of T. W. Manson* (1959), 1–18.

15 Cf. G. Mussies, *The Morphology of Koine Greek as Used in the Apocalypse of St John: A Study in Bilingualism* (1971), 186–9; F. Blass, A. Debrunner, F. W. Funk, *A Greek Grammar of the New Testament and Other Early Christian Literature* (1961), para. 252.

16 Cf. supra, 161–4.

17 H. K. McArthur, *NTS* 18 (1971–2), 81–6.

18 Supra, 201–13.

19 Cf. supra, 216–17.

20 Supra, 208–9.

21 Cf. supra, 203–5, 211; E. Sjöberg, *Der verborgene Menschensohn in den Evangelien* (1955), 241; P. M. Casey, *JSJ* VII (1976), 12–14.

22 Supra, 168–71, 178, 183, 187, 190, 196–7; cf. 197–8.

23 For a preliminary attempt to do this, see my forthcoming essay in one of the NT volumes of *Aufstieg und Niedergang der Römischen Welt*, ed. H. Temporini and W. Haase: for good recent work still handicapped by difficulties over the Son of man, B. Lindars, *BJRL* 57 (1974–5), 366–87; id., *NTS* 22 (1975–6), 52–72.

Select Bibliography

I PRIMARY SOURCES

1 Old Testament

Biblia Hebraica. Ed. R. Kittel. Stuttgart, Württembergische Bibelanstalt. ⁹1954.

Biblia Hebraica Stuttgartensia. Editio funditus renovata. Ed. K. Elliger and W. Rudolph. Stuttgart, Württembergische Bibelanstalt. 1968–77.

Septuaginta. Ed. A. Rahlfs. 2 vols. Stuttgart, Württembergische Bibelanstalt. 1949.

Septuaginta. Vetus Testamentum Graecum Auctoritate Societatis Litterarum Gottingensis editum. Vol. XVI, pars 2. *Susanna. Daniel. Bel et Draco.* Ed. J. Ziegler. Göttingen, Vandenhoeck & Ruprecht. 1954.

Der Septuaginta-Text des Buches Daniel, Kap. 5–12, zusammen mit Susanna, Bel et Draco, sowie Esther, Kap. 1, 1a–2, 15 nach dem Kölner Teil des Papyrus 967. Ed. A. Geissen. *Papyrologische Texte und Abhandlungen,* 5. Bonn, Habelt. 1968.

Translatio Syra Pescitto Veteris Testamenti ex Codice Ambrosiano Sec. fere vi photolithographice edita, curante et adnotante A. M. Ceriani. 2 vols. Milan, Croce. 1976–83.

The Old Testament in Syriac according to the Peshitta Version. Ed. P. A. H. de Boer and W. Baars, on behalf of the International Organization for the Study of the Old Testament by the Peshitta Institute of the University of Leiden. Leiden, E. J. Brill. 1973– .

The Bible in Aramaic. Ed. A. Sperber. 5 vols. Leiden, E. J. Brill. 1959–73.

Neophyti I. Targum Palastinense MS de la Biblioteca Vaticana. Ed. A. Diez Macho. Madrid, Consejo Superior de Investigaciones Científicas. 1968– .

Hagiographa Chaldaice. Ed. P. de Lagarde. Lipsiae, Teubner. 1873.

The Targum to Job from Qumran Cave XI. Ed. and Tr. M. Sokoloff. Ramat Gan, Bar Ilan University. 1974.

2 Other Jewish Sources

Die Texte aus Qumran. Ed. E. Lohse. Munich, Kösel-Verlag. ²1971.

Vermes, G., *The Dead Sea Scrolls in English*. Harmondsworth. Penguin. ²1975.

The Genesis Apocryphon of Qumran Cave I. Ed. J. A. Fitzmyer. Biblica et Orientalia 18A. Rome, Biblical Institute Press. ²1971.

Discoveries in the Judaean Desert. III. *Les 'Petites Grottes' de Qumran*. Ed. M. Baillet, J. T. Milik, and R. de Vaux. 2 vols, 1962. V. *Qumran Cave 4*. *I*. 4Q158–4Q186. Ed. J. M. Allegro. 1968. O.U.P.

The Books of Enoch. Aramaic Fragments of Qumran Cave 4. Ed. J. T. Milik, with the collaboration of M. Black. Oxford, Clarendon. 1976.

Baillet, M., Milik, J. T., Cross, F. M., Jr., Skehan, P., Allegro, J. M., Strugnell, J., Starcky, J., Hunzinger, C.-H., 'Travail d'édition des fragments manuscrits de Qumran', *RB* 63 (1956), 49–67.

Strugnell, J., 'The Angelic Liturgy at Qumran, 4Q Serek Šîrôt 'Olat Haššabât', *VT.S* VII (1960), 318–45.

Milik, J. T., '4Q Visions de 'Amram et une citation d'Origène', *RB* 79 (1972), 77–97.

——, 'Milkî sedeq et Milkî-reša' dans les anciens écrits juifs et chrétiens', *JJS* 23 (1972), 95–144.

The Apocrypha and Pseudepigrapha of the Old Testament. Ed. R. H. Charles. Oxford, Clarendon. 2 vols. 1913.

The Ethiopic Version of the Book of Enoch. Ed. R. H. Charles. Anecdota Oxoniensia, Semitic Series 11. O.U.P. 1906.

Apocalypsis Henochi Graece—Fragmenta Pseudepigraphorum. Ed. M. Black and A.-M. Denis. P.V.T.G.I. Leiden, Brill. 1970.

The Greek Versions of the Testaments of the Twelve Patriarchs. Ed. R. H. Charles. Oxford, Clarendon. 1908.

Testamenta 12 Patriarchum. Ed. M. de Jonge. P.V.T.G.I. Leiden, Brill. 1964.

The Testament of Abraham. Ed. M. R. James. Texts and Studies II, 2. C.U.P., 1892.

The Apocalypse of Abraham. Ed. G. H. Box and J. I. Landsman. TED I, 10. London, S.P.C.K. 1918.

Die Oracula Sibyllina. Ed. J. Geffcken. GCS VIII. 1902.

Nikiprowetsky, V., *La troisième Sibylle*. Etudes Juives, IX. Paris, Mouton. 1970.

The Fourth Book of Ezra. Ed. R. L. Bensly, with Introduction by M. R. James. Texts and Studies III, 2. C.U.P. 1895.

Apocalypsis Baruchi, Ed. M. Kmosko, in *Patrologia syriaca*, ed. R. Graffin, vol. 2, cols 1056–1306. Paris, Firmin-Didot et Socii. 1907.

3 Enoch, or The Hebrew Book of Enoch. Ed. H. Odeberg. C.U.P. 1928.

Die hebräische Elias-Apokalypse. Ed. M. Buttenwieser. Leipzig, Pfeiffer. 1897.

Beth ha-Midrash. Ed. A. Jellinek. 6 vols in 2. Jerusalem, Bamberger & Wahrman. ²1938.

Josephus, with an ET by H. St. J. Thackeray, R. Marcus, and L. H. Feldman. Loeb Classical Library. 9 vols. London, Heinemann. 1926–65.

Talmud Yerushalmi. With full commentaries, etc. Reproduction of the Piebrotvi and Wilna editions. New York, M.P. Press. 5719 A.M.

Le Talmud de Jérusalem, traduit de M. Schwab. 11 vols. Paris, Geuthner. 1932–3.

Talmud Babli. Der Babylonische Talmud, mit Einschluss der vollstaendigen Mischna, hrsg von L. Goldschmidt. 9 vols. Haag, Nyhoff. 1933–5.

The Babylonian Talmud. Tr. under the editorship of Rabbi Dr I. Epstein. 35 vols. London, Soncino Press. 1935–52.

Mekilta de Rabbi Ishmael. Ed. J. Z. Lauterbach. 3 vols. Schiff Library of Jewish Classics. Philadelphia, Jewish Publication Society of America. 1933–5.

Midrash Rabbah. With full commentaries. 2 vols. Vilna, 1878–87.

Midrash Rabbah. Tr. under the editorship of Rabbi Dr H. Freedman and M. Simon. 10 vols. London, Soncino Press. 1951.

Bereshith Rabbah. Ed. J. Theodor and Ch. Albeck. Veröffentlichungen der Akademie für die Wissenschaft des Judentums. 1903–29.

Midrash Tehillim. Ed. S. Buber. Wilna, Romm. 1891.

The Midrash on Psalms. Tr. G. Braude. 2 vols. Yale Judaica Series, vol. XIII. New Haven, Yale U.P. 1959.

Pesiqta Rabbati de Rab Kahana. Ed., with two commentaries, by E. Z. Margoliot. New York, Menorah Institute. 5719 A.M.

Pesikta Rabbati. Tr. W. G. Braude. Yale Judaica Series, XVIII. New Haven, Yale U.P. 1968.

Aggadath Bereshith. Ed. S. Buber. Romm, Vilna. ²1925.

Midrash Haggadol. Sepher Bereshith. Ed. M. Margolioth. Jerusalem, Haraw Kook. 1967.

Miqraoth Gedoloth. Ed. J. Levensohn. 12 vols. Warsaw, 1860–6. This contains the *textus receptus* of the commentaries on Daniel by Rashi, Ibn Ezra (longer recension) and Ps-Saadia.

Daniel, avec commentaries de R. Saadia, Aben Ezra, Raschi etc., et variantes des versions arabe et syriaque, traduits par A.-F. Gallé. Paris, 1900. Only selected excerpts are translated.

Jephet Ibn Ali: Commentary on Daniel. Ed. D. S. Margoliouth, with an ET. *Anecdota Oxoniensia* I, 3. Oxford, Clarendon. 1889.

R. Salomonis Jarchi Commentarius Hebraicus . . . in Prophetas latine versus . . . a J. F. Breithaupto. Göttingen, 1714. This contains a Latin translation of Rashi's Commentary on Daniel.

Midraš Daniel et Midraš Ezra auctore R. Samuel b. R. Nissim Masmuth (Saec. XIII). Ed I. S. Lange et S. Schwartz (in Hebrew). Jerusalem, Sumptibus Mekitze Nirdamim. 1968.

Joseph Albo, *Sepher ha-Ikkarim: Book of Principles*. Ed .I. Husik, with an ET. Schiff Library of Jewish Classics. New York, Jewish Publication Society of America. 1929.

3 New Testament

The Greek New Testament. Ed. K. Aland, M. Black, B. M. Metzger, A. Wikgren. London, British and Foreign Bible Society. ³1975.

Synopsis Quattuor Evangeliorum. Ed. K. Aland. Stuttgart, Württembergische Bibelanstalt. ⁵1968.

Synopsis of the First Three Gospels. Ed. A. Huck, rev. H. Leitzmann. English edn by F. L. Cross. Oxford, Blackwell. 1959.

Evangelion da-Mepharreshe. Ed. F. C. Burkitt. 2 vols. C.U.P. 1904.

The Coptic Version of the New Testament in the Southern Dialect. Ed. G. W. Horner. 7 vols. Oxford, Clarendon. 1911–24.

4 Patristic Sources

Patrologiae cursus completus, series graeca. Ed. J.-P. Migne. 161 vols. Paris, Migne. 1857–66.

The Ante-Nicene Christian Library. Ed. A. Roberts and J. Donaldson. 24 vols. Edinburgh, T. & T. Clark. 1866–72. Vol. 25, Ed. A. Menzies. 1897.

The Apostolic Fathers. Ed. J. B. Lightfoot. 5 vols. London, Macmillan. 1885–90.

Corpus Apologetorum Christianorum Saeculi Secundi. Ed. J. C. Th. Otto. 7 vols. Wiesbaden, Sündig. 1847–72.

Acta apostolorum apocrypha. Post C. Tischendorf denuo ed. R. A. Lipsius et P. Bonnet. 2 vols. in 3. Lipsiae, Mendelssohn. 1891.

New Testament Apocrypha. Ed. E. Hennecke and W. Schneemelcher. ET ed. R. Mcl. Wilson. 2 vols. London, Lutterworth. 1963–5.

Scriptorum Veterum Nova Collectio. Ed. A. Mai. Vol. I (containing the only published edition of comments by Polychronius on Daniel, and a collection of comments on Daniel by various patristic writers). Rome, In Collegio Urbano apud Burliaeam. 1825.

Aphrahat, *Demonstrations*. Ed. I. Parisot in *Patrologia Syriaca*, ed. R. Graffin, vol. I. Paris, Firmin-Didot et Socii. 1894.

Epître de Barnabé. Ed. R. A. Kraft and P. Prigent. Sources Chrétiennes, 172. Paris, Editions du Cerf. 1971.

Cosmas Indicopleustes, *Topographie chrétienne.* Ed. W. Wolska-Conus. SC 141 & 159. 1968–70.

Sancti Cypriani Episcopi Opera, Pars I. Ed. R. Weber and M. Benevot. CChr. SL III. 1972.

Sancti Ephraem Opera Omnia Quae Exstant. Ed. J. S. Assemanus, P. Benedictus and S. E. Assemanus. Vol. 5. Rome, Ex Typographia Pontifica Vaticana. 1740.

Hippolytus Werke. Erster Band. Exegetische und homilietische Schriften. Hrsg. G. N. Bonwetsch und H. Achelis. GCS I. 1897.

Hippolytus, *Commentaire sur Daniel.* Introduction de M. Bardy, Texte établi et traduit par M. Lefevre. SC 14. 1947.

Nautin, P., *Hippolyte contre les hérésies: fragment.* Etude et édition critique. Paris, Editions du Cerf. 1969.

Irénée de Lyon, *Contre les Hérésies* III–V. SC 210–11, 100, 152–3.

Commentaire d'Išoʿdad de Merw sur l'Ancien Testament. V. Jérémie, Ézéchiel, Daniel. Ed. et trad. C. Van den Eynde. 2 vols. CSCO 328–9, SS 146–7. 1972.

S. Hieronymi Presbyteri Opera. Pars I. *Opera Exegetica. 5. Commentariorum in Danielem Libri III (IV).* Ed. F. Glorie. CChr. SL LXXVA. 1964.

Jerome, *Commentary on Daniel.* Tr. Gleason L. Archer. Grand Rapids, Baker Book House. 1958.

L. Caeli Firmiani Opera Omnia: Pars I. *Divinae Institutiones et Epitome Divinarum Institutionum.* Ed. S. Brandt. CSEL XIX. 1890.

Origenes Mathäuserklärung. Ed. E. Klostermann. 3 vols. GCS 38, 40, 41. 1933–41.

Q.S.F. Tertulliani Opera. CChr. SL I–II. 1954.

Theodorus bar Koni, *Liber Scholium.* Ed. A. Scher. CSCO LV, SS XIX. 1910.

5 Other Sources

Ancient Near Eastern Texts relating to the Old Testament. Ed. J. B. Pritchard. Princeton U.P. ³1969.

Sophocles, *The Plays and Fragments.* Ed. R. C. Jebb. Part I. *The Oedipus Tyrannus.* C.U.P. 1883.

C. Vellei Paterculi *Historiae Romanae.* Ed. and Tr. F. W. Shipley. Loeb Classical Library. Heinemann and Harvard U.P. London and Cambridge, Massachusetts. 1924.

P. Vergili Maronis Opera. Ed. R. A. B. Mynors. Scriptorum Classicorum Bibliotheca Oxoniensis. Oxford, Clarendon. 1969.

II SECONDARY LITERATURE

Ackroyd, P. R., and Evans, C. F., eds. *The Cambridge History of the Bible*. 3 vols. Cambridge University Press, 1970.

Allenbach, J., Benoît, A., Bertrand, D. A., Hanriot-Coustet, A., Maraval, P., Pautler, A., and Prigent, P., *Biblia Patristica. Index des citations et allusions dans la littérature patristique*. I. *Des origines à Clément d'Alexandrie et Tertullien*. II. *Le troisième siècle (Origène excepté)*. Paris, Editions du Centre National de la Recherche Scientifique. 1975, 1977.

Anastos, M. V., 'Porphyry's attack on the Bible', in *The Classical Tradition. Literary and historical studies in honor of H. Caplan*, 421–50. Ithaca, Cornell University Press. 1966.

Ashby, E., 'The Coming of the Son of Man', *ExpT* LXXII (1960–61), 360–3.

Ashby, G. W., *Theodoret of Cyrrhus as Exegete of the Old Testament*. Grahamstown, Institute of Social and Economic Research, Rhodes University. 1972.

Balz, H. R., *Methodische Probleme der neutestamentlichen Christologie*. WMANT 25. 1967.

Barnard, L. W., 'The origins and emergence of the church in Edessa during the first two centuries', *VigChr* 22 (1968), 161–75.

Barr, J., 'Jewish Apocalyptic in Recent Scholarly Study', *BJRL* 58 (1975–6), 9–35.

Barrett, C. K., *Jesus and the Gospel Tradition*. London, S.P.C.K. 1967.

——, 'The Background of Mark 10.45', in *New Testament Essays: Studies in Memory of T. W. Manson*, ed. A. J. B. Higgins, 1–18. Manchester U.P. 1959.

——, 'Stephen and the son of man', *BZNW* 30 (1964), 32–8.

Baumgartner, W., 'Ein Vierteljahrhundert Danielforschung', *ThR* 11 (1939), 59–83, 125–44, 201–28.

Beardslee, W. A., 'New Testament Apocalyptic in Recent Interpretation', *Interp.* 25 (1971), 419–35.

Beasley-Murray, G. R., *Jesus and the Future*, London, Macmillan. 1954.

Beck, E., 'Symbolum-Mysterium bei Aphrahat und Ephräm', *OrChr* 42 (1958), 19–40.

Bentzen, A., *Daniel*. HAT. Tübingen, J. C. B. Mohr (Paul Siebeck). 1952.

——, *King and Messiah*. Tr. by the author. London, Lutterworth. 1955.

Black, M., *An Aramaic Approach to the Gospels and Acts*. O.U.P. ³1967.

——, 'The Son of Man in the Old Biblical Literature', *ExpT* LX (1948–9), 11–15.

——, 'The Son of Man in the Teaching of Jesus', *ExpT* LX (1948–9), 32–6.

——, 'The Eschatology of the Similitudes of Enoch', *JThS* NS III (1952), 1–10.

——, 'The Servant of the Lord and the Son of Man', *SJTh* 6 (1953), 1–11.

——, 'The Son of Man problem in recent Research and Debate', *BJRL* 45 (1962–3), 305–18.

——, 'The "Son of Man" Sayings in the Gospel Tradition', *ZNW* 60 (1969), 1–8.

——, 'The Christological Use of the Old Testament in the New Testament', *NTS* 18 (1971–2), 1–14.

——, 'The "Parables" of Enoch (1 En. 37–71) and the "Son of Man"', *ExpT* LXXXVIII (1976–7), 5–8.

——, 'The Throne-Theophany Prophetic Commission and the "Son of Man": a Study in Tradition-History', in *Jews, Greeks and Christians*, Essays in Honor of W. D. Davies, ed. R. Hamerton-Kelly and R. Scroggs, 57–73. Leiden, Brill. 1976.

Boers, H., 'Where Christology is real: A Survey of Recent Research on New Testament Christology', *Interp.* 26 (1972), 300–27.

Borsch, F. H., *The Son of Man in Myth and History*. London, S.C.M. 1967.

——, *The Christian and Gnostic Son of Man*. SBT 25. London, S.C.M. 1970.

Bowker, J., 'The Son of Man', *JThS* XXVIII (1977), 19–48.

Bowman, J. W., 'The Background of the Term Son of Man', *ExpT* LIX (1947–8), 283–8.

Bravermann, J., *Rabbinic and patristic tradition in Jerome's Commentary on Daniel*. Diss., Yeshiva University, 1970. Michigan, Ann Arbor. 1971.

Breech, E., 'These Fragments I have shored against my Ruins: The Form and Function of 4 Ezra', *JBL* 92 (1973), 267–74.

Brekelmans, C. H. W., 'The Saints of the Most High and their Kingdom', *OTS* XIV (1965), 305–29.

Brown, J. P., 'The Son of Man: "This Fellow"', *Bib* 58 (1977), 361–87.

Bruce, F. F., 'Josephus and Daniel', *ASTI* IV (1965), 148–62.

——, 'The Book of Daniel and the Qumran Community', in *Neotestamentica et Semitica*, Studies in Honour of Matthew Black, ed. E. E. Ellis and M. Wilcox, 221–35. Edinburgh, T. & T. Clark. 1969.

——, 'The Oldest Greek version of Daniel', *OTS* XX (1977), 22–40.

247

Caquot, A., 'Sur les quatre bêtes de Daniel', *Sem* V (1955), 5–13.

——, 'Les Quatre Bêtes et le "fils d'homme" (Dan. 7)', *Sem* 17 (1967), 37–71.

Casey, P. M., 'Porphyry and the Origin of the Book of Daniel', *JThS* NS XXVII (1976), 15–33.

——, 'The Use of the Term "son of man" in the Similitudes of Enoch', *JSJ* VII (1976), 11–29.

——, 'The Corporate Interpretation of "one like a son of man" at the Time of Jesus', *NT* 18 (1976), 167–80.

——, 'The Son of Man Problem', *ZNW* 67 (1976), 147–54.

Catchpole, D. R., 'The Son of Man's Search for Faith (Luke xviii.8b)', *NT* 18 (1977), 81–104.

Charles, R. H., *A Critical and Exegetical Commentary on the Book of Daniel*. O.U.P. 1929.

Collins, J. J., *The Sibylline Oracles of Egyptian Judaism*. SBL Dissertation Series, 13. Society of Biblical Literature and Scholars Press, Missoula, 1974.

——, 'The Son of Man and the Saints of the Most High in the Book of Daniel', *JBL* 93 (1974), 50–66.

——, 'The Court-Tales in Daniel and the Development of Apocalyptic', *JBL* 94 (1975), 218–34.

——, 'Jewish Apocalyptic against its Hellenistic Near Eastern Environment', *BASOR* 220 (1975), 27–36.

Colpe, C., 'ὁ υἱὸς τοῦ ἀνθρώπου', *TDNT* VIII (1972), 400–77.

——, 'Der Begriff "Menschensohn" und die Methode der Erforschung Messianischer Prototypen', *Kairos* 11 (1969), 241–63; 12 (1970), 81–113; 13 (1971), 1–17; 14 (1972), 241–57.

Coppens, J., 'Le Messianisme sapiental et les origines littéraires du fils de l'homme daniélique', *VT.S* III (1955), 33–41.

——, 'Le Fils d'homme Daniélique, vizir céleste', *EThL* 40 (1964), 72–80.

——, 'Les Origines du symbole du Fils de l'Homme en Daniel VII', *EThL* 44 (1968), 497–502.

——, 'La Vision daniélique du Fils d'Homme', *VT* XIX (1969), 171–82.

——, and Dequeker, L., *Le Fils de l'Homme et les Saints du Très-Haut en Daniel VII, dans les Apocryphes et dans le Nouveau Testament*. ALBO III, 23.

Cortès, J. B., and Gatti, F. M., 'The Son of Man or The Son of Adam', *Bib* 48 (1968), 457–502.

Crafer, T. W., 'The Work of Porphyry against the Christians, and its Reconstruction', *JThS* XV (1913–14), 360–95, 481–52.

Creed, J. M., 'The Heavenly Man', *JThS* XXVI (1925), 113–36.

Cullmann, O., *The Christology of the New Testament*. Tr. S. C. Guthrie and C. A. M. Hall. London, S.C.M. ²1963.

Dalman, G., *Die Worte Jesu*. Leipzig, Darmstadt. ²1930.

Debrunner, A., 'Über einige Lesarten der Chester Beatty Papyri des Neuen Testaments', *Coniectanea Neotestamentica* XI (1947) in honorem Antonii Fridrichsen sexagenarii, 33–49.

Delcor, M., *Le Livre de Daniel*. Sources Bibliques. Paris, Gabalda. 1971.

Denis, A.-M., *Introduction aux pseudépigraphes grecs d'Ancien Testament*. Leiden, Brill. 1970.

Dequeker, L., 'The "Saints of the Most High" in Qumran and Daniel', *OTS* XVIII (1973), 108–87.

Dhanis, E., 'De filio hominis in Vetere Testamento et in Judaismo', *Gregorianum* 45 (1964), 5–59.

Di Lella, A. A., 'The One in Human Likeness and the Holy Ones of the Most High in Daniel 7', *CBQ* 39 (1977), 1–19.

Dodd, C. H., *According to the Scriptures*. London, Nisbet. 1952.

Doeve, J. W., *Jewish Hermeneutics in the Synoptic Gospels and Acts*. Assen, von Gorcum. 1954.

Downing, J., 'Jesus and Martyrdom', *JThS* NS XIV (1963), 279–93.

Dupont, J., 'Le Logion des douze trônes', *Bib* 45 (1964), 355–92.

Ellis, E. E., *Paul's Use of the Old Testament*. Edinburgh, Oliver & Boyd. 1957.

——, 'Midrash, Targum, and New Testament Quotations', in *Neotestamentica et Semitica*. Studies in Honour of Matthew Black, ed. E. E. Ellis and M. Wilcox, 61–9. Edinburgh, T. & T. Clark. 1969.

Emerton, J. A., 'The Origin of the Son of Man Imagery', *JThS* NS IX (1958), 225–42.

Fahey, M. A., *Cyprian and the Bible: a study in third-century exegesis*. BGBH 9. 1971.

Feuillet, A., 'Le Fils de l'Homme de Daniel et la tradition biblique', *RB* 60 (1953), 170–202.

Fitzmyer, J. A., 'Methodology in the Study of the Aramaic Substratum of Jesus' sayings in the New Testament', in *Jésus aux origines de la christologie*, BEThL XL, 73–102. Leuven University Press. 1975.

Flusser, D., 'The four empires in the Fourth Sybil and in the Book of Daniel', *Isr Or St* II (1972), 148–75.

Ford, J. M., ' "The Son of Man"—A Euphemism?', *JBL* 87 (1968), 275–67.

Formesyn, R. E. C., 'Was there a Pronominal Connection for the Bar Nasha Selfdesignation?', *NT* 8 (1966), 1–35.

France, R. T., *Jesus and the Old Testament*. Downers Grove, Illinois, Inter-Varsity Press. 1971.

Frassinetti, P., 'Porfirio esegeta del profeta Daniele', *Istituto Lombardo: classe di lettere e scienze morale e storiche* 86 (1953), 194–210.

Freed, E. D., 'The Son of Man in the Fourth Gospel', *JBL* 86 (1967), 402–9.

Frend, W. H. C., 'The Old Testament in the Age of the Greek Apologists', *SJTh* 26 (1973), 129–50.

Frost, S. B., *Old Testament Apocalyptic*. London, Epworth. 1952.

Fuller, R. H., *The Foundations of New Testament Christology*. London, Lutterworth. 1965.

Gammie, J. G., 'The Classification, Stages of Growth, and Changing Intentions in the Book of Daniel', *JBL* 95 (1976), 191–204.

Gaster, M., 'The Son of Man and the Theophany in Daniel, Ch. VII: A New Interpretation', *The Search* I (1931), 15–30.

Gaston, M., *No Stone on Another: Studies in the Significance of the Fall of Jerusalem in the Synoptic Gospels*. *NT.S* XXIII. 1970.

Gerson, D., 'Die Kommentarien des Ephraem Syrus im Verhältnis zur jüdischen Exegese', *MGWJ* 17 (1868), 15–33, 64–72, 98–109, 141–9.

Gertner, M., 'Midrashim in the New Testament', *JSS* 7 (1962), 267–92.

Giles, P., 'The Son of Man in the Epistle to the Hebrews', *ExpT* LXXXVI (1974–5), 328–32.

Ginsberg, H. L., *Studies in Daniel*. Texts and Studies of the Jewish Theological Seminary of America, 14. New York, Jewish Theological Seminary. 1948.

——, 'The Composition of the book of Daniel', *VT* IV (1954), 246–75.

Glasson, T. F., *The Second Advent*. London, Epworth, [3]1963.

——, 'Mark xiii and the Greek Old Testament', *ExpT* LXIX (1957–8), 213–5.

——, 'The Reply to Caiaphas (Mark XIV.62)', *NTS* 7 (1960–1), 88–93.

——, 'The Ensign of the Son of Man (Matt. XXIV.30)', *JThS* NS XV (1964), 299–300.

——, 'The Second Advent—25 years later', *ExpT* LXXXII (1970–1), 307–9.

——, 'The Son of Man Imagery: Enoch xiv and Daniel vii', *NTS* 23 (1976–7), 82–90.

Grelot, P., 'La Légende d'Hénoch dans les Apocryphes et dans la Bible: Origine et signification', *RechScR* 46 (1958), 5–26, 181–210.

——, 'Le Livre de Daniel et le Nouveau Testament', *BCES* 45 (1964), 14–32.

Gressmann, H., *Der Messias.* FRLANT 43, NF 26. 1929.

Hahn, F., *The Titles of Jesus in Christology.* Tr. J. Knight and G. Ogg. London, Lutterworth. 1969.

Haller, M., 'Das Alter von Daniel 7', *ThStKr* 93 (1920–21), 83–7.

Hanhart, R., 'Die Heiligen des Höchsten', *VT.S* XVI (1967), 90–101.

Hanson, P. D., 'Jewish Apocalyptic against its Near Eastern Environment', *RB* 78 (1971), 454–79.

Hartman, L., *Prophecy Interpreted.* The Formation of Some Jewish Apocalyptic Texts and of the Eschatological Discourse Mark 13 Par. Tr. N. Tomkinson with J. Gray. *Coniectanea Biblica*, NT Series 1. Lund, Gleerup. 1966.

Hasel, G. F., 'The Identity of the "Saints of the Most High"', in Daniel 7 *Bib* 56 (1975), 173–92.

Haufe, G., 'Das Menschensohn-Problem in dem gegenwärtigen wissenschaftlichen Diskussion', *EvTh* 26 (1966), 130–41.

Hay, D. M., *Glory at the Right Hand. Psalm 110 in Early Christianity.* Soc Bib Lit MS 18. 1973.

Heaton, E. W., *The Book of Daniel.* London, S.C.M. 1956.

Higgins, A. J. B., *Jesus and the Son of Man.* London, Lutterworth. 1964.

——, 'Son of Man Forschung since the Teaching of Jesus', in *New Testament Essays.* Studies in Memory of T. W. Manson, ed. A. J. B. Higgins, 119–35. Manchester University Press. 1959.

——, 'Is the Son of Man problem insoluble?', in *Neotestamentica ed Semitica.* Studies in Honour of Matthew Black, ed. E. E. Ellis and M. Wilcox, 70–87. Edinburgh, T. & T. Clark. 1969.

Hölscher, G., 'Die Entstehung des Buches Daniel', *ThStKr* 92 (1919), 113–38.

Hooker, M. D., *The Son of Man in Mark.* London, S.P.C.K. 1967.

——, 'Christology and Methodology', *NTS* 17 (1970–71), 480–7.

Jeremias, J., *New Testament Theology*, vol I. *The Proclamation of Jesus.* Tr. J. Bowden. London, S.C.M. 1971.

——, 'Die Älteste Schichte der Menschensohnlogien', *ZNW* 58 (1967), 159–72.

Kallarakkal, A. G., *The Peshitto Version of Daniel—A Comparison with the Massoretic Text, the Septuagint and Theodotion.* Diss., Hamburg, 1973.

251

Keulers, J., *Die eschatologische Lehre des vierten Ezrabuches.* BSt(F) XX, Heft 2–3. 1922.

Kilpatrick, G. D., 'Acts vii.56: Son of Man?', *ThZ* 21 (1965), 209.

Kraeling, C. H., *Anthropos and the Son of Man. A Study in the Religious Syncretism of the Hellenistic Orient.* Columbia Univ. Oriental Studies, 25, 1927.

Kraeling, E. G. H., 'Some Babylonian and Iranian Mythology in the Seventh Chapter of Daniel', in *Oriental Studies in Honour of C. E. Pavry*, ed. J. D. C. Pavry, 223–32. London, 1932.

Krauss, S., 'The Jews in the Works of the Church Fathers', *JQR* 5 (1893), 122–57; 6 (1894), 82–99, 223–61.

Kümmel, W. G., *Promise and Fulfilment.* Tr. D. M. Barton. SBT 23. London, S.C.M. ²1961.

Lacocque, A., *Le Livre de Daniel.* Comm. de l'A.T.XV. 1976.

Lamy, T., 'L'Exégèse en Orient au IVe siècle, ou les commentaires de saint Ephrem', *RB* 2 (1893), 5–25, 161–81, 465–86.

Lataix, J., (pseudonym for Loisy, A.), 'Le Commentaire de s. Jérôme sur Daniel', *Revue d'histoire et de littérature religieuses* II (1897), 164–73, 268–77.

Lebram, J. C., 'Perspektiven der gegenwärtigen Danielforschung', *JSJ* V (1974–5), 1–33.

Le Déaut, R., *La Nuit Pascale.* Analecta Biblica XXII. 1963.

Leivestad, R., 'Der apokalyptische Menschensohn als theologisches Phantom', *ASTI* VI (1967–8), 49–105.

——, 'Exit the Apocalyptic Son of Man', *NTS* 18 (1971–2), 243–67.

Lenglet, A., 'La Structure littéraire de Daniel 2–7', *Bib* 53 (1972), 169–90.

Lietzmann, H., *Der Menschensohn: ein Beitrag zur neutestamentlichen Theologie.* Freiburg/Leipzig. 1896.

Lindars, B., *New Testament Apologetic.* London, S.C.M. 1961.

——, 'The Son of Man in the Johannine Christology', in *Christ and the Spirit in the New Testament*, Studies in honour of C. F. D. Moule, ed. B. Lindars and S. S. Smalley, 43–60. C.U.P. 1973.

——, 'The Apocalyptic Myth and the Death of Christ', *BJRL* 57 (1974–5), 366–87.

——, 'Re-enter the Apocalyptic Son of Man', *NTS* 22 (1975–6), 52–72.

——, and Borgen, P., 'The Place of the OT in the Formation of NT Theology: Prolegomena and Response', *NTS* 23 (1976–7), 82–90.

Loader, W. R. G., 'Christ at the right hand—Ps. cx.l in the New Testament', *NTS* 24 (1977–8), 199–218.

McArthur, H. K., 'Mark XIV.62', *NTS* 4 (1957–8), 156–8.
——, 'On the Third Day', *NTS* 18 (1971–2), 81–6.
McCown, C. C., 'Jesus, Son of Man. A Survey of Recent Discussion', *JR* 28 (1948), 1–12.
Maddox, R., 'Methodenfragen in der Menschensohnforschung', *EvTh* 32 (1972), 143–60.
——, 'The Function of the Son of Man in the Gospel of John', in *Reconciliation and Hope*, New Testament Essays on Atonement and Eschatology presented to L. L. Morris on his 60th birthday. Ed. R. Banks, 190–204. Exeter, Paternoster Press. 1974.
Manson, T. W., 'The Son of Man in Daniel, Enoch and the Gospels', *BJRL* 32 (1950), 171–95 = *Studies in the Gospels and Epistles*, ed. M. Black, 123–45.
Marlow, R., 'The Son of Man in Recent Journal Literature', *CBQ* 28 (1966), 20–30.
Marshall, I. H., *The origins of New Testament Christology*. Illinois, Intervarsity Press. 1977.
——, 'The Synoptic Son of Man sayings in Recent Discussion', *NTS* 12 (1965–6), 327–51.
Mearns, C. L., 'The Parables of Enoch-Origin and Date', *ExpT* LXXXIX (1977–8), 118–9.
Mertens, A., *Das Buch Daniel im Lichte der Texte vom Toten Meer*. SBM 12. 1971.
Michel, O., 'Der Menschensohn', *ThZ* 27 (1971), 81–104.
Miller, M. P., 'Targum, Midrash and the Use of the Old Testament in the New Testament', *JSJ* II (1971), 29–82.
Moe, O., 'Der Menschensohn und der Urmensch', *StTh* 14 (1960), 119–29.
Montgomery, J. A., *A Critical and Exegetical Commentary on the Book of Daniel*. ICC. Edinburgh, T. & T. Clark. 1927.
Moore, A. L., *The Parousia in the New Testament*. NT.S. XIII. 1966.
Morgenstern, J., 'The "Son of Man" of Daniel 7.13f. A New Interpretation', *JBL* 80 (1961), 65–77.
Mørkholm, O., *Antiochus IV of Syria*. Classica et Mediaevalia, Dissertationes VIII. Copenhagen, Gyldenhal. 1966.
Moule, C. F. D., *The Origin of Christology*. C.U.P. 1977.
——, 'From Defendant to Judge—and Deliverer', *BSNTS* 3 (1952), 40–53. Reprinted in C. F. D. Moule, *The Phenomenon of the New Testament*. SBT second series, 1. 1967.
——, 'Neglected Features in the Problem of "the Son of Man" ', in *Neues Testament und Kirche*. Für Rudolf Schnackenburg. Hrsg von J. Gnilka, 413–28. Freiburg, Herder. 1974.

Mowinckel, S., *He that Cometh*. Tr. G. W. Anderson. Oxford, Blackwell. 1956.

Muilenberg, J., 'The Son of Man in Daniel and the Ethiopic Apocalypse of Enoch', *JBL* 79 (1960), 197–209.

Müller, K., 'Beobachtungen zur Entwicklung der Menschensohn-vorstellung in den Bilderreden des Henoch und im Buche Daniel', *Östliche Christentum* 25 (1971), 253–61.

——, 'Menschensohn und Messias. Religionsgeschichtlichen Vorüberlegungen zum Menschensohnproblem in den synoptischen Evangelien', *BZ* 16 (1972), 161–87; 17 (1973), 52–66.

Müller, M., 'Uber den Ausdruck "Menschensohn" in den Evangelien', *StTh* 31 (1977), 65–82.

Müller, U. B., *Messias und Menschensohn in jüdischen Apocalypsen und in der Offenbarung des Johannes*. Studien zum NT, 6. Gütersloh, Gerd Mohn. 1972.

Mussies, G., *The Morphology of Koine Greek as Used in the Apocalypse of St. John: A Study in Bilingualism*. *NT.S* XXVII. 1971.

Noth, M., 'Zur Komposition des Buches Daniel', *ThStKr* 98–9 (1926), 143–63.

——, 'Die Heiligen des Höchsten', *NTT* 56 (1955). Festschrift S. Mowinckel. 146–61. ET 'The Holy Ones of the Most High', in *The Laws in the Pentateuch and other Essays*, Tr. D. R. Ap-Thomas, 215–28. Philadelphia, Fortress. 1967.

Orchard, J. B., 'Saint Paul and the Book of Daniel', *Bib* 20 (1939), 172–9.

Otto, R., *The Kingdom of God and the Son of Man*. Tr. F. V. Filson and B. Lee-Wolf. London, Lutterworth. ²1943.

Perrin, N., *Rediscovering the Teaching of Jesus*. London, S.C.M. 1967.

——, *A Modern Pilgrimage in New Testament Christology*. Philadelphia, Fortress. 1974.

Plöger, O., *Das Buch Daniel*. KAT XVIII. 1965.

Pollard, T. F., 'Martyrdom and Resurrection in the New Testament', *BJRL* 55 (1972), 240–51.

Porteous, N. W., *Daniel*. London, S.C.M. 1965.

Poythress, V. S., 'The Holy Ones of the Most High in Daniel VII', *VT* XXVI (1976), 208–13.

Prigent, P., *Les Testimonia dans le christianisme primitif: l'Epître de Barnabé I–XVI et ses sources*. Etudes Bibliques. Paris, Gabalda. 1961.

——, *Justin et l'Ancien Testament*. Etudes Bibliques. Paris, Gabalda. 1964.

Rhodes, A. B., 'The Kingdoms of Men and the Kingdom of God: A Study of Daniel vii.1–14', *Interp.* 16 (1961), 411–30.

Robinson, J. A. T., *Jesus and his Coming*. London, S.C.M. 1957.

Rogerson, J. W., 'The Hebrew Conception of Corporate Personality. A Re-examination', *JThS* NS XXI (1970), 1–16.

Rollins, W. G., 'The New Testament and Apocalyptic', *NTS* 17 (1970–1), 454–76.

Rost, L., 'Zur Deutung des Menschensohns in Daniel 7', in *Gott und die Götter*. Festgabe für E. Fascher, BZAW 101 (1958), 41–3.

Rowley, H. H., *Darius the Mede and the Four World Empires*. Cardiff, University of Wales Press Board. 1935.

——, *The Relevance of Apocalyptic*. London, Lutterworth. ³1963.

——, 'The Unity of the Book of Daniel', *HUCA* XXIII (1950–1), 233–79. Reprinted in *The Servant of the Lord and Other Essays*, 235–68. London, Lutterworth. 1952.

——, 'The Composition of the Book of Daniel', *VT* V (1955), 272–6.

Russell, D. S., *The Method and Message of Jewish Apocalyptic*. London, S.C.M. 1964.

Sahlin, H., 'Antiochus IV Epiphanes und Judas Maccabaeus. Einzige Geschichtspunkte zum Verständnisse des Daniel-buches', *StTh* 23 (1969), 41–68.

Sant, C., *The Old Testament Interpretation of Eusebius of Caesarea*. Malta Royal University, 1967.

Schippers, R., 'The Son of Man in Matt. xii.32 = Lk. xii.10, compared with Mk.iii.28', *StEv* IV, TU 102 (1968), 231–6.

Schmid, H., 'Daniel, der Menschensohn', *Judaica* 27 (1971), 192–220.

Schmidt, N., 'Was בר נשא a Messianic Title?', *JBL* 15 (1896), 35–53.

——, 'The Son of Man in the Book of Daniel', *JBL* 19 (1900), 22–28.

——, 'Recent Study of the Term Son of Man', *JBL* 45 (1926), 326–49.

Schnackenburg, R., 'Der Menschensohn im Johannesevangelium', *NTS* 11 (1965), 123–37.

Schweizer, E., 'Der Menschensohn', *ZNW* 50 (1959), 185–209.

——, 'The Son of Man', *JBL* 79 (1960), 119–29.

——, 'The Son of Man again', *NTS* 9 (1963), 256–61.

Scott, R. B. Y., 'Behold, he cometh with the clouds', *NTS* 5 (1958–9), 127–32.

Seitz, O. J. F., 'The Future Coming of the Son of Man: Three Midrashic Formulations in the Gospel of Mark', *StEv* VI, TU 112 (1973), 478–94.

Sharman, H. B., *Son of Man and Kingdom of God*. New York, Harper. 1943.

Shotwell, W. A., *The Biblical Exegesis of Justin Martyr*. London S.P.C.K. 1965.

Silver, A. H., *A History of Messianic Speculation in Israel*. New York, Macmillan. 1927.

Sjöberg, E., *Der Menschensohn im äthiopischen Henochbuch*. Skrifter Utgivna Av Kungl. Humanistika Vetenskapssamfundet I Lund, XLI. Lund, Gleerup, 1946.

——, *Der verborgene Menschensohn in den Evangelien*. Skrifter Utgivna Av Kungl. Humanistika Vetenskapssamfundet I Lund, LIII. Lund, Gleerup. 1955.

——, בן אדם und בר אנש im Hebräischen und Aramäischen', *Acta Orientalia* XXI (1953), 57–65, 91–107.

Smalley, S. S., 'The Johannine Son of Man sayings', *NTS* 15 (1968–9), 278–301.

Smith, M., 'What is Implied by the Variety of Messianic Figures?', *JBL* 78 (1959), 66–72.

Sokoloff, M., ' 'amar nĕqē', "LAMB'S WOOL" (DAN. 7:9)', *JBL* 95 (1976), 277–9.

Stauffer, E., 'Messias oder Menschensohn', *NT* I (1956), 81–102.

Stinespring, W. F., *The Use of the Old Testament in the New and Other Essays. Studies in Honor of W. F. Stinespring*, ed. J. M. Efird. Durham, N. Carolina, Duke University Press. 1972.

Stone, M. E., *Features of the Eschatology of IV Ezra*. Diss, Harvard. 1965.

Stott, W., ' "Son of Man"—A Title of Abasement', *ExpT* LXXXVIII (1971–2', 278–81.

Swain, J., 'The Theory of the four Monarchies', *CP* XXXV (1940), 1–20.

Taylor, V., *The Names of Jesus*. London, Macmillan. 1953.

——, 'The "Son of Man" Sayings Relating to the Parousia', *ExpT* LVIII (1946–7), 12–15.

Teeple, H., 'The Origin of the Son of Man Christology', *JBL* 84 (1965), 213–50.

Theisohn, J., *Der auserwählte Richter. Untersuchungen zum traditionsgeschichtlichen Ort der Menschensohngestalt der Bilderreden des äthiopischen Henoch*. StUNT 12. 1975.

Thompson, G. H. P., 'The Son of Man: The Evidence of the Dead Sea Scrolls', *ExpT* LXXII (1960–1), 125.

——, 'The Son of Man: Some Further Considerations', *JThS* NS XII (1961), 203–9.

Tillman, F., 'Hat die Selbstbezeichnung Jesus "der Menschensohn" ihre Wurzeln in Dan., VII, 13?', *BZ* 5(1907), 35–47.

Tödt, H. E., *The Son of Man in the Synoptic Tradition*. Tr. D. M. Barton. London, S.C.M. 1965.

Torrey, C. C., 'Notes on the Aramaic part of Daniel', *Transaction of the Connecticut Academy of Arts and Sciences* XV (1909), 241–82.

Trudinger, L. P., 'Some Observations Concerning the Text of the Old Testament in the Book of Revelation', *JThS* 17 (1966), 82–8.

Ullendorf, E., 'An Aramaic "Vorlage" of the ethiopic text of Enoch?', *Atti del Convegno Internazionale de Studi Etiopici, Accad. naz. dei Lincei, Problemi attuali di scienza e di cultura*, quad. 48 (1960), 259–68.

Vermes, G., *Jesus the Jew*. London, Collins. 1973.

——, 'The use of בר נשא/בר נש in Jewish Aramaic', App. E in M. Black, *An Aramaic Approach to the Gospels and Acts* (³1967), 310–28.

Vielhauer, P., 'Gottesreich und Menschensohn', in Festschrift für Günther Dehn, ed. W. Schneemelcher, 51–79. Neukirchen, Kreis Moers. 1957.

——, 'Jesus und der Menschensohn', *ZThK* 60 (1963), 133–77.

——, 'Ein Weg der neutestamentliche Theologie? Prüfung der Thesen F. Hahns', *EvTh* 25 (1965), 24–72.

Vögtle, A., 'Das christologische und ekklesiologische Anliegen von Mt. 28, 18–20', *StEv* II, TU 87 (1964), 266–94.

——, *Jesus und der Menschensohn*. Für Anton Vögtle. Hrsg. von R. Pesch und R. Schnackenburg, in Zusammenarbeit mit O. Kaiser. Herder, Freiburg/Basel/Wien. 1975.

Völter, D., 'Der Menschensohn in Dan. 7, 13', *ZNW* 3(1902), 173–4.

Volz, P., *Die Eschatologie der jüdischen Gemeinde im neutestamentlichen Zeitalter*. Tübingen, Mohr. ²1934.

Walker, W. O., 'The Origin of the Son of Man Concept as applied to Jesus', *JBL* 91 (1972), 482–90.

Wifall, W., 'Son of Man—A Pre-Davidic Social Class?', *CBQ* 37 (1975), 331–40.

Zevitt, Z., 'The Structure and Individual Elements of Daniel 7', *ZAW* 80 (1968), 385–96.

ADDENDUM

The following works are among those which have come to my notice since the completion of the revised manuscript of this book. Those which I have read have not caused me to alter my views to any significant extent.

Achtemeier, P. J., ed., *Society of Biblical Literature 1978 Seminar Papers*, vol. i. Missoula, Scholars Press 1978.

Barr, J., 'Aramaic-Greek Notes on the Book of Enoch (I)', *JSS* 23 (1978), 184–98.

Berger, K., *Die Auferstehung des Propheten und die Erhöhung des Menschensohnes*. StUNT 13. Göttingen, Vandenhoeck und Ruprecht, 1976.

Black, M., 'Jesus and the Son of Man', *JSNT* 1 (1978), 4–18.

Bowker, J., *The Religious Imagination and the Sense of God*. Oxford, 1978.

Braverman, J., *Jerome's Commentary on Daniel: A Study of Comparative Jewish and Christian Interpretations of the Hebrew Bible*. CBQ Monograph Series 7. Washington, 1978.

Caquot, A., 'Remarques sur les chapitres 70 et 71 du livre éthiopien d'Hénoch', in M. Delcor *et al.*, *Apocalypses et théologie de l'espérance: Congrès de Toulouse* (1975). Lectio Divina 95. Paris, Cerf. 1977, 111–22.

Charlesworth, J. H., 'The SNTS Pseudepigrapha Seminars at Tübingen and Paris on the Books of Enoch', *NTS* 25 (1978–9), 315–23.

Coke, P. T., 'The Angels of the Son of Man', in A. Fuchs (hrsg), *Probleme der Forschung*. Studien zum Neuen Testament und seiner Umwelt 3. Herold, Wien/München 1978, 99–113.

Collins, J. J., *The Apocalyptic Vision of the Book of Daniel*. Harvard Semitic Monographs, 16. Missoula, Scholars Press 1977.

Coppens, J., 'Le chapitre VII de Daniel. Lecture et commentaire', *EThL* 54 (1978), 301–22.

Fitzmyer, J. A., *A Wandering Aramaean*. Collected Aramaic Essays. SBL Monograph Series. Missoula, Scholars Press 1979.

Greenfield, J. C., and Stone, M. E., 'The Enochic Pentateuch and the Date of the Similitudes', *HThR* 70 (1977), 51–65.

Hartman, L. F., and di Lella, A. A., *The Book of Daniel*. Anchor Bible. New York, Doubleday 1978.

Hooker, M. D., 'Is the Son of Man problem really insoluble?', in *Text and Interpretation*. Studies in the New Testament presented to Matthew Black, ed. E. Best and R. McL. Wilson. C.U.P. 1979, 155–68.

Kearns, R., *Vorfragen zur Christologie* I. Tübingen, Mohr 1978.

Kilpatrick, G. D., 'Again Acts VII. 56: Son of Man?', *ThZ* 34 (1978), 232.

Klein, M. L., 'The Messiah "That Leadeth upon a Cloud" in the Fragment-Targum to the Pentateuch', *JThS* 29 (1978), 137–9.

Knibb, M. A., *The Ethiopic Book of Enoch*. 2 vols. O.U.P. 1978.

Knibb, M. A., 'The Date of the Parables of Enoch: A Critical Review', *NTS* 25 (1978–9), 345–59.

Kvanvig, H. S., 'Structur und Geschichte in Dan 7, 1–14'. *StTh* 32 (1978), 95–115.

Legasse, S., 'Jésu historique et le Fils de l'homme aperçu sur les opinions contemporaines', in M. Delcor *et al.*, *Apocalypses et théologie de l'espérance: Congrès de Toulouse* (1975). Lectio Divina 95. Paris, Cerf 1977, 271–98.

Lust, J., 'Daniel 713 and the Septuagint', *EThL* 54 (1978), 62–9.

McDermott, J. M., 'Luke, XII, 8–9: Stone of Scandal', *RB* LXXIV (1977), 523–37.

McDermott, J. M., 'Luc, XII, 8–9: Pierre angulaire', *RB* LXXV (1978), 381–401.

Mearns, C. L., 'Dating the Similitudes of Enoch', *NTS* 25 (1978–9), 360–69.

Stone, M. E., 'The Book of Enoch and Judaism in the Third Century B.C.E.', *CBQ* 40 (1978), 479–92.

Vermes, G., 'The Present State of the "Son of Man" Debate', *JJS* 29 (1978), 123–34.

Wilson, F. M., 'The Son of Man in Jewish Apocalyptic Literature', *Studia Biblica et Theologica* 8, (1978) 28–52.

Wittstruck, T., 'The Influence of Treaty Curse Imagery on the Beast Imagery of Daniel 7', *JBL* 97 (1978), 100–2.

Zevitt, Z., 'The Exegetical Implications of Daniel VIII, 1, IX, 21', *VT* 28 (1978), 488–92.

Index of Primary Sources

I OLD TESTAMENT

Gen.
I 25
2.17 229
5.21-4 106
13.16 116
15.12 71
28.12 197-8
49.10 80

Exod.
12.42 90, 92
15.3 87
20.2 87

Lev. 6.2 77

Num.
19.8-9 197
24.7 139
24.17 85, 139

Deut.
30.3f 170
32.2-4 33
33.2 133

1 Sam. 2.8 78

2 Sam. 7.13-16 193

1 Kings 22.19 23

Isa.
4.3 23
6 75
6.1 113, 149
9.7 193
10.12 73
13.10 171
17.12f 18
27.1 18
34.4 169-70
40.6-8 229
45.17 89
51.9-10 18
53 203, 206, 210
60.8 153

66.1 87

Jeremiah 93-4

Jer.
4.7 19-20
5.6 19
10.11 13
30.21 81-2
46.7f 18
49.19 20
49.22 20
49.36 18
50.17 20

Ezek.
1 32, 75, 109, 113
1.1 201
1.4 113
1.5 125
1.10 145
1.26 32, 37, 113, 125, 144
1.27 113
8.2 113
9.2 144
10.14 145
17.3f 20
29.3f 19

Hosea 144

Joel
2.10 171
3.12 22

Amos
5.19 72
9.11 91

Obad.
1.4 77
1.21 76, 89

Hab.
1.8 20
2.3 162

Zeph. 1.3 186
Hag. 2.22 76

Zech.
2.6 18, 170
2.10 170
6.5 18
9.9 85
12.10-12 168-70, 178
12.10 83, 143-4, 168, 197
12.12 143, 177
14.2 170
14.5 22-3, 170

Mal. 3.16 23

Ps.
2 36
8 28, 152, 155, 182
8.5 152, 154
8.6-8 25
8.6 28, 152
34.10 44
47.4 76
47.5 76
47.9 76
62.13 164
68.31 19
69.29 23
73.21f 26
74.13f 18
75.4 109
80 182
80.14 19
80.16 90
80.18 90-1
82 23
89.10-11 18
96.13 22
104.25-6 18
110.1 80, 83-4, 152, 169, 178, 181-2, 200, 211
110.2f 182

Ps.—(*contd.*)
118.2 23
145.13 43, 135

Job
1 23
25.3 75
25.6 116
35.8 116

Eccl. 12.5-7 229

Lam.
1.16 83
4.19 20

Daniel 7-10, 142, 151

Dan.
1 9, 11
2-7 7-10, 17, 20
2 7-9, 12-13, 15, 17,
   44-5, 48, 55, 62, 68,
   120-2, 128
2.4 10
2.31-3 73
2.31 12
2.34 68
2.35 63
2.38 28
2.39 30
2.40-3 73
2.44 44, 46, 68
3 7, 17
3.25 31
3.33 43, 135
4 7, 12-13, 17, 20, 26
4.7 12
4.10 12
4.14 192
4.31 135
5 7, 17
5.21 28
6 7, 17
6.27 135
7 passim, *see* Table of
   Contents
7.1 8, 122
7.2-14 17
7.2-8 15, 17, 22, 122,
   147
7.2 13, 18, 122, 124,
   126, 142, 146
7.3-8 18-19, 142
7.3 13, 18-19, 52, 122,
   142, 147

7.4 19-20, 26-7, 52, 73,
   86
7.5 13, 15, 20, 27, 52, 72
7.6 20, 27, 52
7.7-8 20-1, 26, 71, 74-5,
   107, 109
7.7 11, 13-15, 52, 71,
   122, 142, 147
7.8 11-15, 23, 38, 46-7,
   53, 67, 147
7.9-10 12, 14-16, 22-3,
   29, 33, 36, 38, 43, 53,
   75-7, 84, 86-8, 99,
   107-10, 113-14, 119,
   122, 130-1, 133, 135,
   142, 146, 149-50, 158,
   188-9, 192-3
7.11 11-12, 16, 23-4, 53,
   68, 77, 107, 109, 111-12,
   122-3, 142, 147, 149
7.12 16, 24, 68, 107,
   109, 111-12
7.13-14 passim, especi-
   ally 24-40, 58, 62-70,
   80-112, 124-9, 131-2,
   136-9, 142-5, 148-9,
   157-219
7.15 122
7.16 53, 107, 109
7.17ff 27
7.17-18 26, 40-1, 47
7.17 16, 30-1, 53
7.18 24, 32, 42, 53, 67,
   79, 107, 119, 142, 158,
   194
7.19 26, 86, 107, 109
7.20 11, 14, 26, 46-7,
   142, 147
7.21 11, 14, 26, 38-42,
   53, 57, 67, 142, 147,
   158, 164
7.22 11, 14, 22, 24, 26,
   32, 38-41, 53, 78, 107-8,
   132-3, 142, 149, 151,
   158-60, 188, 194
7.23 47, 107, 109, 122-3
7.24 11, 14-15, 20, 47,
   57, 142, 147, 149
7.25 11, 14-15, 40, 42,
   47-8, 53, 57, 67, 107,
   121, 142, 147
7.26 14, 31, 42-3, 75,
   107, 142, 149
7.27 24, 31-2, 40-3, 47,

53, 67, 78, 80, 107, 129,
   135, 142, 147, 149, 158,
   194-5
7.28 8, 48, 113, 122
8-12 7, 9-10, 14-15, 27-8,
   32, 46-8
8.1 113
8.8 18
8.9f 46
8.10 109
8.11 47
8.14 121
8.15 28, 31-2
8.16 31-2
8.17 34
8.21 30
8.24 44
8.25 45
9 25, 47
9.21 31-2
9.24-6 115
9.26f 47
9.27 48
10.5 31-2, 144
10.6 144, 192
10.16 31, 144-5
10.18 31, 125, 144
10.21 32
11-12 113, 115
11.4 18
11.21 21
11.31 47
11.40-12 11, 61-2
11.44 62-3
12 30, 44, 46, 61
12.1-3 45, 110
12.1 32, 44
12.6 31-2
12.7 31, 44, 48, 146-7
12.11 47

4Q Dan^a 113

4Q Dan^b 113

1 Chron.
3.10ff 82
3.24 82, 166

LXX 11, 29, 41, 63,
   131-3, 169-71, 178, 192,
   200

Theodotion 11, 41, 133,
   158, 178

Peshitta 11, 52-3, 63

Targums 90-2

II OTHER JEWISH SOURCES

Agg. *Ber.*
14, 3   80
23, 1   80

Apoc. Abraham 11   135

2 Baruch   5, 99, 129-30
24.1   129
39-40   129
39.3   130
39.5-7a   129
40   128
40.3   129
53.8   129-30

CD XX, 8   114

Eccl. R. 10, 8   225-6

1 Enoch
1.2   103
1.3-9   22
1.9   133
12.4   103
13   106
13.10   103
14   109
14.1   103
14.8-25   133-4
14.8   111
15.1   103
18.2f   133
18.5   133
25.3   22
37-71 (The Similitudes)
  16, 35-7, 99-112, 122,
  130, 137-9, 205, 214,
  238
38.4   108, 110
38.5   108
39.4f   106
39.4   108
39.6   100
39.7   110
40.1   107, 110
40.5   100
41.9   107-8
43.4   108-10
45.3   107
46   108-9, 124
46.1   99, 107, 110
46.2   99-104, 107, 109,
  214
46.3   102-7, 109

46.4   102, 107
46.5   107
46.6   107
46.7   107, 109
46.8   107
47.2   107-8, 110
47.3   107, 109-11
47.5   111
48.2   102, 107
48.5   107
48.7   107-8
48.8   107
48.9   107-8
48.10   107, 111
49.2   100, 107
49.4   100
50.1   110
51.3   100, 107
51.5   100
52.4   107, 111
52.5   100-1
52.6   100
52.9   100
53.6   107
55.1   107
55.4   107
56.5f   110
56.8   110
60.1-2   107
60.2   110
60.10   102, 107
61.1   109
61.5   100
61.6   110
61.8-9   107
61.9   107
61.10   100
62.1   100, 102, 107
62.2-16   107
62.5   102, 104
62.6   111
62.7   102, 104-5
62.9   102
62.10-16   110
62.10   100-1
62.14   102
63.11   102, 107
65.12   107-8, 111
69.26-9   107
69.26   102, 104-5
69.27   102, 104-5, 107-8
69.29   102, 105

70-71   105, 111
70.1   102, 105, 107
70.4   106
71   102, 105, 107, 109-11,
  133-4
71.1   107, 110
71.2   107
71.13   100-1, 106
71.14-17   105-6
71.14   102, 104-6
71.17   102, 106
78.17   33
80.2   31, 174
90   134
90.20   22, 134
90.37   134
108.12-13   189

3 Enoch   99, 130-1
15   88
18.19   130
28.7   130
30.2   130
35.4   130
36.1   130

Esth. R.
Proem 5   72
1, 6   86
3, 7   225-6
4, 12   86

Ezra   99, 122-9
1-9   122
3.1-2   122
4.21   122
5.4ff   174
5.14-15   122
6.20   122
7.26   128
7.29   127
9.38   122
10.25   122
10.30   122
11-12   27, 122-4, 127-8
11.1   122
11.2   122
11.39   122-3
11.40-2   122
12.3   122-3
12.11-12   122-3

Ezra—(contd.)
12.13 **122**
13 37, 88, 122, 123-9,
  136-9
13.2 **124**
13.3 **124-7**
13.4 **127**
13.5 **124-7**
13.6-7 **127**
13.10-11 **127**
13.12 **124-5, 127**
13.13 **127**
13.25 **124, 126-7**
13.27f **127**
13.32 **124**
13.33 **127**
13.51 **124, 126-7**
13.52 **126-7**
14 **122**
14.29 **127**

Galipapa 51-3, 55, 64,
  69, 146

Gen. R.
13, 11 **80-1**
13, 12 **80-1**
61, 18 **197**
76, 6 **74**
79, 6 **224-6**

Ibn Ezra 73, 84-5, 87,
211

Jephet 73, 76

Josephus 99, 120-1
  B.J. I, 19 **121**
  I, 32 **121**
  A.J. X, 188-281 **120**
    X, 208 **120**
    X, 267 **120**
    X, 269-76 **121**
    X, 271 **121**

Jub. 10, 17 **103**

Lev. R. 13, 5 **71, 86**

1 Macc. 1, 41ff **47**

Mekh. *Bah.* IV, 24ff
  (Exod. 20.2) **87**

Mekh. *Shir.* IV, 23ff
  (Exod. 15.3) **87**

Midr. Haggadol Gen.
  49.10 **80**

Midr. Ps.
2, 9 **80, 83**
4, 4 **88**
21, 5 **80-2, 86, 89, 162,
166**
47, 2 **76, 88**

Midr. Wayosha' **83**

Ms MICH 9, fol 67b **88**

Mysteries of R. Simeon
83

Num. R. 11, 1 **78**

Talmuds
bT *AZ* 2b **72**
bT *Hag* 13b **75**
bT *Hag* 14a **87-8**
bT *Meg* 72 **72**
bT *Qid* 72 **82**
bT *San* 38b **87-8**
  96b **90-2**
  97b **74**
  98a **80, 85-6**
  98b **83**
pT *Sheb* IX, 1 **224-5**
pT *Ta anith* 2, 65, 69 **90-
91**

Pes. R. I, 3 **153**

Philo **99**

Ps-Saadia **80, 83-4**

1QApGen **12, 228**
XXI, 13 **116**
XXI, 16 **18**
XXII, 2 **12**

1QH III, 21 **41**

1QpHab
IV, 30 **116**
V, 3-6 **115-16**
V, 4 **151, 188**

1QS
V, 6-7 **115**
IX, 3-5 **115**
XI, 20 **116**

1QSa I, 1-3 **115**

2Q24 **16-17**

4Q174 **113, 115, 136**

4Q184 **116**

4Q 'Amram^b I, 10-14
14

4Q Giants **12, 22, 113**

4QOrNab **114, 229**

4Qps-Dan **114**

4Q Serekh Sîrôt **113**

11Q Melchizedek **115,
238**

11QTgJob **12, 228**
IX, 9 **116**
IX, 12 **116**

Rashi **74, 84-5, 211**

Samuel ben Nissim **80**

Sib. Or. **117-20**
II, 241-4 **120**
III, 49-50 **120**
III, 388-400 **117-20, 136**
III, 397-400 **117-20, 136**
IV, 47f **119, 129**
V, 414-33 **37**
V, 414 **119-20, 139**

Tanch.
Mis. **88**
Tol. 20 **80-3, 86, 89,
166**
Ts. 4 **77**
Qed. 1 **87-8**

Test. Abr.
7 **139**
13 **198-9**

Test. Dan 5.6 **103**

Test. Jos. 19.11-12 **135**

Test. Levi 10.5 **103**

Wisd.
3.8 **41, 151, 188**
4 **103**
5.16 **194**

III NEW TESTAMENT

Matt.
4.17 158
5.11 200
8.20 229, 236
9.6 158-9
9.8 161, 229
10.1 204
10.23 158, 163, 185-6,
  197, 201, 213, 216, 218,
  236
10.32 162, 194, 208, 231
10.33 162-3, 231-2
10.40 191
10.42 77, 191
11.19 229, 234
12.32 229-31, 236
12.36 76
12.40 236
13.37 236
13.41 158, 186-7, 202,
  209, 236
16.13 236
16.18 67
16.19 195, 204
16.27 158, 161, 164, 190,
  201, 232
16.28 158, 163, 186-8,
  201, 209-10, 213, 216,
  235-6
17.12 158, 164
18.5 191
18.18 204
18.23f 77
19.28 41, 119, 158, 175,
  187-90, 192, 202, 236
20.21 187
20.28 158, 164
21.43 194
24.27 158, 189, 236
24.30 77, 93, 143-4, 158,
  163, 165, 169, 177, 183,
  185, 187, 191, 201, 213,
  218, 236
24.37 236
24.39 236
24.42 163, 216
24.44 158, 163, 190,
  197, 201, 213, 216, 236
25.31 119, 158, 163, 175,
  190-2, 201, 210, 213,
  216, 232, 236
25.32 190

25.34 191, 195
26.2 236
26.64 158, 163, 178, 180,
  183-5, 187, 191, 201,
  213, 218
28.3 158, 192
28.18-20 158, 192-3

Mark
1.15 158-9
2.10 98, 158-60, 204,
  208, 212, 228-9, 236
2.28 227-8, 236
3.15 204
6.7 204
8.31 212, 232, 236
8.38 158, 161-4, 201,
  208, 210, 213, 216, 232,
  236
9.1 187, 208
9.9 236
9.12 158, 164, 233, 236
9.31 232, 236
9.37 191
9.41 191
10.15 195
10.33 232, 236
10.34 232
10.45 158, 164-5, 206,
  229, 236
11.28 193
13 172-3, 215
13.2 172-3
13.4 172-3
13.14 202
13.24-7 169-71, 173-4
13.26 158, 162-3, 166-
  178, 184-5, 196-7, 201,
  213-18, 236
13.27 166-7, 186
13.29 209
13.30 173
13.32 173
13.35 163, 216
14.21 227, 229-30, 233,
  236
14.25 184
14.41 236
14.62 83-4, 158-9, 162-
  163, 168-9, 175, 178-85,
  191, 196-7, 200-1, 203,

211, 213, 215-16, 218,
  236
14.63 180

Luke
1.32-3 158, 193
1.33 158, 187, 193
5.24 97, 158-9
6.22 200, 236
7.34 228, 236
9.1 204
9.26 158, 162, 164, 201
9.48 191
9.58 228, 236
10.16 191
10.19 204
11.30 236
12.8 158, 162, 193-4,
  208, 210, 232, 236
12.9 162-3, 210, 232
12.10 162, 210, 229-31,
  236
12.32 158, 194-5, 208
12.40 158, 163, 184,
  190, 197, 201, 213, 216,
  236
17.22 158, 195-6, 200,
  202, 236
17.24 158, 189, 236
17.25 236
17.26 236
17.30 200, 236
18.1 196
18.8 158, 163, 184, 196-
  197, 200-1, 213, 216,
  235-36
18.17 195
19.10 236
21.27-31 208-9
21.27 158, 163, 165,
  177, 184, 196, 200-2
21.36 197, 200, 236
22.29 194
22.30 158, 187-9, 202
22.48 229, 236
22.69 158, 178, 180,
  183-4, 197, 200-2
23.42 187
24.7 197, 200, 236

John
1.12 204
1.51 158, 197-8, 202, 235

John—(contd.)
3.14 **197**
5.27 **158, 198-9**
6.27 **204**
12.34 **199-200, 208, 234**
14.3 **163**
14.10-11 **197**
14.18 **163**
14.28 **163**
17.22 **204**
19.37 **143-4, 168, 197**
20.23 **204**
21.22 **163**
21.23 **163**

Acts **201, 213**
1.6 **195**
1.9 **177, 184**
1.11 **158, 162, 177, 199**
3.20 **162**
7.55 **201**
7.56 **158, 197, 199-202, 209, 234**

Epistles **151-5, 201, 213-214**

Rom. 8.18 **204**

1 Cor.
4.5 **162**
6.2 **31, 151, 188**
6.3 **151**
6.9-10 **195**
11.26 **162**
15.23-8 **152**
15.24 **187**
15.47 **151-2**
15.50 **195**

2 Cor. 5.10 **76**

Gal. 5.21 **195**

Eph.
3.5 **212**
5.5 **187, 195**

Phil.
2.7 **152-3**

3.20-1 **152**

Col.
1.13 **187**
3.4 **152**

1 Thess.
4.16 **77, 79, 152**
4.17 **77, 153-4**
5.2 **162**

2 Thess.
1.7 **152**
1.10 **162**
2 **154**
2.3-5 **79**

2 Tim.
4.1 **187**
4.18 **187**

Heb.
1.8 **187**
2.6 **154-5**
10.37 **162**

Jas.
2.5 **195**
5.7-8 **155**

1 Pet. 1.11 **204**

2 Pet.
1.11 **187**
3.10f **155**

1 John
2.18 **155, 162**
4.13 **155, 162**

2 John 7 **155**

Jude 14 **162**

Revelation **142-50, 213**

Rev.
1.7 **142-4, 168, 177-8, 197, 213, 215**
1.13 **142, 144-5**

1.14 **142, 146**
1.15 **145**
2.18 **145**
2.26f **204**
3.21 **189**
4.3 **145**
4.6 **145**
4.7 **145**
5.11 **142, 146**
7.1 **142, 146**
9.7 **145**
9.10 **145**
9.19 **145**
11.1 **145**
11.2 **142, 146-7**
11.3 **145, 147**
11.7 **142, 147**
11.15 **142, 147, 187**
12.3 **142, 147**
12.6 **147**
12.8 **142, 147**
12.14 **142, 146-7**
13.1-8 **142, 147-8**
13.2 **145**
13.4 **145**
13.5 **146**
13.11 **145**
14.14 **142, 144-5, 148-9**
14.15 **149**
14.17-19 **149**
17.3 **142**
17.7 **142**
17.8 **142**
17.12 **142, 149**
17.16 **142**
18.8 **145**
19.14 **31**
20.4 **41, 142, 149**
20.11 **142**
20.12 **142, 149**
21.11 **145**
21.18 **145**

Syriac **179-80, 205-6**

Sahidic **180**

IV PATRISTIC SOURCES

Acts of Peter **xxiv 92**

Anon., *Dialogue on the Orthodox Faith* **XXV 93**

Anon. on Dan. 7.7 **52-3**

Apoc. of Peter 1, 6 **93**

Aphrahat,
Dem. V **52-70, 73**
XXII **55, 57**

Barnabas
IV, 4-5 **74, 96**
XII, 9 **96**

Chrys. *Hom. de Res.* 1 **119**

1 Clement 34 **76**

Clem. Alex., *Paedagogus* III, 16, 4 **76**

Cosmas Indicopleustes, *Christian Topography*
II, 66-73 **52-3, 66, 68-9**
V, 131-2 **52, 68**

Cyprian, To Quirinus *Testimonia* II, 26 **93-7, 161, 172**

Didache 16.8 **93**

Ephraem, Comments on Daniel **52-5, 64-6, 68-69, 146**

Eusebius
Prophetic Extracts III, 44 **93**
Ecclesiastical History I, 2 **93**
Demonstration of the Gospel IX, 17, 4-7 **93**
XV **72, 93**
Against Marcellus II, 1, 4-5 **93**
On the Theology of the Church III, 17 **93, 97**
On the Lives of the Prophets, s.v. Daniel **93**
Commentary on the Psalms, 96.1 **93**

Eusebius—(*contd.*)
Commentary on Luke 9.26; 19.12; 21.28 **93**
Catena comment on Dan.
7.13 **93**
7.14 **93**
7.18 **79, 93**

Hippolytus
On Christ and Antichrist
XXII **93**
XXVI **93**
XLIV **93-4**
On Daniel IV **59, 72, 74, 78-9, 93-5**
Syntagma, p. 243 **93**

Irenaeus
Against Heresies **94**
III, 19, 2 **92**
IV, 20, 11 **92**
IV, 33 **92**
V, 25-6 **74-5**

Isho 'dad of Merw, *Commentary on Daniel* **52-4, 65, 69, 189**

Jerome, *On Daniel* **52, 59-64, 71, 77, 95**
Justin, *Apology* I, 51, 9 **92-4**
Dialogue
14, 8 **92, 144**
31-2 **92, 94**
76, 1-2 **92, 96**
79, 2 **92**

120, 4 **93**
126, 1 **92**

Lactantius
Div. Inst. IV, 12-21 **93, 95**
Epitome 42, 4 **93**

Origen
On Matthew XIV, 8-9 **76-7**
Comm. Ser. 111 (Matt. 26.64) **180**

Polychronius, *Commentary on Daniel* **52-5, 66-9, 211**

Tertullian
Against Marcion
III, 7, 4 **93-4**
III, 24, 11 **93**
IV, 10, 9-14 **93, 97, 206**
IV, 39, 11 **93**
IV, 41, 4 **93**
Against the Jews XIV **93**
On the Flesh of Christ XV **93**
On the Resurrection of the Flesh **93**

Theodore bar Koni *Questions and Answers, Daniel* **52-4, 65, 69**

Theodoret, *Commentary on Daniel* **54, 73, 77, 96-7**

V OTHER SOURCES

Aemilius Sura **71**

Enuma Elish IV, 40 **19**

Porphyry, *Against the Christians*, XII **52-4, 59-64, 69**

Sophocles, *Oedipus Tyrannus* 1080 **239**

Velleius Paterculus, *Roman History* I, vi, 6 **71**

Vergil, *Aeneid* IX, 638-40 **148**

Index of Names and Subjects

Abba Jose son of Dosai 75
Abbahu, R. 91
Akiba, R. 86-8
Albeck, C. 226
Alexander Balas 118
Alexander the Great 15, 20-1, 52, 54, 56-7, 60-1
'Anani 82-3, 166
Ancient of Days 22-4, 27, 32, 53, 55, 62, 64, 76, 81-8, 99, 110-11, 113, 130, 132-3, 135, 146, 179
Angels 31-2, 40-5, 53, 66-7, 75-6, 79, 82-4, 88, 94, 102-3, 110-11, 123, 130, 134, 139, 145-6, 148-9, 151, 162, 164, 166, 170-1, 186, 192, 197
Antichrist 61, 74-5, 77-9, 131
Antigonus 21
Antiochus I Soter 20
Antiochus II Theos 20
Antiochus III the Great 20
Antiochus IV Epiphanes 10, 20-1, 25, 40-8, 53-7, 59-62, 64, 67-8, 71, 112, 117-18, 135-6, 147, 154
Antiochus V Eupator 117
Antiochus VI Epiphanes 117-19
Antiochus, son of Seleucus 20-1, 117
Aramaic: of Daniel 11-15, 19, 21, 23, 27-30, 32-3, 39-48; in sayings of Jesus 157-71, 178, 182-5, 190, 193-7, 205-8, 212-13, 218-19, 224-39; בר אנש 1, 28, 90-2, 96-7, 99-107, 115-16, 124-6, 139, 157-239 passim
Assyria, Assyrians 19 71-2, 119

Babylon, Babylonians 7-9, 17-20, 24, 35, 52, 55, 68, 71-2, 114-15, 119-20, 123, 129-31
Barrett, C. K. 50n, 222-3nn, 240n
Baumgartner, W. 49n
Beasley-Murray, G. R. 220nn
Belshazzar 7, 17
Ben Neszer 74
Bentzen, A. 36-7, 50n
Billerbeck, P. 134, 141n

Black, M. 32-3, 49n, 140n, 219n, 223nn, 239nn
Blass, F. 240n
Borsch, F. H. 239n
Boussett, W. 141n
Bowker, J. 227, 240n
Bowman, J. W. 140-1nn
Breech, E. 126, 141n
Brekelmans, C. H. W. 40, 42, 50nn, 140n
Broadribb, D. 49n
Bruce, F. F. 116, 140-1nn, 156n

Caesar, Julius 74
Caquot, A. 49n
Casey, P. M. 70n, 98nn, 140nn, 220-222nn, 240nn
Catchpole, D. R. 222n
Charles, R. H. 100, 140-1nn, 147, 150nn
church: exegesis of 51-80, 92-8, 142-156, 157-219 passim, 232, 234-8; sayings of Jesus produced by 157-219 passim, 234-8
clouds 28-9, 34, 37-8, 58, 62-4, 66, 68, 81-4, 90-2, 111, 124, 129-34, 142-3, 148, 153-4, 165, 174, 176-8, 180-4, 189, 199, 204
Collins, J. J. 31-2, 49-50nn
Colpe, C. 239-40nn
Colwell, E. C. 199
Conzelmann, H. 223n
Coppens, J. 48n, 50n
corporate personality 30, 211
Cranfield, C. E. B. 223n
Cross, F. M. 140n

Dalman, G. 141n, 150n, 222n
Daniel 7-48 passim; see also index of primary sources, s.v.
Darius the Mede 17, 54, 61
David 86-8
Debrunner 240n
Dehn, G. 223nn
Delcor, M. 13, 49n

269

Demetrius I Soter   20-1, 118
Demetrius II Nicator   118-19
Dequeker, L.   11-16, 40-4, 48-50nn
Dhanis, E.   30-1, 49n, 98n
Dodd, C. H.   156n, 193, 203, 219nn, 221-2nn
Doeve, J. W.   215, 219n, 221n, 223n
Driver, S. R.   28, 49-50nn
Dupont, J.   221n

Edessa   59-9
Edom   71, 73
Eleazar son of Azariah, R.   86
Ellis, E. E.   151, 155n
Emerton, J. A.   37, 50nn
Enoch   16, 88, 90, 99-112, 133-4, 137-9, 214-15, 238-9; see also index of primary sources, s.v. 1 Enoch, 3 Enoch
Esau   56, 71, 74
exegesis: Jewish   1-3, 51-5, 58-60, 62-65, 69, 71-92, 97-139, 143, 146, 153, 165-6, 174, 197, 206, 211, 214-15; Christian   1-3, 51-80, 92-8, 142-56, 157-219 passim, 232, 234-8

Farrer, A. M.   159-61, 219n
Feuillet, A.   32-3, 49n, 219n
Fitzmyer, J. A.   49n, 227, 239n
Flusser, D.   49nn, 98n
four kingdoms   8-9, 19, 40, 46, 55-62, 71-4, 76-9, 112, 114-15, 119-20, 123, 128-31, 202; see also Babylon, Greece, Media, Persia, Rome
France, R. T.   170-6, 220nn
Freed, E. D.   222n
Fuller, R. H.   223n
Funk, R. W.   240n

Gabriel   32
Gaster, M.   33-4n, 50n
Gaston, L.   98n, 164-5, 203-5, 220-2nn
Geffcken, J.   119, 140n
Gelston, A.   221n
Giles, P.   156n
Ginsberg, H. L.   13, 48-9n
Glasson, T. F.   83, 133-4, 141nn, 169-170, 175, 179-80, 220-1nn, 223nn
Goudge, H. L.   155n
Grässer, E.   156n
Greece, Greeks   19-21, 24, 30, 52-69, 71-3, 115, 117-21, 123, 129-31, 135-6
Grelot, P.   221n
Gundry, R. H.   192, 220-1nn
Gunkel, H.   35, 50n

Hahn, F.   223n
Haller, M.   15, 48n
Hanhart, R.   50n
Hartman, L.   108-9, 140nn, 220n
Hasel, G. F.   40, 42, 44-5, 50nn, 140n
Hay, D. M.   188, 220-1nn
Heaton, E. W.   50n
Hill, D.   221n
Hölscher, G.   11-15, 48n
Hooker, M. D.   39, 49-50nn, 140n, 164, 205-6, 219n, 222-3nn
Hunter, A. M.   155n

Isaac, R.   91
Israel: land of   17-19, 22; people of   8-11, 24-34, 39-48, 53-5, 57-60, 62-5, 67-9, 76, 78, 81-3, 85, 114-15, 121, 124, 127, 151, 191, 195, 198, 205, 216

Jaoel   135, 139
Jeremiah son of Abba, R.   75
Jeremias, J.   190, 219-21nn, 223n, 239-40nn
Jesus of Nazareth: birth   68; teaching   157-239 passim; death   206, 213, 217-18, 229-30, 232-3, 237; Resurrection and Ascension   68, 94-6, 152, 161, 175, 179-82, 184, 193, 213, 217-18, 232-3, 237-8; parousia   58, 77-9, 93-4, 143-4, 150, 152-4, 161-91, 196-7, 199, 202, 210-18, 234-5, 238; as the man-like figure (Dan. 7.13)   58, 62-6, 69, 77-9, 92-7, 142-4, 148-9, 150-219 passim; see also Son of man
Jews   passim; see Israel. Jewish exegesis   1-3, 51-5, 58-60, 62-5, 69, 71-92, 97-139, 143, 146, 153, 165-6, 174, 197, 206, 211, 214-15; see also Son of man
Johanan, R.   74, 81, 86
Jose the Galilean, R.   86-7
Joseph, R.   72
Joshua son of Levi, R.   85-6
Judaism   see Jews, Son of man
Judas Maccabaeus   34, 63-4, 69

Keulers, J.   141n
Kiddle, M.   150n
Kingdom of God   24-5, 29, 43, 58, 76-79, 159, 186-7, 194-5, 208-9, 217, 234
Kraeling, C. H.   36, 50n
Kümmel, W. G.   219n, 221n

Lagrange, M.   98n
Le Déaut, R.   90, 98n

Leivestad, R. 198, 222-3nn
Levy, J. 98n
Lindars, B. 150n, 240n
literary dependence 1-6, 90-3, 99-100, 107-35, 142-219 passim, 229-30, 234-8
Loader, W. R. G. 220n
Lohmeyer, E. 152-3, 155n, 221n
Lohse, E. 239n
Loos, H. van der 219n

McArthur, H. K. 220n, 240n
Macedonia, Macedonians see Greece
Mai, A. 70n
Mann, C. S. 140n
Manson, T. W. 191-2, 219n, 221-3nn, 240n
Marshall, I. H. 239n
Martin, R. P. 155n
Mattathias 55, 146
Media, Medes 9, 19-20, 24, 54-6, 60-61, 68, 71-2, 119-20, 123, 129-31, 136
Melchizedek 90, 139, 238
Mertens, A. 140nn
Messiah 30-1, 65, 69, 77, 80, 82-92, 114-16, 119-20, 124-33, 136-9, 143, 166, 176, 193, 206, 211; see also Jesus of Nazareth
Metatron 88, 110, 130, 139
Michael 31-2, 35, 90, 134-5, 139
Milik, J. A. T. 113, 140-1nn
Miller, M. P. 222-3nn
Montefiore, C. G. 221n
Montgomery, J. A. 13, 48nn, 141nn
Mørkholm, O. 49n
Moses 33-4, 90, 238
Moule, C. F. D. 38-9, 50n, 164, 203, 205-6, 219n, 222-3nn
Mowinckel, S. 23, 37-8, 49-50nn
Müller, K. 48n
Müller, U. B. 48n, 141nn
Muroaka, T. 239n
Mussies, G. 145, 150nn, 240n

Nachman, R. 91
Nathan, R. 74
Nebuchadnezzar 7-8, 17, 20, 26, 54, 192
Nikiprowetzsky, V. 140nn
Noth, M. 11, 15-16, 40-2, 44-5, 48n, 50nn

Odeberg, H. 88, 98n
Odenathus 74
Oepke, A. 204, 222nn
Orchard, J. B. 154, 156n

Perrin, N. 22, 49n, 83, 181-2, 200-1, 220-2nn
Persia, Persians 9, 19-20, 24, 52, 55-7, 60-1, 68, 71-2, 115, 119-20, 123, 129-31, 136
Plöger, O. 13
Poythress, B. S. 50n
Ptolemy VI Philometor 118
Ptolemy VII Euergetes 118-19

Rab 74-5
Rabbi 75
Rawlinson, A. E. 155n
Ridderbos, H. 219n
Robinson, J. A. T. 179, 220-1nn, 223nn
Rogerson, J. W. 49n, 223n
Rome, Romans 55-7, 71-4, 77, 115, 117, 119-23, 129-31, 135-6, 147-8, 150, 202
Rowley, H. H. 12-13, 48-49nn
Russell, D. S. 140n

Sahlin, H. 34, 50n
Saints 24-32, 38-48, 53-5, 57-8, 62-5, 67-9, 71, 78-9, 108, 114-15, 132-3, 147, 149, 151, 159-60, 195, 198, 202, 211
Samuel son of Nachman, R. 86
Schaeder, H. H. 49n
Schmid, H. 34, 48n, 50n
Schmidt, N. 31-2, 35, 49-50nn
Schnackenburg, R. 219n, 222nn
Schneider, G. 222n
Schweizer, E. 223n
Seitz, J. F. 170, 220n
Seleucids see Antiochus, Demetrius, Seleucus
Seleucus I Nicator 20-1
Seleucus II Callinicus 20
Seleucus III Ceraunus 20
Seleucus IV Philopator 20-1, 117-18
Sharman, H. B. 223n
Simeon, R. 224-6
Sjöberg, E. 100, 140n
Sokoloff, M. 49n
Son of man passim, see table of Contents; in Daniel 24-40; in the Similitudes of Enoch 99-107; in Judaism 24-40, 90-2, 99-107, 115-116, 119-20, 124-9, 137-9, 144; in the Gospels 157-239; in patristic theology 96-7, 199; suffering son of man 1, 38-9, 70, 164, 203, 205-6

Stone, M. E.   126-8, 141nn
Strack, H. L.   141n
Strugnell, J.   113, 140n
suffering Servant   203, 206, 210
Suhl, A.   223n
Swain, J.   49n, 98n, 141n
Swete, H. B.   148, 150nn

Taylor, V.   212, 223n
Theisohn, J.   140nn
Theodor, J.   226, 243
Titus 74
Tödt, H. E.   221-2nn
Torrey, C. C.   143, 150n
Trudinger, L. P.   150n
Trypho   118-19

Ullendorf, E.   100-1, 140n
Vanhoye, R.   150n
Vermes, G.   49n, 98n, 189, 219nn,
   221-3nn, 224-7, 239-40nn
Vespasian   74
Vielhauer, P.   186, 208-9, 221nn,
   223nn, 234
Vögtle, A.   48-9nn,156n, 192, 221-2nn
Walker, W. O.   221n
Weimar, P.   48n
Whiteley, D. E. H.   155n
Winter, P.   223n
Zevitt, Z.   49n
Ziegler, J.   141n
Zutra son of Tobiah, R.   75